THE
PREACHER'S
HANDBOOK

EDITED BY
GREVILLE P. LEWIS
B.A., B.D.

NUMBER FIVE

THE EPWORTH PRESS

THE EPWORTH PRESS
(FRANK H. CUMBERS)
25–35 City Road, London, E.C.1

MELBOURNE   CAPE TOWN
NEW YORK   TORONTO

PRINTED AND BOUND IN ENGLAND BY
HAZELL WATSON AND VINEY LTD
AYLESBURY AND LONDON

LOCAL PREACHERS DEPARTMENT
THE STUDIES BOARD
1956–1957

Rev. E. RALPH BATES
  ,, JOHN C. BOWMER, M.A., B.D.
  ,, CHARLES A. CLARK, B.D.
  ,, HORACE CLEAVER, B.D.
  ,, RONALD CRAWFORD, B.D.
  ,, J. CYRIL T. DOWNES, M.B.E., M.A., B.D.
  ,, BENJAMIN DREWERY, M.A.
  ,, GEORGE ELVIDGE, B.A., B.D.
  ,, J. ALLAN FLETCHER, B.D.
  ,, KENNETH I. FORD, B.A., M.Th.
  ,, H. TREVOR GREEVES
  ,, G. LESLIE HOLDSWORTH, B.D.
  ,, RICHARD L. J. KAYE
  ,, ALFRED C. LAMB, M.A., B.Sc., B.D., Ph.D.
  ,, ALFRED H. S. PASK, M.A., Ph.D.
  ,, ARTHUR N. ROSE, M.A.
  ,, GARFIELD WADE, M.A.
Mrs ROBERT J. BARTLETT, B.Sc.
Miss DOROTHY H. FARRAR, B.A., Ph.D.
Mr CECIL O. MACKLEY, M.A.
Mr GEORGE H. VALLINS, B.A.
Mr G. GILBERT YATES, M.A.
Rev. GREVILLE P. LEWIS, B.A., B.D. (*Secretary*)

PREFACE

The Preacher's Handbook (*Number One*) was published in July 1949 as a venture of faith and in the hope that it might prove of some service to the preachers of Methodism. In particular, it was planned to meet the needs of our great lay ministry—those 24,000 Local Preachers and 3,500 Local Preachers on Trial who have all too little leisure for the preparation of sermons, and even less for the study of those scholarly reinterpretations of the Gospel and the Faith which enable the modern preacher to challenge the minds and meet the spiritual needs of the men and women of today.

It was also hoped that it would be of some help to the preachers of other communions who have not time for the reading of many books.

The sales of the Handbook—almost 40,000 copies of the first four issues have been sold—suggest that we did not underestimate the need, and that the Studies Board of the Local Preachers Department was wise in its decision to authorize the publication of a new issue of the Handbook every two years.

We are glad to know that many Preachers' Fellowships use it as a textbook for corporate study and discussion.

We hope that new readers will buy the previous issues of the Handbook, while they are still available. If a subject of vital importance to the preacher is absent from any particular Handbook, it has probably been dealt with in earlier books of the series.

ABBREVIATIONS

AOT = *An Approach to the Old Testament* (Horace Cleaver)
ANT = *An Approach to the New Testament* (Greville P. Lewis)
ACD = *An Approach to Christian Doctrine* (Ed. Greville P. Lewis)
RVmg = Margin of the *Revised Version.*
RSV = *Revised Standard Version.*
MHB = *Methodist Hymn-book.*
PH = *The Preacher's Handbook.*

EDITORIAL

BEFORE I present *The Preacher's Handbook* (*Number Five*) to you and introduce its contributors, will you permit me, kind reader, to indulge in a brief swan-song ?* Because I am retiring from the secretaryship of the Local Preachers Department at the 1958 Conference, it will be my duty to gather the material for the 1959 Handbook, but my successor will prepare it for publication. As I write my last editorial, therefore, I would express my deep gratitude to those who have made this venture possible, and who are so largely responsible for its continuing success.

Throughout the past eleven years, I have enjoyed close and happy colleagueship with every member of the Studies Board of the Department. In the planning of each issue of the Handbook, as in so many other matters, I have owed much to their counsel and encouragement.

From the day when I first suggested this venture, I have received the most generous support of the Book Steward of the Methodist Publishing House, Dr Frank H. Cumbers, and of the Connexional Editors, first Dr Leslie F. Church, and later Dr J. Alan Kay. My cordial thanks are due to them; nor do I forget the efficient work of the managerial and editorial staff of the Epworth Press.

And now a word about our past contributors. Every one of them had many other commitments and could easily have 'begged to be excused'; obviously, none of them did! Many of them had already established themselves as scholars of repute. Some of these are no longer with us: Henry Carter, Fred A. Farley, F. Warburton Lewis, Dr C. Ryder Smith, Winship Storey and George Vallins (whose recent death has brought a deep sense of loss to his many friends). Others are still enriching the life of the Church with their scholarship: Dr Eric W. Baker, N. Allen Birtwhistle, Dr Kenneth H. Crosby, Rupert E. Davies, Dr Maldwyn L. Edwards, Dr Dorothy Farrar, Kenneth Grayston, Frederic Greeves, Dr C. Leslie Mitton, Dr Walter J. Noble, Prof. Cecil H. Pawson, Edward Rogers, Dr W. Edwin Sangster, Dr Norman H. Snaith, and Ronald V. Spivey. It has also been

* Non-Methodist readers are advised to jump to the other side of the asterisks on page viii.

my privilege to persuade quite a number of preachers to venture on the joys and agonies of authorship for the first, or almost the first time, and they have made a very real contribution to the four previous Handbooks. All these contributors laboured without thought of prestige or royalties, that they might serve the Church through serving its preaching ministry.

* * *

Part One of this Handbook consists of three Introductory Articles on subjects of great importance to preachers.

'Whether we like it or not, our way of life is becoming increasingly scientific.' The truth of that statement cannot be denied by any intelligent student of the modern scene, but how few of us—especially the older of us—let this truth fully influence our preaching ministry. In introducing the Warrack Lectures for 1953 (*Preaching in a Scientific Age*), Dr A. C. Craig tells us that, early in his ministry, a theological professor said to him, 'Preaching is not difficult, man; it's impossible!' This 'bracing hint to a callow preacher' should certainly remind us of the new demands which are made on the preacher in a scientific age. Much wise counsel is needed by the modern preacher as he prepares himself to face congregations which, to an increasing degree, consist of people whose thinking and daily work are conditioned by the tremendous advance of pure and applied science. The author of the article on 'Science and the Preacher' is Dr Charles A. Coulson, the Rouse Ball professor of Mathematics in the University of Oxford, and he is well qualified to write on this subject. Outstanding both as preacher, lecturer, and scientist, Professor Coulson has already made many valuable contributions to the thought of the Church, and every reader of this Handbook is advised to study and re-study what he has written for their guidance.

English-speaking preachers throughout the world are deeply indebted to Dr W. Edwin Sangster, and in particular for his books which deal in such masterly fashion with the preacher, his task and his message. I have often heard him speak to preachers about the folly and tragedy of 'marginal preaching', and he himself never seems to indulge in either marginal preaching or marginal thinking. His previous contributions to *The Preacher's Handbook* had as their titles 'The Gospel Message' and 'I Believe in Preaching'; again, in his present article, 'A Plea for Practical Preaching', his message is both central and challenging. I imagine that very few of us, as we read it, will not have a sense of personal guilt in this matter. How often we have committed the sin of vagueness! How often, as we have concluded our sermons, we have ignored that question which comes from the eager inquirer, 'How, preacher? How?'! How often we have failed really to be effective in our preaching because we have forgotten that 'doctrines must be preached practically, and duties doctrinally'! If every reader puts Dr Sangster's counsel into practice, there will be a vast uneasiness among the dark angels, for more and more people, as they go home after divine worship, will be saying to themselves: 'Now I know what I must be and do, and *how*. Now I know what to believe, and *how* to translate my belief into Christian behaviour.'

In 1954, the Methodist Conference published a new lectionary of Scripture lessons for use in public worship, authorizing its use for a trial period of two years. It is an ironic fact that most of the preachers of the Church which has the greatest need of such a lectionary ignore or almost ignore it! In Methodism—and in many of the smaller nonconformist chapels—the Sunday Services are conducted by at least ten, and in its rural circuits by more than twenty different preachers each quarter, in the latter case the majority being Local Preachers. In such circumstances, if every preacher chooses his own lessons, a large number of familiar Bible passages will be read again and again in the course of a few years, but whole areas of the Bible will be completely ignored. Now and then I preach in country chapels, and I have often noticed how soiled and worn are certain pages of the pulpit Bible, but how significantly unsoiled are most of them. It is a matter of real urgency that the case for the widespread use of an authorized lectionary should be strongly presented, and this has been done by Mr Russell Clegg, in his article on 'The Preacher and the Lectionary'. Mr Clegg belongs to that 'glorious company' of schoolmasters who are also Local Preachers. He writes as an authority on this subject, for he has taken a keen interest in Church Lectionaries for a number of years. He frankly answers the familiar arguments against the use of a lectionary, makes out a strong case for its widespread use, and at the same time offers valuable suggestions for the improvement of our present forms of public worship.

Part Two is quite different in subject-matter from the central section of previous Handbooks. In the first four volumes, the

Study Articles dealt with the great doctrines which are preached during the chief Festivals of the Christian Year—Advent, the Incarnation, the Cross, the Resurrection, the Ascension and the Holy Spirit—and also with the preacher's message on other special Sundays. In future issues, *Part Two* will be devoted to general Study Articles which will provide the preacher with much preaching material.

In this Handbook, the first Study Article is concerned with 'The Life and Work of Moses' and is written by J. Yeoman Muckle. He occupies the A. S. Peake chair in Old Testament Language and Literature at Hartley-Victoria College, Manchester, and he contributed a short Preacher's Commentary on *Genesis* 1–11 to the previous Handbook. The importance of the work of Moses, both to Judaism and to Christianity, is being re-emphasized by modern scholars, and Mr Muckle reminds us that 'the account of the life and work of Moses set out in the Pentateuch provides material of the highest value for the preacher'. From *Exodus* to *Deuteronomy* we are dealing with what is 'fundamentally history', and though we need not accept as 'literal history' all the details of the story, even the later additions, which express the religious experience and convictions of a later age, are not without religious value. The author then studies the work of Moses as prophet, leader, and law-giver, and shows how great a contribution to the life of his people, and to our life, has been made by this great man who, in all things, was guided and empowered by Yahweh, the Living God of Israel.

At a time when preachers are being urged to return to the classical form of preaching, that of Biblical exposition, it is imperative that all possible help should be given to them as they strive to understand the timeless and always relevant truth of the Word of God. It is to provide such help that two series of Commentaries for Preachers are now being produced: the massive *Interpreter's Bible*, published in 12 volumes by the Abingdon-Cokesbury Press, U.S.A.; the smaller (and cheaper) *Epworth Preacher's Commentaries*, of which three volumes are already available—*Romans* by Dr Vincent Taylor, *Amos, Hosea, and Micah* by Dr Norman H. Snaith, and *Mark* by Dr C. Leslie Mitton. Another kind of book for the expository preacher is being written. Its purpose is to give him a deeper understanding of those great key words and phrases of the Bible which he must use whenever he expounds the Scripture. What may be called the 'prototype' of this sort of book is G. Kittel's *Theologisches Worterbuch zum Neuen Testament*,

selections from which are now available in an English translation.
A Theological Word Book of the Bible (ed. Alan Richardson) is
an indispensable book of reference for the preacher, and I strongly
recommend it. Many students who are already deeply indebted
to William Barclay's excellent devotional commentaries, are also
using *A New Testament Wordbook* by the same author. It is to
give more help of this kind to preachers that 'Great Words of the
Gospels for Preachers' has been written by George A. E. Corn-
forth, a minister in the Richmond and Barnes Circuit. In examining the key words of the Gospels, he first deals, and at some length,
with the Kingdom of God, the central theme in Jesus's message,
and with thirteen other 'great words' in the Synoptic Gospels.
He then studies four phrases which are at the heart of the message
of *John*, and the seven great 'I am's' of that Gospel. This is no
mere academic exercise. The writer carefully selects and examines
the texts which, taken together, reveal the full meaning of each
word, lights up that meaning with apt illustrations and well-
chosen quotations, and shows how relevant that meaning is to
the needs of today and (therefore) to the message of the preacher.

The author of 'An Outline of Church History' is Norman P.
Goldhawk, tutor in Church History and History of Doctrine at
Richmond College. In this Handbook, he shows us 'the broad
sweep of events' of the Church's life, from its beginning down to
'the high Middle Ages'; he has promised, in our next issue, to
deal with the modern period, from the Reformation to today. In
this article, he first shows the significance of the fact that the
Church was born within the great Roman Empire, and that it
had a Jewish background and heritage. Then, in masterly fashion,
and using a broad brush, he paints the picture of the Church's
life (1) during the first three centuries (the 'Martyr Period'),
(2) after Constantine, and into the 'Dark Ages', and (3) from
AD 950-1350. He concludes with a brief study of Monasticism.
Under his expert guidance, we shall appreciate the significance
of the Church's successes and failures in the crises of its history;
we shall also better understand the great personalities of the
Church whom we meet in this brief survey, because we shall be
able more exactly to 'place' them in their true context. The reader's
one complaint will be that he will have to wait until 1959 for the
completion of this most helpful outline.

Preachers who have never worked in, or even visited, the
'Kingdom Overseas' may be tempted to avoid preaching missionary sermons. This is playing into the hands of the Devil! Nor is

it enough for the 'home' preacher to deliver an occasional sermon whose purpose is to remind his hearers of our work in what we used to call 'the foreign field'. The work of the Church, at home and abroad, is *one*, just as the world is *one*. The motive that inspires Home Missions and Overseas Missions is identical; our Gospel is for all or none. This has been brought home to us in the Report on 'The Missionary Obligation of the Church' which was presented to the 1955 Conference. The Secretary of the commission which prepared this report, N. Allen Birtwhistle, has written the next article, and under that same title. He entered the ministry after seven years as a lay missionary in Nigeria. During the past sixteen years, he has done splendid work in the fields of publicity and missionary education as the Home Organization secretary of the Methodist Missionary Society. Taking the Report as his text, the author brilliantly develops its main themes. He challenges us with the vision of the Church on the move in a changing world, proclaiming God's final word to humanity and in God's chosen way. What he has written will inspire many sermons, and his excellent illustrations will often be quoted—appropriately, I hope!

Part Three again contains two brief Commentaries for Preachers. That on '*Isaiah* 40–55' is written by Garfield Wade, now of Bournemouth. This is his second contribution to a Handbook, and by his present study of the message of Isaiah of Babylon he again places every reader in debt to him. He first explains the political context in which Isa 40–48 and 49–55 were written, and summarizes the message of the prophet about his contemporaries, God and the Servant. In the Commentary itself, he does not expound the meaning of each section, but concentrates on the most important passages in this sublime prophetic book, giving particular attention to Isa 40 and 53. Can a preacher faithfully proclaim the Gospel as he expounds an Old Testament text? Mr Wade convincingly answers that question. He starts from a word of Second-Isaiah, in a few sentences brings us into the presence of Christ, and then to the modern scene; thus he shows us how the faith and promises of Isa 40–55, deepened and ful- filled in Christ, meet the desperate needs of man today. He quotes from the two Jowetts, W. Russell Maltby, H. H. Farmer, George Adam Smith, L. P. Jacks, C. R. North and A. E. Whitham; and most effectively.

The New Testament Commentary is on '*John* 1–4', by Owen

E. Evans, tutor in N. T. Language and Literature in Hartley-Victoria College, Manchester, and he has made a special study of the Fourth Gospel. After noting the most helpful modern books on *John*, he briefly summarizes his convictions as to the person and purpose of the evangelist. In the Commentary, he amply justifies the claim that this Gospel is pre-eminently 'the preacher's Gospel'. He does not deal with these four chapters verse by verse, losing those who follow him in a maze of critical and exegetical trivialities; he is writing for preachers, not for potential B.D.s! He divides his material into nine substantial sections, and devotes two or more pages to each of them. In his expositions, he concentrates on the main preaching themes of each passage, thus providing us with an almost embarrassing number of sermon suggestions. In every paragraph, he impresses on us the truth that Christ is indeed the Way, the only Way, along which men may rise from earth to heaven. To quote Mr Evans: 'As a result of the Incarnation, Ministry, Death, and Resurrection of Jesus, "Jacob's ladder" is now "pitched betwixt heaven and Charing Cross"—and every other corner of the earth as well.'

Here it is then—*Number Five*—and may it help you more effectively and fervently to offer Christ to all as sufficient Saviour and sovereign Lord, and to Him be all the glory!

GREVILLE P. LEWIS

CONTENTS

---

1. Science and the Preacher

By PROFESSOR C. A. COULSON, M.A., PH.D., F.R.S.

WHETHER we like it or not, our way of life is becoming increasingly scientific. Yet relatively few of us who preach, whether ministerial or lay, have any professional scientific training. There is little wonder that we feel confused about the part that science should play in our preaching. We know that science affects all parts of the community with its gadgets and its inventions: we know too that the influence of these discoveries spills over from our 'doing' to our 'thinking', so that Professor Oppenheimer was quite right to say at the beginning of his Reith lectures for the BBC a few years ago: 'Science has changed not only the things men do, but also the way men think about themselves and the world.' So also was Sir Francis Simon, professor of physics in Oxford, when he wrote in a recent book, *The Neglect of Science*, that 'in the last resort our world is moulded by science'. We may perhaps wish to modify the first few words of this remark, but there is certainly a sufficient degree of truth in what he wrote for us to feel that this situation ought somehow to affect our preaching. Must ideas like those of atomic energy, automation, the expanding universe, the physical basis of life and personality, figure nowhere in our sermons? They certainly are part of the background of our congregation's thinking; and if the Word of God has got no relevance to the new ways of life and thought which science is provoking, then the Word of God will seem almost totally irrelevant to the younger and more thoughtful generation.

Most of us would agree with this, even though we are so uncertain about the way that we should behave in relation to it. It may be well, therefore, to begin by reminding ourselves of some of the mistakes which those of us who go into the pulpit are most tempted to make. After that we can turn to the more positive side, and consider the attitude and type of approach which seem to be most necessary, if we are to 'play fair' with this new and exciting influence.

Our first temptation is to pay no attention to science. I have already stressed the dominating influence of science in our behaviour and our background of thought. To neglect it entirely in our preaching, even if we have no specialist scientific knowledge, is therefore to fail to do justice to an important part of human life. The Christian Church has always been tempted to try to escape the painful thinking which any great change in a people's way of life makes ultimately inescapable, and our Christian tradition in the last 150 years has too often encouraged us to flee from the implications of the Industrial Revolution into a form of pietism. I do not wish to deny the value of true pietism: but I do believe that the Christian Church, and the Christian preacher, have to enter the painful process of rethinking their attitude towards an increasingly complex industrial set-up. To leave aside from our preaching any reference to science and technology is to back out of that responsibility.

A second temptation, particularly for those who are ignorant of science, is to see its bad effects—on society and in the matter of peace and war—and to belittle it, to pour scorn on it, to deride it. A few weeks ago I was invited to speak to a group of preachers about Science and the Christian doctrine of Creation. In the discussion which followed, one preacher got up and said that it seemed to him that the Church should denounce science as being the fountain-head of materialism, and for being so impersonal that it could not be other than alien to the ways of a personal God. Another preacher got up to say that, since science is only concerned with what you can weigh or measure, it cannot be of much interest to the Christian. Now as a matter of fact neither of these two assertions is true. For example, to say that science is only concerned with the measurable is to miss nearly all the excitement of discovery, always a creative act; and in any case the most significant single scientific notion of the nineteenth century—the theory of evolution—is not really measurable at all. Nor are most of the fundamental particles of modern physics, such as the electron and neutron; yet we believe in them, and out of them we construct atomic bombs and nuclear energy reactors. What matters in science is form and symmetry and pattern, just as much as fact. This means that the old charge of rank materialism is quite out of date, and we ought not to use it. Indeed we shall see later that the element of materialism in science is something for which we should be grateful. For we must never forget that ours is an incarnational faith. God was translated into human terms, accepted those very conditions of hot and cold, hunger and thirst whose nature science seeks to understand. Christians above all others ought to concern themselves with the material order, since it is God's creation, and becomes sacramental, mediating God to us according to its power. We may remember some words of the historian of science, Georges Sartan: 'Most people know science only by its technical achievements, and are unaware of its intrinsic beauty and of the beauty which it extracts from the bosom of Nature.' I am prepared to say that, unless science helps us to understand the universe in which we live, we can never understand the real, deep, full meaning of the Incarnation. Never let us say that Science is the Devil's trump card. No one would be better pleased than the Devil!

The third of our temptations in the misuse of science is to try to parcel out human experience into those elements which are spiritual and Christian, on the one hand, and those which we can give over to science, on the other hand. This is, of course, merely the old division into sacred and secular, which has done so much harm to the faith. It is fatally easy to say that science will rule and regulate in certain parts from the sum total of human experience, and religion in the others—rather like the way in which we used to colour some parts of the earth's surface red on our maps of the world, and then say that the British Empire had authority in the red areas, and other governments in the rest. This particular mistake has a hoary past, and can be traced right back into history for about as long as the Christian has tried to give an apologia for his faith. But it fails. The chief reason for its failure is that it is only in a world that is static and dead that you can put a hedge between one part of a man's experience and another part. You cannot say: 'Thus far science, and after that religion' or 'science can explain some things, but there are others that it cannot explain, and it is here that religion comes in'. For if you plant that hedge, it will not be long before science discovers something new, and the hedge has got to be uprooted and transplanted somewhere else. Whatever we may say about science, it is alive and growing, and it is daily extending the compass of its control and understanding. The rate of increase of scientific knowledge is almost frightening, and should warn us against the mistake of supposing that there are any fixed boundaries. For example, in every twelve months professional chemists publish no less than 100,000 scientific articles in the chemical journals, describing their new results. This means that each year there are at least 100,000 pieces of chemical research sufficiently advanced and perfected to be worth publication. In the whole field of science the figure is probably at least a million. And each one of these may take a man three years of research: it may even be a monograph of fifty or more pages of writing, tightly packed with information. It is staggering to contrast this with the amount discovered in other branches of human knowledge. I myself had the good fortune to be educated at school in the classics, but I have now very little hesitation in saying that the scientific period in which we are living utterly transcends anything that this world has known before—and in no other period of time has there been any human activity with such scope and variety and such daring quality of thought as in the scientific thinking of today. If this is so, it cannot be kept within bounds. We can no longer tolerate the gentlemen's agreement of the latter half of the nineteenth century, that each party shall keep off the grass that belongs to the other. Some of us would say that we did not particularly want any such agreement. For if this earth is God's earth, then His glory is to be found in every part of it, and we shall not be playing fair with science unless we admit that it is, in some sense, a revelation of God. Then we shall see that the temptation to parcel out human experience into sacred and secular is an insult to the majesty of God. It is not surprising that the gentlemen's agreement is unworkable and has failed. For sacred and secular are two words which we ought to hesitate before using together in the same sentence.

And now to the *last of our possible mistakes*. Instead of decrying science, it is an easy temptation to use it for our own purposes. I am thinking of the way in which, when someone has made a scientific discovery which we think we can make use of, we pounce upon it and cite it as evidence for the Christian faith. I believe this is a dangerous thing to do. The reason for this belief is not merely that scientific theories change with time, so that in a few years we may find our foundations pulled away from under us; for although theories do change, the changes are nothing like so dramatic and revolutionary as many people would believe. The real reason is that, because science is a way of talking about things, it has its own field of working, its own language, its own thought-forms, its own concepts; and we must be careful not to mix concepts from one way of talking with concepts appropriate to another.

Let me illustrate what I mean. A little while ago, at the World Methodist Conference in America, one of the speakers was talking about science: and he used an argument that a good many others have used. His intention was to show that science had not really disproved the existence of free-will. Most of us will remember the old type of argument often brought against the Christian, to the effect that if only there were some super-mathematician, who could write down the equations that govern the movement of all the many atoms of which our universe is composed, and could then solve them, he would be able to foresee the future. Determinism of that kind would rule out all free-will, or human decision; and one chief plank in the Christian edifice would be removed. Now it happens that there are logical objections even to the proposal which I have just outlined—no one can ever describe absolutely everything in a universe of which he who describes is himself a part. But let us disregard this point and pass to the main argument. In the late 1920s, Professor Heisenberg in Germany showed that there were certain hitherto unsuspected difficulties in measuring, not the positions of all the atoms in the universe, but the position and the velocity of any one of them. In its baldest terms, if we think of an atom as a very tiny particle, then we can never know exactly where it is and how fast it is going. There is an essential imprecision about all measurement, and this imprecision is inherent in nature: it is not the fault of our measuring instruments. It followed from all this that strict determinism was quite impossible, for if you could not measure the position and velocity of one single atom at this present moment, how could you hope to predict its later behaviour? Christians were not slow to welcome this Uncertainty Principle, and some of them hailed it as a gift from God in the fight against atheistic scientists! How foolish they were! This is not because the Uncertainty Principle has been abandoned—for it has not—but because this principle really says nothing at all about free-will. Without trying to become too technical, what it does is to warn us that if we try to represent an atom as if it were a tiny billiard ball, we shall run into the trouble of not being able simultaneously to say where it is and where it is going. It suggests to us that perhaps it is not completely adequate to represent an atom in this way, and that some other model may do better. In short, the Uncertainty Principle sends us back to think much more deeply and imaginatively about our science; and the words of a well-known physicist are totally irrelevant, that 'the electron leads us to the gateway of religion'.

I have dwelt on this particular illustration at some length because it has figured so much in discussions of this type. Determinism may or may not be 'disproved', according as you do or do not 'accept' the particle account of an atom. It belongs to the concepts and ideas and language of science. But free-will is a concept that belongs to my own personal experience of myself. I am never really aware of your free-will, but only of my own. Let us be careful, therefore, how we use ideas in one field of experience to support conclusions in another.

There is another aspect of this particular illustration which links it with my previous temptation to allot a region to science and another region to religion. The writer of a book a little while ago was anxious to show that science allowed room for God within its world; and he fell back on the same Uncertainty Principle. If it is true, he said, that we can never know the exact motion of a particle, then by deft touches here and there God can alter, or adjust, its motion in such a way that we, with our human limitations of measurement, will never be able to detect. So God can intervene in life without scientific laws being broken. If you could accept this kind of argument, you would soon come to accept any kind of miracle as not really anti-scientific at all. But my point is that a God who is kindly permitted to come into our human experience in this slippery fashion is more like a little mouse scuttling in and out along the wainscoting and escaping us whenever we look too closely at him, than the God of the Old Testament or the New. If the only basis on which we can talk about God's activity is the loophole left when the Uncertainty Principle has told us all it can, then we deny the glory and the majesty of God. The Christian does not really need to be some sort of suppliant, timidly begging for any available crumbs at the laboratory back door. Let us not preach about science like this.

It is time to turn to something more positive. What are we to say about science as we preach? It may help us to have in mind some mixed congregation. In the front there a few elderly ladies who do not and never will know much of the technicalities of science, except human biology. In the middle are some professional people, perhaps including a few scientists: in the gallery or at the back are a few apprentices, very full of their recently acquired ability to use a lathe and understand a radio circuit diagram. These latter are going to be pretty sceptical, and rather critical, and if we pretend to a scientific knowledge which we do not possess, the old ladies may not spot it, but they will. The professional people may look down a little condescendingly upon our attempts to appear more knowledgeable than we are, but the apprentices will quite frankly have no use for us whatever. Like many of their predecessors they will leave the Church. Here at any rate the golden rule is: do not try to preach what you do not really know. This is one reason why what is sometimes called the 'scientific sermon' has only a rather limited role. Quite clearly we shall be obliged to talk in relatively general terms. A church sermon is not for a university student's study circle.

I grow increasingly certain that the best place to begin is precisely where the Book of *Genesis* begins, by asserting that this is God's universe, so that as we study it in whatever way we can, we are in fact studying God. Such an approach cuts right away from the unhappy division into sacred and secular that we considered earlier. This implies that every scientific study, whether physics, chemistry, geology, or medicine, is a kind of description of God. It may be that we do not yet see in detail how these various descriptions fit together, for each of them is partial in the sense that any photograph of a person is partial, leaving out all that could be seen in the many other photographs that could be taken from different angles and different distances: but until we claim that the 'whole show' is His, I do not see how we are going to tackle the major problems of new thought today. Such a claim is not new. As early as the thirteenth century, at the very dawn of science, St Thomas Aquinas could say that when we consider what God has made, we catch a glimpse of the divine likeness which has expressed a certain image of itself upon the created world.

The complete image of God is too big to be comprehended within any one such glimpse; there is more of God than we shall ever see in the natural order; but let us not be afraid to say that this natural order does mediate God to His children. Ours is a deeply sacramental faith, not just in the conventional sense of that phrase, but in the wider sense: 'Raise the stone and thou shalt find Me, cleave the wood and I am there.' We shall never come to terms with science except within that framework. But with it we shall not be tempted any more to reject science, for we shall see it as one of the modes of God's revelation. And we shall be prepared to understand Paul's great phrase about God's intention 'to sum up all things in Christ, both things on earth and things in heaven'. It is things, earthy things and not spiritual people, of whom Paul is writing here.

One corollary of this is that there ought to be some aspects of God which are properly revealed only in science, and that therefore God will not be fully known until He is recognized in a fully developed science. The professional man in the middle of the Church will appreciate this. But both he and the young apprentice will look for an example. For myself I should claim that atomic and nuclear physics had shown me, as nothing else could, what is meant by the words 'Almighty God'. We use them at the beginning of about half our prayers, but if the physicist had never told me how, as I looked into the evening sky and counted the stars, every one of which was a burning sun like our own, I was watching God stoking his giant fires—and the light and the heat from one of them gave me life—I should never have known what the word Almighty really meant. Or again, I should never have known what the 'Ancient of Days' could mean, if I had not been taught something about the pattern and scale of the universe, and that I must learn to think in light-years, if I would do justice to all this splendour. Indeed I should not even recognize the full implications of the first chapter of *Genesis* without science. How odd it is that this should have been considered one of the stumbling-blocks, when the true fact is that, thanks to the scientist, creation has taken on a far more luminous aspect than ever before! I do not think the elderly ladies in the front pews will make much of all this; but never mind.

The second positive point is more practical. We believe that we are in this earth to redeem it, and to express its redemption in the pattern of human relationship and human life. It follows that the task of converting this earth into something more closely resembling the Kingdom of Heaven is an undoubted Christian responsibility. Such a task needs all the technological ability and 'know-how' that we possess. Technology and invention—which grow out of scientific knowledge—are the indispensable tools of the Kingdom.

Two or three years ago I travelled to Japan by air. As I flew over South-east Asia in one of the ill-fated Comets, I looked down from a height of some eight miles. I could see 300 miles in each direction. I could view the unending forests, and the jungles ravaged by malaria and the tsetse fly; I could trace the great delta of the Ganges and the sparse habitation of man, an occasional little rudimentary village. There came over me an enormous feeling that here is some indication of the size and scope of our Christian job—the job which we share with others, but in which we ought not to be behind. We have got to make that part of the earth habitable, so that malaria and cholera no longer ravage it. We have got to build there something of the same order as our western civilization, but without its evils. We have got to see that there should no longer be two-thirds of the world's population who must live in a condition of under-nourishment, surrounded by squalor, ignorance, misery, and death, and having an average age of life only a bare half of our own. To put this right is a task of unbelievable scope and grandeur: to do it properly will call forth from us the best that we have—of science, atomic energy, automation, machinery, and all other technological equipment. In a phrase used shortly before his death, the American Senator MacMahon spoke of his hope for the future, and of the time when even the grisly forces of hydrogen fusion could be used creatively, and he said that before that could be true, we needed dedicated men, dedicated scientists and technologists in taking over this kind of development, and putting it within the Christian framework. We are showing the young apprentice at the back of the church that his lathe is part of the armoury of God's kingdom, and his understanding of radio circuit diagrams an essential element in building that kingdom.

So let us say that the houses men live in, and not just the people who live in them, are of concern to God; and the food men eat and not just the men who do the eating, are offerings for His glory. Until we can give our young people some vision that the discoveries of science and technology are to be used in a holy and sacred fashion, we shall have left a major part of the background of their working life unrelated to our church worship. A little science may lead away from God. But more science leads back to Him, and is needed to fulfil His commanding purpose. It is not accidental that ever since the fifth century BC the doctors have subscribed to a Hippocratic oath, and that every version of that oath, from the first pagan one of the Greeks down to the latest post-war one of the World Medical Association, is essentially religious. The same kind of inner feeling inspires the scientist, though there is no corresponding scientific oath. I sometimes feel that, if only we could relate our Christian faith in this way to the needs of the world and the practical skill of ordinary people in factories and workshops, we might be able to sweep up and canalize this deep desire for human betterment, which runs right through the scientific movement of today.

The last point to make concerns the professional man near the middle of the church. He may be a lawyer, or a teacher, or an accountant, but from the nature of his training he knows how to think. It is to this that I want to appeal. For if Christ is the Lord of all life, He is Lord of the mind; and so whenever we see true and genuine thinking, we are seeing something of Him and His Spirit. Now it is one of the glories of our Christian faith that we have asserted its rationality: we believe that despite all its imperfections, the human mind can understand something about God. Quite clearly there are many other different ways of knowing God, but that is no excuse for neglecting this particular way. And at a time like the present, when many people are tempted to distrust the mind, it is important that we should be able to emphasize our belief in rationality. I believe that within the scientific movement there is something of great value in this respect. No one who knows anything of some of the larger scientific theories—such as the atomic theory, nuclear theory, genetics, evolution—will be disposed to disagree with Dr J. B. Conant, at one time President of Harvard and later U.S. High Commissioner in Germany, when he said of these great conceptual schemes of modern science, that 'they were fit to be compared with the Parthenon of Ancient Greece, and the great Gothic cathedrals of the Middle Ages, as witnesses to the flowering of the human mind'. In its passion for truth, in its vivid use of the imagination, and in its capacity for sustained thinking, I believe there is nothing in the whole of human history that is to be compared with the last fifty years of science. If this is so, it is something for the glory of God.

This is a time when we often hear the phrases: 'Haven't a clue', 'Couldn't care less'. I believe we ought to be profoundly grateful that a group of people as universal as the scientists can hold the traditions, and do the thinking, that I have described: and I believe that it is in the mercy and providence of God that all this has happened. It underlines something which I believe to be important, and with which I shall conclude. This attempt of science to make a meaningful pattern out of nature is at rock bottom a religious activity. If indeed we are understanding the nature of God as we see it expressed in our surroundings, then our science is a work of holiness. So also the attitudes of mind that go with it—reverence for the created things that the scientist studies, zeal for truth, patience and humility before scientific laws which he did not make and to which he is subject—these are essentially religious. God moves in mysterious ways, and the scientific movement of today may be one of the ways in which He has kept before the human race the value of clear, straight, honest thinking. This does not mean that the scientist is the only High Priest of the new order. For his insight into the nature of God is only one of the many insights that are vouchsafed to human minds, and the artist, the poet, the historian and the man of letters each have their contribution to make. What it does mean is that we want scientists to join with us in our search for the truth that liberates. So our attitude to them should not be one of conflict, but of co-operation: we make a mistake in ever speaking of a supposed conflict between science and religion. How can there be a fundamental conflict, if science is one element in the fullness of religion? If indeed all things are to be summed up in Christ, then the work of the laboratories is a part of that purpose, and Christ Himself must shine not only in the eyes of those who label themselves Christians, but—though sometimes as in a glass darkly—even in the eyes of some who do not openly know Him. So it seems that our attitude of mind must be much more open than it has sometimes been, prepared to recognize that scientists will see things rather differently from ourselves, but that they can help us to understand the grandeur and the mystery of Him whom we worship. Conversely, we may be able to help them to open their eyes so that they can see that there are other thought-forms than their own. We are in this together. It was Max Planck, one of the most distinguished German physicists of the last fifty years, who put it in these words: 'Science and faith are fighting a joint battle against scepticism and against dogmatism . . . and the rallying cry in this great crusade is, and always has been "On to God".' Or, as Einstein said about his work in the last years of his life, 'Our chief business is to set God properly in the centre of science'.

Preaching which avoids the errors that I described at the beginning, and follows the principles which I have just explained, may not make many converts. But it will be a reconciling ministry, which will satisfy the thoughtful members of our congregations, helping them to see the total oneness in all experience and will help the technician to see his work in a new light. This indeed is one of the many functions of our preaching the Word of God.

2. A Plea for Practical Preaching:
How to 'Earth' Our Message

By the Rev. Dr W. Edwin Sangster, M.A.

So much preaching ends in the air. The people do not know what the preacher was after and sometimes doubt if the preacher himself knows. The sermon concludes and the congregation disperses, but with no clear idea of what has to be done about the topic the preacher has discussed.

I

How does it happen that this vagueness hangs over the con-cluston of many sermons and leaves the people with no practical tasks to be performed?

1. In some instances, no doubt, for the reason the people themselves suspect.

Because the message has not been thoroughly thought out.

Because it has not aimed to do one clear thing. Because the structure was not taut, and clear, and firm. Because the end was not clearly in view from the start. Because, in preparation, the preacher gave a disproportionate amount of time to the earlier part of the sermon and was driven to scamp his conclusion.

All this amounts to saying that he himself did not really know what he was after; and how, then, could he make the people know? The suspicions of the people were well founded. They did not know the practical conclusions because *he* did not know them. The man who aims at nothing in particular will hit it every time.

2. In other instances, the preacher *does* know what he is after—*but in a vague way*. He is certain that 'all problems are solved in Christ', and that an 'outpouring of the Holy Spirit is our great need', and that 'we have to go forward and upward'.

But what do those phrases amount to, when honestly examined in the keen mind of a business man?

In his heart, the business man says: 'So what?' If Christ is the answer, how does He work in this present practical world? If we need an outpouring of the Holy Spirit, what are the plain conditions laid down in the Bible by which He may come in power? If we have to go forward and upward, may we know precisely what it is that we have to go forward and upward *to—and how?*

Discerning writers on homiletics have long known that the neglected word in preaching is the word *how*. No amount of eloquence is a substitute for plainness in a conclusion. 'Though I speak with the tongues of men and of angels and have not *clarity*, I am become as a sounding brass or a tinkling cymbal.'

It is a hard task as we shall see in a moment—and harder with some types of sermons than others—but a preacher should steadily hold before himself the ambition of sending away his hearers saying quietly to themselves: 'This is what I have to do.'

3. Still other sermons come to a vague conclusion, not because the preacher does not know what he is after, and not because he could not put it into plain and practical terms if he wished, but he is hindered by a disinclination to expose his heart in public on matters that are private by their very nature.

There is a healthy reticence in most men of spiritual sensitivity against displaying the secrets of their souls in public. They feel that their intercourse with God is a very personal thing. If a man has no close communion with God, well . . . , he has nothing to hide; but if a man has a deep and secret devotional life, he may rightly fear to display spiritual pride, or claim an intimacy with God he does not possess, or pose as an expert on the spiritual life when he knows himself to be but a beginner.

All this is healthy and humble.

But there is a kind of spiritual reticence which is not healthy and humble, and which can militate against the purposes of God in our lives. How loath Christian people are to talk to one another, for instance, about their methods in private prayer. How hesitant preachers are—even with their fellow preachers—to pass on any technique they have learned in aiding God to subdue the sin in their souls. They are all pilgrims of time to eternity, with a serious responsibility to help one another to heaven, and yet this dumbness is common and men conceal the most important thing they know as though it were a guilty secret.

No wonder, then, that the silence extends to the pulpit as well, and many sermons are preached, e.g. on the importance of prayer, or on the necessity of imitating Christ, or on the duty of outwitting temptation, or on the privilege of being filled with Divine Love . . . but the *how* of it is barely touched. The more successful the sermon is in establishing the necessity of any of these important things, the more sharp is the disappointment of the congregation when it ends without the preacher getting down to ways and means. Every intelligent and heart-warmed hearer is saying in his heart: 'How, Preacher? How? How do I learn to love prayer? How imitate my Lord? How outwit the Devil? How open myself to the Divine Love? How?'

No man can answer those mute questions without drawing on his own spiritual experience. If he has little experience to draw upon, he may wonder how he became a preacher at all, but if (as is almost certainly the case) he has learned many things of his Lord through the years, he must overcome his shyness and tell it out.

He need not always put it into the first person. Much that he has learned, he has found also in the practice of the saints (and may, indeed, have learned it from them) and he can step behind a great name as he sets it forth. 'It was a custom of Fletcher of Madeley . . .'; 'St Teresa tells us . . .'; 'In the Journal of Henry Martyn . . .'; but his power to select the particular reference, and his glowing heart in telling it, will tell his people more than he knows. 'Our minister knows that also,' they will feel.

At other times he must be most plain. 'I have found in my own life . . .' So he exposes his heart and, in fulfilment of his solemn responsibilities as an under-shepherd of the flock, tells them all he knows: presses forward himself on the way to heaven and beckons and enheartens them as he goes.

He cannot say everything he knows. No one—not even the saint—is able to put into plain words all the secret intercourse of God with his soul. But it is important to say, when God directs, as much as we can. It is not easy, but it is most necessary. The omission of these practical aids in preaching is a common and serious defect of the modern pulpit and gives an 'airy-fairy' conclusion to many sermons which should have come out sharp and clear and challenging.

Let a young preacher in his sermon preparation—especially when he is dealing with ethical sermons (holding up a virtue for emulation, or denouncing some vice to his people's face)—let him pin up the word HOW in front of him, and let him count that sermon unfinished until he has wrought out in himself, and in his prayer-thought with God, all that he can say under that. 'This is the way forward . . .'. 'I suggest that you do this and this . . .'.

Of such a man it may be confidently affirmed that, as his skill grows, the people will never disperse after worship saying in bewilderment: 'How does he expect us to achieve all that?'

II

It will be said, however, by some who have followed me until now that certain sermons cannot possibly have a practical conclusion and it would be frank to admit that with some of them it is hard.

Doctrinal sermons, for instance. What practical conclusion, it may be asked, follows from a well-wrought sermon on the Deity of Christ, or the Doctrine of Assurance, or the element of truth in Predestination?

The word 'practical' has not to be interpreted too narrowly. A new, healthy, positive way of thinking is a practical thing: in some circumstances the most practical thing of all.

But perhaps the most important thing here to remember is the dictum of the early Protestant theologians that doctrines must be preached practically and duties doctrinally.

It would be hard to exaggerate the deep wisdom of that dictum. The sad hiatus that has come between duties and doctrine explains many of the unhappy features of modern life. The absence of sound doctrine has reduced religion in the mind of many people to some vague sentimentalism which you can have or not have according to the fancy of the moment. God, if He can be said to exist in their mind at all, is an upright blur. Jesus is an archaic name, slightly embarrassing. Talk about the Holy Spirit is as unsubstantial to them as talk about 'spooks'. Incarnation, atonement, and grace are meaningless counters they cannot intelligently exchange, and nothing in all the realm of ideas seems related to the duties of daily life.

Not understanding doctrine, the duties of daily life have no real basis in reality for these people. Morality is convention. If, under duress, they connect it with God at all, they do so with hesitation and confusion. If they have tried to think the matter through, they have concluded that 'morals' are what people in time past have found socially convenient, but they have no real and ultimate sanction. At a pinch, they can be jettisoned. Tired of the same face over the breakfast table, you can go off with someone else. If what has proved socially convenient in time past proves now to be personally inconvenient, well . . you need not be held by it. Nothing has eternal meaning. 'What's right or wrong but thinking makes it so?'

So think the way you like! Let changing desire be your erratic guide and recognize in your rare moments of lucidity that you are like a mariner lost on an uncharted ocean, without a compass or a rudder.

To what a pass do people come who lose a firm grasp on doctrine and whose only basis for duty is that it is 'the done thing'!

How clear it is, therefore, that doctrines and duties must be bound together, and how plain that the old dictum which required doctrines to be preached practically and duties doctrinally is deeply sound and urgently needs recovery. It holds together things which should never be put asunder. It shows duties rooted in the reality of God and doctrines underpinning the plain tasks of every day. Paul is our guide here as in so much else. Strong doctrine and plain morals are always tightly bound together by him. *Ephesians* and *Colossians* would both illustrate it. Clear Christology, a high doctrine of the Church, a strong warning against the current heresies—and it all issues at the last in 'walk worthily'. Be what you were meant to be! Live up to your new status! Sound doctrine shows you who and what you are. Let daily life confirm it!

What answer can be made to two married people involved in a guilty liaison and planning each to desert their loyal partner and advertise their incontinence and disloyalty to the world? They protest that they love each other: that their feelings for the one they promised 'to love and to cherish till death do us part' have changed: they conceive of love only as an emotion and not as a set will. What kind of argument is likely to prevail with them unless the fact of God, and the reality of God, and the will of God have been built into their nature, and unless they are made to feel that God forbids this deceitful thing and that the fiat of the Almighty is against it? What hope have we in an age of shameless theft, when many people have ceased to be sorry for stealing and only sorry to be found out . . . ? What hope have we of making them honest in the dark, unless we make God a reality to them, and prove that the difference between 'thine and mine' is embedded in His purposes and intended by Him for all people through all time?

How clear it is, then, that an awful responsibility rests upon the preacher to bind together doctrine and duty, and how plain that the doctrines must be preached practically and the duties doctrinally. 'If this dogma be true, plainly based and broadly set in the Scriptures, does it not follow as an irresistible inference that we *ought* . . .?' Or, beginning with the duty, is not the preacher under the obligation of his divine calling not merely to exhort people to the moral imperative, but to show them that it is a divine imperative too? The duty follows as a necessary inference from God's nature and His revealed will. So life takes wholeness! Human personality has meaning and eternal worth; human duties are buttressed by the commandments of the Lord of Creation, and life has unity from the Mighty God behind all things to a child struggling against the temptation to tell a lie.

But divorce those two, and there is chaos. Dogma becomes academic lumber—the dry-as-dust speculation of doctrinaires; and human duties are social conventions which we may accept or reject at our fancy. The ten commandments do not apply East of Suez, and 'scientifically' examined prove to be no more than outworn Jewish taboos! Immoral night descends upon the world and, losing grip on God, we are perilously near to losing grip on all things.

III

How, then, can a preacher 'earth' his message? He is trans-mitting the word from God, and it came to him through the Book, and through his prayer, and through his prayer-thought, and through the long experience of the Church. How can he show its day-to-day significance to men?

Let him work in the way we have suggested. When his sermon is mainly ethical in character, let him be careful to show how the high moral demand roots in the character and will of God; but when he is dealing with doctrine, or plain Bible exposition, or it is a sermon classified as 'philosophic' or 'apologetic', let him hold before his mind the special responsibility to be as practical in his conclusions as he possibly can.

There is, perhaps, no need today to warn intelligent men against laboured moralizing. 'Now the lesson of all this . . .' 'The moral I want to draw out . . .' One can still recall the extra bore-dom which spread over us as children when the preacher got to that point. One recalls, also, the little girl who said: 'Our vicar is fine: he has no morals . . .' Not many men are guilty today of those sententious 'stuck-on' conclusions which signify that all interest is now over and only the heroic can be expected to listen any more.

Moreover, this kind of moralizing is *not* the practical conclusion we are pleading for. It is usually a bit more theory and a lot more exhortation. In a practical conclusion a preacher aims to get right into the context of his hearers' lives, and shows them plain things they can do and clear things they can live on in their thinking. He is never afraid to be elementary and he hates unnecessary vagueness as he hates the devil. He does not *over-face* the people, putting upon them in any one sermon so many things to do that they cannot even remember them, much less feel exhilarated in translating them into life. And the over-all impression the people have is that the preacher is living their life with them, sensing and, indeed, experiencing their own difficulties, and sharing with them his discoveries on the road to holiness. He shows them what helps he has found in avoiding mind-wandering in prayer: how they may learn to love people they do not like: how to hold the children to religion when they enter their difficult 'teens: how to cling to God in great trouble when all things cave in: how to walk by the little light of duty when the thrill and joy of the Christian adventure fade for a while from the mind.

Now and then, no doubt, the preacher may soar above the heads of his average hearer. The rapture of religion will carry him away and he will come near to saying things that, as Paul said, it is not lawful for a man to utter.

The people will allow him that. The more spiritually mature among them will follow his flight and he will remember that the most advanced of all have outflown *him*. But he will not soar away from the people every week. A leader who leads so far ahead that he passes out of vision no longer leads.

The normal sermon will end with down-to-earth practical things for the people to do, and those who are serious in the pursuit of holiness will know the next steps they have to take.

3. The Preacher and the Lectionary

By RUSSELL CLEGG, M.A.

METHODISM has always had a lectionary, or rather two lectionaries. Wesley used and commended the lectionaries of the Book of Common Prayer, the Epistle and the Gospel of the Communion Service, still retained in our Methodist *Book of Offices* but rarely used in our churches, and the First and Second Lessons of Morning and Evening Prayer. The Table of Lessons for Morning and Evening Services has undergone changes, both in the Church of England and in Methodism, but through the years the principle of a lectionary, authorized by Conference and printed in the Epworth Press Diaries and in many Circuit Plans, has been maintained. In the past thirty years, great interest has been shown in the problem of lectionary-making and there have been a large number of experiments. New lectionaries have been adopted by the Church of England and the Church of Scotland. Two years ago our own Church published *The Methodist Church Lectionary* and this is now in use for a trial period.

But, although we have, and always have had, an authorized lectionary, there is no rule which compels preachers to read the appointed lessons, and it is true to say that the very existence of the lectionary is ignored by many, if not most, of those who lead the Services of the Church. The reason for this lies in the circumstances in which Methodism originated. As is well known, the preaching Services of Methodism were at first supplementary to those of the local parish church. It was assumed, in many cases somewhat optimistically, that on the Lord's Day good Methodists would attend Morning and Evening Prayer and the Holy Communion at their parish church, and that the evangelistic Service in the open air or in the Methodist Chapel would be an additional exercise of the Methodists in their capacity as an activist group within the Church of England. At such Methodist Services, the essential features were Wesley's hymns and the sermon. Duplication of the Scripture reading, the psalm singing and the comprehensive intercession of the parish church Services would have been unnecessary and out of place. It was not long, however, before this system broke down. Methodists ceased to go to the

parish churches, often because they found there abuse and dis-
order. Wesley endeavoured to meet the situation by ordaining
that in such circumstances the Prayer Book Services, with some
modifications, should be held in the Methodist chapels. This
plan was never wholly effective. In some places the hostility of the
people to the persecuting vicar was translated into dislike for the
forms of Service which he represented. At a later period, also,
Methodism was much influenced by Protestant Non-conformity.
Now, after two hundred years, the position is that Evening Prayer
has altogether disappeared from Methodism, and Morning Prayer
is read in only about forty of our churches. The Occasional
Offices have been retained, although with large modifications. The
Communion Service remains substantially as it was in the Prayer
Book, but in most of our churches the first part of the Service,
which contains the Scripture reading, is invariably omitted.
The final result is that, in the vast majority of our churches,
the normal Sunday Service follows a form—hymns, lesson,
extempore prayer and sermon—which was intended merely as
an evangelistic supplement to the regular acts of Christian worship, and which in its contents may fail to meet the full needs
of the spiritual life of our people. In this respect, as in some
others, Methodism has never fully faced up to the implications
of her decision to declare herself a Church in her own right, and
independent of the Church of England.

It is not to be supposed, however, that Conference was wholly
blind to what was going on. For something like one hundred
and fifty years, it continued to recommend the retention of
Morning Prayer; and the full order of the Communion Service,
including the Epistle and the Gospel, has always been printed in
the *Book of Offices*. As has been said, it was largely a forlorn hope.
The position, however, was partly met by the recommendation
that, when Morning Prayer was not read in full, at least the lessons appointed should be read. The dangers of the situation were
thus recognized, even though the steps taken to meet them were
hardly effective.

This is not, of course, the place to enter upon a full discussion
of the many problems of Methodist worship; nor is it suggested
that a wholesale return to the 'liturgical' forms of worship of
Wesley's day should be attempted. Sufficient has been written,
it is hoped, to explain the cause of the desuetude of the lectionary in most of our Services. It is true to say that many, if not
most, of our preachers regard the Scripture reading as little

more than a subsidiary of the sermon. Is it not high time that we considered afresh the problem of the use of Scripture in our Services, and, in particular, the case for the observance of the discipline of a lectionary?

A well-arranged lectionary gives the regular worshipper a wide general acquaintance with the content of the Bible. In a two-year cycle of lessons, it is possible to include the greater part of the New Testament and a wide selection of Old Testament passages. If the *Methodist Church Lectionary* is followed, each lesson is preceded by a short explanatory Introduction, which gives help in difficult places and briefly emphasizes the teaching of the passage. Those of us who take a 'high' view of the value of Scripture as the authentic Word of God must find the case for the use of a lectionary almost unanswerable. Apart from it, the choice of lessons in churches which are served by a variety of preachers is dictated by the needs of one particular Service, without reference to those which precede and follow it, and without regard to the need for comprehensiveness in the content of Scripture read. Favourite passages are repeatedly heard, but the total amount of Scripture read to the people in a year is pitifully small. The result is that our people are woefully ignorant of the Word of God. Especially is this true of the Old Testament, upon which our understanding of the Teaching of Jesus so greatly depends. Much of our preaching loses in effectiveness because our frequent references to Scripture are not understood. They are not understood because the people are unfamiliar with the passages which we quote. Much as we regret it, we must face the fact that many of our people do not read their Bibles at home. Dare we continue to leave them in ignorance of the Scriptures? They will remain ignorant so long as we leave the choice of lessons to the individual preacher. Only by the use of a lectionary can we ensure that our people get the wide general acquaintance with Scripture which is needed if they are to be built up in their holy Faith.

The 'Reading of the Word' should form an essential element in Christian Worship. In the inspired Scriptures, God speaks directly to the human mind and heart. As the sacred Word is read, the very Light of God shines into our souls. We hear in faith the very tones of the Saviour's voice. The Comfort of the Scriptures confirms us in the Christian Hope. For the instructed Christian, this part of the service is full of the richest blessing. How dreadful it is when, as so often happens, the Scripture reading is attenuated into a mere subsidiary of the sermon, without an assured place in the Service in its own right, competing unsuccessfully for worship-time with inflated announcements, 'collection voluntaries' and children's addresses which, important as they are in themselves, must be considered as derivative and therefore secondary to the reading of the Word of God!

The use of a lectionary is an antidote to the narrowing subjectivity which endangers our Methodist worship. We rightly condemn sacerdotalism but, while we eschew it in word, we tolerate it in practice. We allow the individual preacher to dominate our worship to an extent which is positively harmful to the spiritual life of our churches. The preacher chooses the hymns. He prays extempore. He chooses the lesson or lessons. The children's address and the sermon are his. The whole Service—hymns, lessons, prayers, and sermon—is often focused on a single theme of the preacher's choice. This is excellent, no doubt, for a single Service in an evangelical mission, but it is inadequate as the norm of regular worship. In these days, our congregations, for the most part, are confronted with an endless series of subjects, entirely unco-ordinated and unrelated. They simply do not add up into a complete presentation of the Christian faith. In practice, popular themes of the day are repeated by preacher after preacher, and large areas of Scripture and doctrine are utterly neglected. If all our Services found place for the appointed lessons, this excessive subjectivity in our services would be greatly mitigated, and those for whom the preacher's choice of subject was inappropriate might not go away unfed.

At this point, a few words as to the mechanism of the lectionary may not be out of place, since there will be some preachers who have no experience of its use. Although the lesson references are in the *Local Preacher's Diary*, the Epworth Press Diaries, and in the *Minutes of Conference*, it will be advisable for the preacher to procure a copy of the booklet *The Methodist Church Lectionary* (Epworth Press: 1s. 6d.). Here he will find the lessons for each Sunday in the Christian Year and for certain other great festivals (e.g. Christmas Day) and special occasions. There are two series of lessons, read in alternate years to form a two-year cycle of readings. On special occasions, these lessons are superseded by those appointed for the occasion concerned (e.g. Church Anniversary, Remembrance Sunday). It is important, however, to note that on great festivals, such as Easter Day or Whit Sunday, the lessons for the festival should always be read.

The booklet gives a short Introduction to be read before each lesson. It is advisable to announce the lesson in some such a way as 'The First Lesson is written in the Book of . . . in the . . . chapter at the . . . verse'. Then read the Introduction. After the Introduction, some preachers may prefer to repeat the reference for the benefit of folk who are slow to apprehend, but who wish to follow the reading in their Bibles. Others will begin the actual reading without more ado. The custom of concluding the reading by 'Here endeth the Lesson' is a relic of Morning Prayer in which the words are a necessary signal to the Choir to begin singing the *Te Deum* or *Benedictus*. The words are unnecessary in most of our services. There is much to be said for the reverent custom of the Presbyterians in concluding the Second Lesson with an ascription of Praise. 'Here endeth the present reading of the Word of God. To His Name be praise and glory.'

The question as to what version should be used in Public Worship is too involved and controversial for full discussion here, but it seems advisable to use a *translation* rather than a *paraphrase*. We should read to the people, so far as is possible in English, the actual words of the Bible. Paraphrastic versions, such as those of Moffatt and Phillips, are most valuable for private devotion, especially where there is not access to the original languages, but they are apt to give us, not the words of the Bible itself, but the author's interpretation of its meaning. Their text is often far removed from the wording of the original, and for this reason it is better not to use them in public reading.

Where the service is followed by the Holy Communion, some ministers substitute the Epistle and Gospel of the Day for the appointed lessons in the lectionary. This is one way of bringing in the most ecumenical of all lectionaries, for the Epistles and Gospels appointed in our *Book of Offices* are common to the Communion Services of most Christian churches. It may lead eventually to the restoration in more of our churches of the full order of Communion, instead of the truncated service which is now so usual among us.

In all but a very few of our churches, the lessons are read by the preacher from the pulpit or the rostrum. This practice has the great advantage of ensuring that the reading is done by men and women who are committed to the study of Scripture and have received training in its use. It is disastrous where, from the motive of encouraging the young to take part in the conduct of worship, or for other reasons, the lessons are read by people who, like the

Ethiopian eunuch, do not understand what they are reading and are therefore incapable of communicating to the congregation the intimate riches of the Biblical phrases. Of course, in Young People's Services and the like, there must be apparent exceptions to this rule, but they need not be real exceptions, if the opportunity is taken to select intelligent young people and to train them carefully, so that they are able to read clearly and with the correct emphases. So often the reading of a lesson at a Sunday School Anniversary has been the first step on the way to a young person's Call to Preach. The important thing is to ensure that, when the Scriptures are read, the Word of God comes to people with vividness and power, and this is impossible, unless the lesson has been first received by the reader as a message to himself from God, and its every phrase pondered and made his own. As has been said, in most churches this is best achieved by maintaining the practice whereby the lessons are read by the preacher. There are, however, not a few churches in which at every service there are others present who are able to undertake this work competently and with a due sense of dedication. In some circuits, for instance, few appointments are available for circuit local preachers and they are found, Sunday by Sunday, in their own places of worship. In these circumstances there is much to be said for having regular lesson-readers who relieve the preacher of his duty in this part of the Service. They will not read better than the preacher, but their participation in the Service will have positive advantages. It will help to solve the difficult problem of *attention*. People get accustomed to the patterns of thought and phraseology which characterize our Services. They feel that they know almost instinctively what is coming next. Especially is this true when the preacher is familiar. There comes the temptation to allow the mind to wander and it may be a real help to introduce a different person as the lesson-reader. There will be a marked gain of interest in the lessons as attention is restored as the result of the change, and the change back to the preacher in the Second Prayer will again raise the level of attention so that there will be a gain here also. The provision of lesson-readers, too, will be a help to some of our older preachers who find the strain of conducting the whole Service almost more than they can manage.

If the lessons are not read by the preacher, some provision for a lectern will be needed in some of our churches, although many will have room on their rostrums for both preacher and reader. Where such arrangements obtain, it will be necessary to adhere strictly to the lectionary. Lay readers can hardly be expected to undertake, without notice, readings specially chosen by the preacher.

Our present lectionary makes some use of the Psalms as passages for reading, but inevitably there is room for only a small selection of the riches of the Psalter. The Hymn Book, however, includes sixty-eight of the Psalms in whole or in part, pointed for chanting. It is much to be regretted that in these days the singing of the Psalms is so generally neglected in Methodism. Thirty or forty years ago, they were sung in hundreds of our churches. Their disuse, one fears, is an index of the decline in the standards of our choral music, for it is difficult to sing Psalms without the leadership of a choir which will take the trouble to study them and sing them with intelligence and devotion. The spiritual value of the Psalms is beyond all computation. They are infinitely precious to every Christian for their own sake, and, throughout the ages until now, they have been sung in Christian churches whenever men have raised their voices in God's praise. They are doubly consecrated to His service through their use by our Saviour and His apostles. It is hoped that a new edition of the *Methodist Lectionary* will include proper Psalms from the Hymn Book selection for the Morning and Evening Services each Sunday, and that, in many churches, they will be regularly sung. Where, however, the Psalms cannot be sung, they need not be neglected. The practice of some preachers of *substituting* a short Psalm for the appointed First Lesson is, of course, not recommended, since it is one of the chief causes of the widespread neglect of the Old Testament in our churches. But there is no reason why a Psalm should not be read *in addition* to the lessons. The writer has often asked a congregation to read a Psalm *with* him, usually in alternate verses. He has never found anything but appreciation from the people, and the children delight in it. It gives them the chance of *activity* in devotion as opposed to the comparatively passive listening of which our services largely consist.

The question must now be asked: '*Ought a preacher to be a slave to the lectionary?*' Are there not occasions in which a change of lessons is desirable? Of course there are! Many of these special occasions are provided for in the lectionary; e.g. Harvest Festival, Temperance Sunday, etc. There will be others—a Day of National Prayer, a Memorial Service—in which a change of reading is called for. But, unless such changes are rare, the whole principle of the lectionary and the great positive values for which it stands will be imperilled. That one intends to preach on a text unrelated to the appointed lessons is not sufficient reason for altering them. This will be made clearer if we consider the relation of the lectionary to the sermon.

How do you make your sermons? Do you make them simply as sermons without thought of a particular day or an individual congregation? I suspect that all of us do this at some time or other. A subject or a text has gripped us and filled our minds until it outflows in a message which we know that we must deliver when the opportunity arises. Do you, on the other hand, begin by thinking of a particular Service you are appointed to take and the needs of the congregation to whom you are to preach? I am sure that we all do this, although in many cases it is easier for ministers than for local preachers, who so often find themselves in churches in circuits other than their own with whose people they have had no previous contact. *In no circumstances should the use of a lectionary interfere in any way with either of the two mental and spiritual processes I have just described.* The message in each case has come to us, as we believe with all our hearts, from God Himself, and woe betide us if we fail to deliver it. There is, however, no compelling reason why the subject of the sermon should be directly related to the lessons which are read. As has been suggested already, there is often a very positive advantage, if a service presents to the people more than one message. Those who may not have been directly helped by the sermon may find in the appointed lesson the word which 'speaks to their condition'. But what if the sermon is expository in character? Surely, then, it may be objected, the passage which included the text should be read as one of the lessons. Of course the passage must be read, but may it not be in addition to, rather than instead of, the passages appointed? The time taken to do this before the text is announced will be very short and the sermons which will necessitate the reading of an extended passage of Scripture in this way will not be numerous. It seems unreasonable, to say the least, to sacrifice the whole principle of the lectionary, with all its possibilities as a means of grace, merely because, occasionally, the form of the sermon may call for an additional reading.

But to most preachers the day-to-day work of sermon-making will seldom derive its inspiration in these ways. The messages will come to us in the normal way through our devotional study of the Scripture, the divine source of all true preaching. Perhaps the preacher's greatest temptation is to preach topical, rather than expository sermons. God will sometimes lead him to preach a topical sermon, but such sermons should be the exceptions to the norm, which is the exposition of the Word of God. People ought not to come to hear our opinions on the questions of the day. They should come to be given a message from God and this will be rooted and grounded in Scripture. It is here, I believe, that the lectionary may be of supreme value to a preacher. It can bring him Sunday by Sunday fresh spiritual pastures for his devout contemplation. It can save his congregations from the peril of constant repetitions of familiar themes. As he looks forward to a service, the preacher will read and ponder the appointed lessons and often, although, of course, by no means always, he will find that a text therein lays hold of his spiritual imagination until he longs to expound its great message to the people to whom he is to read it.

A minister in a single station could conceivably make his own arrangement of Scripture lessons and sermons. This, one supposes, may be practice among Congregationalists and Baptists. It is impossible in Methodism. The only way in which our people can be given a comprehensive view of the riches of the Bible is by the use of a lectionary appointed by the Conference, and by the loyalty to it of our ministers and local preachers. The commonly heard argument, 'It's no use my reading the appointed lessons. The fellow last Sunday didn't read them, and the man next Sunday may not do so either', is mere defeatism. If more and more preachers are loyal to the lectionary, congregations will come to expect it, and to ask for it, and preachers will be more and more disposed to follow it. This is the way in which nearly all reforms have had to begin.

In the standard sermon on 'The Means of Grace', our founder defined them as Prayer, Searching the Scriptures, and the Lord's Supper. Does anyone doubt that, in these days, at least the second of the three God-given ways of receiving the food of the soul is woefully neglected? Is it not therefore the sacred duty of the preacher to see to it that, in the services which he conducts, the reading of the Scriptures has a primary place? How can this be done better than by the use of the lectionary of our Church?

PART TWO

Study Articles

---

1. The Life and Work of Moses

By the Rev. J. YEOMAN MUCKLE, B.A.

THAT the Old Testament is ancient literature is obvious. That parts of it are more ancient than others is not so obvious to everyone, though the simple fact that it includes some Prophetical Books which can only be placed in the eighth century BC, and some that have little meaning except in an Exilic setting, lies before the reader. The truth is that there is much in the Old Testament which is far earlier than the eighth century, and a great deal that is later than the Exile. The period involved is a thousand years at least, and throughout it the religion of Israel was developing and its literature increasing. The older traditions of the faith were not left untouched during those centuries. Men looked back on the stories of the days when the nation had its origin, and they saw them in the light of the knowledge they had more recently received; for example, they often credited the heroes of the past with teachings of the later time. So far as the religious value of the Bible is concerned, this matters very little. But it raises considerable difficulties for the historian of Israel and its religion, for he is frequently confronted with narratives which, though they clearly have their setting in remote antiquity, bear on themselves signs that they have been augmented or modified in a more recent age. It follows that he must again and again be doubtful of what actually happened in the far past, and there have been extremely sceptical scholars who have almost abandoned the attempt to find out.

But in the traditions of Israel there are certain features which can be recognized as hard historical facts. They stand out from the mass of what is or may be the creation of the later centuries, and there is no shaking them. One of them is that an important section of the Hebrew people experienced oppression and persecution in Egypt under one of the great Pharaohs. That is history beyond a doubt, whatever the character of some of the details of the story. The reason for this dogmatic pronouncement is simply that it is the Hebrews themselves who have set down the narrative. It is not the kind of story which people invent about their origins. Later Israel were a small but intensely proud nation, keenly aware of their position as the chosen people of God (though they did not always see the implications of that choice). It is inconceivable that such people would devise an account of their beginnings which shows them as a mob of miserable slaves in the brickyards of Egypt. The thing is true. When proud men tell stories of their descent from kings and heroes, we may well have our doubts until we have seen the indubitable proofs. When they say that their forefathers were serfs and bondservants, the odds are enormously in favour of their speaking the truth, and proof is scarcely necessary. As a tutor of mine pointed out many years ago now, the Crucifixion is a close parallel to this. The best evidence that the Founder of Christianity died on a cross is the fact that His disciples say He did. The followers of Jesus, eager to win Jew and Gentile, preached Christ crucified—blasphemy to the one and rank nonsense to the other! The only possible reason for such a message is that it was true. So, then, with the Egyptian bondage; the people who tell the story are the very people who stand to lose most by telling it. It is to be admitted that we cannot confidently date it, for apparently it never occurred to the ancient writers to mention the names of the Pharaohs concerned; but of the fact there is no uncertainty at all.

The other fact with which we have to do at present is that the man who, under God, was responsible for the deliverance of the Israelites and their subsequent organization into the nucleus of a nation was Moses. There is no doubt that what the Old Testament gives us on that point is neither more nor less than history. The proof of it lies in this, that what certainly happened cannot be explained without him. We begin with a persecuted minority in a strange country, so weak that they cannot do other than submit to the most inhuman commands of their overlord, so dispirited and wearied by their brutal servitude that they expect no release but death. But it is these people who later march out into the wilderness, where they learn to govern themselves and to defend their own against the fierce attacks of other wanderers, until they are ready to invade a country with a developed civilization and take possession of a large portion of it. When we are seeking to explain such circumstances, the first thought that occurs to us is that they must have had a leader of exceptional character. Moreover, it was in the Exodus experience that the really significant religion of Israel began. The faith which produced the Prophets and prepared the way for Christianity takes its rise in the great conception of the God who of His own will becomes the Saviour of Israel. The God of the Hebrews is primarily the Lord who brought them up out of the land of Egypt. In other words, we see at the Exodus the birth of a religion, the truth of which is demonstrated by its existence to this day in Judaism, and by its having inspired both Christianity and Islam. Now it is almost universally true that great religious movements are personally inaugurated; they go back to the experience of men whom God has taken and enlightened. There are ten living organized religions in the world, in addition to Judaism. All but two of them we know to have been personally founded. The exceptions are Hinduism and Shinto, which are fundamentally nature-religions. Yet in the case of Shinto, it is clear that the most significant moments in its history were when there arose within it teachers whom we may justly call inspired; and it is nearly as clear that a similar thing is true of Hinduism. Great religions, then, have their origins in persons. We need a *man* to explain the rise of the Hebrew faith at the Exodus. The Old Testament answers both requirements with Moses. He was both leader and prophet to Israel. There is not the slightest reason to doubt that claim. To place such emphasis on this matter may appear surprising. But sceptics have denied the historicity of Moses, regarding him as an ideal figure created by later generations in explanation of the past. To this the simple answer is that to the best of our knowledge nations are not made and great religions launched by ideal figures, but by living men. If Moses was not the man who did both in the case of Israel, it would be necessary to find someone else who did. An attempt to explain the rise of either, without an historical Moses or his equivalent, is like the play of *Hamlet* without the Prince of Denmark.

When, therefore, we study the books of the Pentateuch from *Exodus* to *Deuteronomy*, we can do so with confidence that what they deal with is fundamentally history. There is much of value in the Old Testament which is not history and was never meant to be taken as such; but here it is of the utmost importance that we should have the assurance that what these books are chiefly concerned with actually happened at certain points in time, to people who, though of different race and environment, were in some ways very like ourselves. We can have that assurance without accepting as literal history all the details of the story. Some of them are later additions, though that does not mean that they have no religious value. But it would indeed be unreasonable to suppose that so famous an epic as this could come down the generations without receiving embellishment here and there. But the main subjects of this literature stand firm on that foundation for which even the most materialistic enemies of religion ought to show respect—hard fact.

The name Moses is not Hebrew, but Egyptian. The attempt of the writer of Exod 2^{10} to explain the name as if it were Hebrew is very unconvincing. But Egyptian names which include the equivalent of the element 'moses' are numerous, though the fact is often concealed by the peculiarities of the English transliteration (Thotmes, Thutmosis, Thutmose; Aahmes, Amose, Ahmosis; etc.). In these cases the expression, which means "son", is compounded with an Egyptian divine name—Thotmes means "son of Thot"—and it is quite likely that the name of the Hebrew hero was originally of such form. If the tradition of his being brought up in Egyptian court circles is accepted, it would be surprising if Moses was not given an Egyptian name. The abbreviated form so familiar to us can be explained without difficulty; Hebrew writers would delete the name of the Egyptian god, whatever it was, on religious grounds, especially as the remainder bears a superficial resemblance to a Hebrew word.

The account of the life and work of Moses set out in the Pentateuch provides material of the highest value for the preacher. And it may now be said that this is true even of many passages concerning the historical accuracy of which there may be some doubt. It still appears to be thought by a considerable number of people that any examination of the Scriptures which leads to the conclusion that there is legendary material incorporated in a history must drastically reduce the field in which the preacher can work. This is not really so. It is right that emphasis should have been placed on the historical character of the Exodus and of Moses himself, for a fundamental belief of Hebrew and Christian religion is that God expresses Himself in history. It is not right to suppose that, unless a particular incident in the story of Moses can be clearly proved to be authentic, it cannot have religious value or authority. It may have a great deal; it may reflect ideas far higher than Moses ever taught, and the preacher ought to take it and use it. He will not, however, want to use every such passage. One of the benefits of the critical study of Scripture is that it makes it possible for us to recognize what are not so much additions as intrusions, of very doubtful value indeed. The uncritical acceptance of everything that is written commits one, presumably, to making something of Exod 4²⁴⁻⁶—an embarrassing task for any-one who believes that the rest of the Moses story gives a revelation of the character of God. How is the conception of the God who has compassion on oppressed Israel, and who encourages a modest man to take up the task of their leadership, to be reconciled with that of a deity who tries to kill the same leader because he is not circumcised? Examination of the passage enables us to recognize it for what it is, a barbarous sanctuary-legend emerging from the underworld of magic, without any original connexion with Moses (there are features of the story which point back to a time centuries before Moses). Why it should have been allowed to survive is, of course, very largely a puzzle, but nothing compared with the puzzle for the theologians if it is taken as an authentic experience of Moses. Possibly it was desired to give the rite of circumcision in Israel Mosaic authority. But as there are two other different traditions in the Old Testament regarding the origin of circumcision, the matter need not detain us long. This is an example of the kind of passage which the wise preacher will leave severely alone, unless, of course, he is dealing with this very subject of difficult sections in the Scriptures.

But, it must be repeated, the religious value of much of the additional material is very great, because it is a consistent development of what we can with confidence ascribe to Moses himself. So true is this that, for purposes of preaching, the story may often be taken exactly as it stands—that is to say, it can be treated like a historical narrative, so far as exposition is concerned. An example of what is meant occurs in Exod 3. Here the ancient writer seeks to explain the divine name Yahweh by using the Hebrew verb 'to be'. In effect, he says Yahweh means 'the God who is' or 'the God who will be'. Now it is extremely doubtful if the explanation is correct; it is far from certain that the name Yahweh is Hebrew at all. But the fact is that this attempt is a happy and indeed an inspired one, for it calls attention to the tremendous truth that Moses discovered when he was called, and that all the later experience of Israel proved, that Yahweh is the Living God—the One who sees, hears, and knows the afflictions of His people, and who acts, and will always act, for them who trust Him. He is the God who is always equal to the situation and who acts in accordance with the needs of it; He speaks by the Prophets; He acts in the coming of Jesus. That is really implicit in Moses' experience of call, and so there is no reason why the story, with its 'explanation' of the name, should not be used just as it is.

Keeping such things in mind, we may now turn our attention to some of the points of chief importance and interest in the records of the life and work of the great Hebrew leader.

Tales of the fortunate preservation of great men in their infancy are widespread in antiquity, and it has been maintained that the story of the casting away of the child Moses in the ark of papyrus stems may have no more foundation in fact than some of these; for example, Cyrus of Persia, Romulus, Sargon of Akkad (a remarkably close parallel to our story). It must be admitted that the incident could have been suggested by the attempted explanation of the name Moses as 'drawn out'. What, however, is also worthy of consideration is the possibility that casting away was a common enough means in Egypt of disposing of children unwanted or in danger. To point out that there is no evidence of this in Egyptian records is no answer, for this is scarcely a matter which could be expected to form the subject of inscriptions or the kind of document which Egyptians commonly wrote. Assuming that there were unwanted children in Egypt, abandonment by the riverside would seem indeed to be a rather obvious way of disposing of them.

The tradition that Moses was reared and educated in Egyptian court circles appears to be strongly supported; as a matter of fact it would be difficult to account for the rise of it if it had not a historical basis. Why should Hebrews invent a story about their champion which shows him a debtor to Egypt for anything? But nothing in the narrative suggests that there was any doubt about his Hebrew origin in the mind of Moses or anyone else. That he took the part of an oppressed Israelite, even to the extent of slaying the persecutor, might be explained entirely by his keen awareness of kinship with the Hebrew slaves, though some of us would prefer to see in the incident an indication of that concern for justice and mercy which is so pronounced in his later history.

The all-too-brief narrative of Moses up to the years of early manhood concludes with his flight from Egypt, in fear of the consequences of his act of defending the helpless. It looks like the end of a promising career. In Egypt his own future would appear to have been assured, and he might have done much, through his Egyptian contacts, to improve the lot of the slaves. But that is irrevocably ended. It looks even more like a tale that is told when, in Midian, the exile finds shelter and friends. He embraces a simpler way of life and is content in his retirement, and the course of his remaining years seems to be set. Yet it was only the beginning, for God had great work to do, and He brought this very man, whose life was apparently settled, from the obscurity of Midian to be His agent. Like Amos centuries later, Moses might have said: 'No prophet was I . . . I was a shepherd . . . but the Lord took me.'

It is scarcely possible to overestimate the importance of the conception of God to which the Hebrews were introduced by Moses. This is the foundation of the highest and noblest teachings of Israel concerning God. Yet to us the idea of the Living God is so familiar that we can easily miss its greatness. If, however, it is seen against the background of the general religious beliefs of the time, its significance stands out. The world of Moses was a very religious one, far more religious than ours. There were gods many and lords many, and they were worshipped. All peoples had their gods, and they meant something. They were regarded as powerful and formidable beings; but to their activity there were certain important limitations. Many of them were nature-gods, chiefly concerned with the maintenance of the processes of the physical world; others were conceived as being inseparably connected with their peoples, whom they must preserve in all circumstances in order to retain their status as gods. It is obvious that there is little promise in such a situation of the development of a highly ethical doctrine of the deities. But Yahweh, the Living God of Israel, is bound neither by nature nor by a necessity to save His people. To put it in homely terms, He has a will of His own. He is above nature, which indeed He rules and uses in order to teach His people. And His existence is not dependent on that of Israel, for His relationship with them is one of His own choice. He has elected to make a covenant with them; they are His people because He has willed it. That He chose them implies that He existed without them, and—a most important truth—can continue to exist without them. In other words, He may reject them if they do not respond in the proper way to His discipline. This is an entirely different matter from the other. On this foundation it is possible for the noblest ethical doctrines of God to arise, and as a matter of fact that is what happened. Moses and his contemporaries may have perceived only dimly the possibilities of this conception, but the teachings of the later centuries showed them clearly. The day came when Hosea, for all his emphasis on the firm love of God for Israel, could contemplate God's destroying Israel rather than allowing her to continue in sin. It may be said with confidence that no such doctrine of God would have been possible on the basis of the usual conception of deity. For Israel, highly ethical ideas of Yahweh were seen as the revealing or 'unfolding' of the character of the God who had first chosen them to be His people; in other words, Israel never outgrew their God. They never had to discard Him, under the pressure of developing moral perception, in favour of a newer God. But that is precisely what happened in the rest of the ancient Near East. Ethical thought took men to positions far beyond the reach of the gods; men had nobler ideals than those gods, by their very nature, could ever set forth. Such deities, outgrown, incapable of satisfying the deep desires of mind and heart, cease to count and fade out, and today we know them only through the literature and the cult-objects which have chanced to survive across the centuries.

But Yahweh, the Living God of Israel, is always ahead of His people, even as in the *Exodus* narrative. He is represented as leading them on through the desert.

It was in the name of this great God, truly living and acting, equal to any situation, that Moses raised up a contemptible little people in the land of the Pharaohs, and began the process which was to make them a nation. The well-known account of the prolonged negotiations with Egyptian authority has much to say of the series of disasters which preceded the escape from the land of bondage. How are we to understand these events? Are we to think of the God of the Hebrews as personally directing a programme of calamitous occurrences intended to force an Egyptian decision to release the slaves? There is no doubt whatever that the narrative as it stands in *Exodus* sets forth this view; the plagues are represented as sensational incidents, brought on with dramatic suddenness and in rapid succession at the command of God. That, however, is a theory not without serious difficulties; why, for example, should the all-powerful God who does such awe-inspiring acts be so long frustrated of His purpose? Why should such mighty deeds make so slight an impression on the Egyptians? It is far from the present writer's intention to deny that, at moments of great crisis in human history, there may be special manifestations of the divine power. But we may well inquire regarding the way in which it is manifested, and examination of this narrative suggests a rather different process from that already mentioned. The *Exodus* story of the plagues is a compilation from at least three sources, which can be identified with some confidence. The interesting thing is that the oldest of them is the least sensational in character, and the latest the most wonderful. It would be reasonable to believe that the earliest version, being nearest to the events described, gives the most faithful account of them. Further, so far as the character of the disasters is concerned, it may be said that every one of them is basically of the type which would admit of explanation in terms of the processes of nature in the land of Egypt; moreover, most of them fall into a sequence which is quite natural. The initial poisoning of the river by decaying vegetation would give rise to five or six of the others. Again, there are indications in the early document that the period involved is quite considerable, possibly eight or nine months. It is the latest document's presentation of the story which creates the impression of breathless haste. In short, the evidence is really that what happened was a series of calamities which, though severe, could be explained away by those with an interest in doing so, and in such circumstances it becomes easier to understand the remarkable stubbornness of the Pharaoh. Especially, we are delivered from the necessity of finding the kind of explanation of it which the Hebrew writers felt obliged to produce, namely, that God deliberately 'hardened Pharaoh's heart', so that He might display a full range of terrible acts before defeating the king. It ought to be a relief to realize that we are not obliged to think of God's action as being rather like that of the boxer who, having knocked his opponent down, picks him up in order to have the pleasure of repeating the process.

But to say that the disasters were natural does not imply that they were not in a real sense a means of revelation used by God. God speaks through what can be accepted and explained as natural, as well as in the startling and sensational event. The very orderliness of the star-spangled heavens led Second-Isaiah straight to the thought of the indescribable majesty of his God, and for Jesus the sending of sun and rain for the benefit of the just and unjust alike was a sign that the love of God reaches out to all men.

And God used these natural events to instruct Israel. For them, the significant thing was that there was a man who interpreted them as the acts of the Living God who had declared His intention of saving them. The most important feature of the story is not that the plagues impressed and influenced Egypt (which they did only to a limited extent), but that they awakened the faith of Israel in their God. This, said Moses, is the Living God in action, and they received his teaching. In so representing the disasters, Moses was guilty of no misinterpretation or deception, for they were indeed a manifestation of the God who has established the natural order, though a less sensational one than has often been supposed.

It was above all as a law-giver that Moses was remembered and venerated in later Israel. So great was his reputation as the one through whom the commands of God were conveyed to the people that all the later legislation, much of it many centuries after his time, was set forth in the form of divine instructions issued to him. This practice, however inconvenient to the historian who would trace the development of law in Israel, means one thing at least: that the historical Moses was certainly a law-giver. And when we turn to the task of determining what legislation may be attributed to Moses, it is seen that he was probably responsible for the famous code known as the Decalogue, or Ten Commandments (Exod 20), though we must think of it in a simpler and briefer form than the familiar one. Research has revealed that ancient law-codes were almost always short, and in the form of prohibitions. What is immediately noticeable is the strong ethical emphasis of the Commandments. This is entirely in harmony with the conception of God which is presented in the idea of the covenant-relationship of God and Israel. Yahweh is setting forth the conditions on which the relationship may be maintained, and since He is the God who has of His own free-will entered into the covenant with Israel, His commands have authority far beyond what would be possible if the relationship were unbreakable. The Decalogue is not, of course, the whole of morality, but it is a sure foundation on which the loftiest morality may rise.

It has been objected that the Decalogue expresses ethical ideas that are too advanced for the time of Moses, and that therefore he cannot be credited with having introduced it. But the researches of recent years have shown that this position cannot be maintained. A good deal is now known about the law of the ancient Near East, and it is clear that, in some of the lands adjoining Israel, there was an interest in similar matters of morality to those that appear in the Hebrew code, even at an earlier date than that of Moses. A famous example is provided by the Egyptian *Book of the Dead*, in which the candidate for eternal life is depicted as affirming in the judgement hall of Osiris that he has not committed theft, adultery, murder, fraud, deceit, and that he has shown mercy and kindness. This is certainly centuries older than the earliest date which could be suggested for Moses.

Indeed, ancient non-Israelite law furnishes a good many parallels to the kind of legislation which appears in the Ten Commandments; perhaps the best-known case is that of the Babylonian law-code of Hammurabi. It is clear that we are not to think of the laws with which the Decalogue is concerned as having been originated by Moses. But, it may be asked, if this is so, wherein lies the importance of Moses as the law-giver of Israel? The answer is in the fact that he selected these laws and presented them as the supreme requirements of Israel's God. Out of all the mass of social and ceremonial laws, cult regulations, and tabu restrictions which lay heavy on the religions of his day and place, he chose a small basic code concerned almost wholly with ethical matters, and set that forth as what was demanded above all else by Yahweh. It might have been otherwise; indeed, there is proof in the Old Testament that other sections and movements in Israel concerned themselves far more with ritual observances. There is, for example, another 'Decalogue' in Exod 34 which prescribes festivals and offerings, and does not include a single ethical commandment anywhere. But Moses perceived what mattered most and, in laying down a sure foundation in laws which declare an unbreakable connexion between worship and righteousness, he is to be seen to this day as the religious genius that the Jews have always claimed him to be. For Moses, the Living God was the One who not only acted, but acted in righteousness, and required that His people also should be righteous.

That Moses died shortly before the arrival of the Israelites in the promised land of Canaan seems to have troubled sorely the writers of the ancient records. They appear to have made a rather desperate search into the traditions of his life, in order to find some fault which would explain the disappointment as a righteous judgement of God. There was not much to find, and they were driven to magnifying an occasion when the severely tried man of God let his anger blaze out against the people. We cannot but feel that he had every justification, and we are not likely to be satisfied with their explanation. Surely we may see the death of Moses as occurring at the time when his great work was well and truly completed. He had laid the foundation, and other men must build thereon; and so truly was it laid that, though in the following centuries there was much apostasy, it remained to provide a sure standing-ground for other teachers whom God raised up to rebuke and exhort His people. We are told that, before the end, Moses was permitted to see the whole extent of Canaan 'from Dan to Beersheba', from the summit of Mt Nebo on the east of Jordan. There is a beautiful old Jewish legend which improves on this by saying that he saw also, in a vision, the whole long pageant of Israel's future, with Saul and David and the Prophets. One would like to think that that is true. Yet in a sense it is true; for one cannot believe that Moses, having brought these people through so many trials and disciplines, could die without realizing that, because of what God had enabled him to do, they had a great future. He found them ready to perish; the word of God raised them to new life. They accepted him as leader and followed him into the wilderness. They sinned continually, but repented and returned to the Lord. They failed times out of number, but they produced some leaders not unworthy to take up the task when Moses laid it down. They began as a rabble, and now they were on the threshold of nationhood. They were full of faults; but surely, after such a beginning, they must attain to greatness.

2. Great Words of the Gospels for Preachers

By the Rev. GEORGE A. E. CORNFORTH, M.A.

THE best preaching is Biblical. The preacher is not commissioned to preach his own views and opinions, but to proclaim the true Word of God. The aim of this article is to draw attention to the key words of the Gospels, to indicate their meaning and significance, and to suggest some methods of exposition.

THE SYNOPTIC GOSPELS*

THE KINGDOM OF GOD

In all the Gospels there is the recurring theme of the *Kingdom of Heaven* or the *Kingdom of God*. A correct understanding of this phrase will help towards the appreciation of what the Gospel of Jesus is about. The first three Gospels unite in attesting that Jesus began His public ministry with a call to repentance and an assertion that the Kingdom was at hand (Mk 1^{15}, etc.). To a modern reader the term 'Kingdom' conveys the idea of a territory, over which the rule of God is especially exercised. There have even been attempts to identify the Kingdom with the Church, but there does not appear to be any scriptural basis for this. For the Jew of the Old Testament period, the Kingdom might well have been in part understood of the nation itself, because their history showed that God had ever been active in the affairs of the Jewish State and the Jewish Church. We approach the meaning of 'Kingdom' when we see it in terms of 'Kingship'.

The Kingdom is dynamic, not static. When Jesus pointed to the evidence for the fact of the Kingdom, He did so by drawing attention to His own activity. 'If I by the finger of God cast out demons, then is the kingdom of God come upon you.' It is not a subject for an academic thesis, but for practical demonstration. As far as Christian living is concerned, the Kingdom is to be known by its fruits. When Paul said, 'I bear branded on my body

*References are chiefly taken from Matthew's Gospel. Parallel references in *Mark* and *Luke* should be obtained from the margin of the AV or RV.

the marks of Jesus' (Gal 6¹⁷), he was thinking of the active and incontrovertible evidence of the Kingdom. The 'marks' were probably a reference to the common practice of branding a slave with the mark of its owner. Signs of the activity of Jesus could be seen in Paul's own life. A Christian is an instrument of the will of God. It is known that God is King, because the Christian is seen to be His subject. The subject of the Kingdom of God, however, may cause some embarrassment to the Kingdom of this world. The first Christians were regarded with some measure of alarm. 'These that have turned the world upside down are come hither also' (Acts 17⁶). The Christian must be prepared for collisions.

There can be no Kingdom without a King. It is not the works of man that make the Kingdom, but the reign of God. Whatever man's reaction is, God still rules. It is conceivable that in an earthly monarchy there will be some citizens who disapprove of the system of government, and who may be in active rebellion against it. But they are still subject to the laws of the kingdom, and are judged by them. No man can contract out of the Kingdom of God. The highest wisdom is to know the King and learn His will, so that within that Kingdom there may be harmony and peace. Harmony with God is the basis of harmony between men. This raises the question of man's dependence upon God. The familiar words, 'Except ye turn, and become as little children, ye shall in no wise enter into the kingdom of heaven' (Mt 18³) are sometimes misunderstood. Jesus is not here thinking of the innocence of a child, nor its gentleness. (These are not qualities which are conspicuous in actuality.) He is thinking of the child's dependence upon his parents. Food, clothing, and shelter must be provided for him until such time as he can provide for himself. There may be times when the child will act as though he were able to fend for himself, but he will need to be retrieved from his mistakes and set again on the right path. He will learn from his own experience that he is not self-sufficient. Life would teach all men that they are dependent upon provisions that have been supplied for them. The raw materials of life have been discovered, but not created, by men. Life in its simplest form is always rubbing in the fact that we are not self-sufficient. In the text quoted, Jesus seems to be appealing for the recognition of the very simple truth that 'It is he that hath made us, and we are his' (Ps 100³). It is out of a sense of dependence that gratitude springs, and from a gratitude, worship.

Other tokens of citizenship of the Kingdom are to be deduced from teaching recorded in *Matthew*. In Mt 18²¹⁻³⁵ we see that the Kingdom is the realm of forgiveness. No grudging heart can find a place there. Any man who is in the Kingdom knows he can be there only because God has given him forgiveness. God has forgiven him greater injuries that he can ever receive. Therefore he must forgive any who have wronged him. Christian charity is the pre-eminent virtue. When we truly know ourselves before God in Christ, there is no limit to that understanding and compassion that make it possible to forgive all wrongs that have ever been done to us. 'Do good to them that hate you, pray for them that despitefully use you.' When we really take these words seriously, it will not be surprising if we feel that they simply cannot be fulfilled. It is not in man to do this thing. Perhaps we are meant to feel that way about the words, for we read in them the law of the Kingdom, which becomes intelligible and realistic only to those who are within the Kingdom already.

In Mt 19²³⁻³⁰ we are reminded that the Kingdom is entered only by those who are whole-hearted in their determination to attain it. Wealth in itself is neither good nor bad. It can be used for beneficent ends, but it can so easily become the object of life. Its quest can become an idolatry which supplants the worship of the true God. The facilities provided for gambling today are to be deplored because they treat the quest for money as being in itself desirable. Where this view is held the service of the Kingdom is not possible. There was a poignant moment in the ministry of Jesus when He was confronted by an eager young man, rich and attractive, who was inquiring about eternal life. The commandments he had observed from his youth. There was only one thing that was detaining him. He had not settled the question of priorities. His worldly wealth meant so much to him that he could not surrender it in order that Jesus might have the first place in his affections (Mt 19¹⁶⁻²²).

Mt 20¹⁻¹⁶ implies that in the Kingdom all are treated alike. There is no favouritism. Obey the call, early or late, and entrance is obtained. There is only one reward God can possibly give, and that is the reward of being with Him and knowing that all is done in obedience to His holy will. Those who obey first, enjoy the reward sooner. The service of God is the perfect freedom. The only real freedom to be enjoyed by anyone is the freedom to choose whom we will serve. Everyone has a master somewhere. Happy indeed is the man whose Master is God.

Mt 20²⁰⁻²⁸ shows how the teaching of Jesus on this subject could be misunderstood, even by one who was in close touch with Him. The natural sense in which to understand the word Kingdom is in the sense of power and authority. The privileged people within the Kingdom are those who see kingship in terms of service. When Jesus stooped to the meanest and most menial task of washing the feet of the disciples, He was doing a deed which was natural to His conception of kingship. This was not a 'stunt', performed because He wished to teach the disciples a lesson. It was a deed that was natural to Him. A direct consequence of the fact that in becoming incarnate He 'emptied himself'. A. E. Whitham tells of a vision in which it seemed that he was being conducted through a heavenly museum where objects connected with the life of our Lord were displayed. He remarks to the angelic guide that he does not see the towel and the basin. 'No,' says the Angel, 'they are not here, for they are still in use.' Those who will sit on the right and left of Jesus in the Kingdom will not be those who feel that they have a right to be there. We should perhaps link with these comments Mt 21⁴³, where Jesus declares that the Kingdom will be given to the nation that brings forth the fruits thereof. In the Kingdom men do not think first and foremost of their rights and privileges, but of their opportunities to serve. Mt 22¹⁻¹⁴ underlines the lesson that to belong to the Kingdom is not a formal or mechanical privilege. The wedding-garment may be taken as the 'outward and visible sign of an inward and spiritual grace'. The true citizen of the Kingdom will bring forth the fruits of the Kingdom. If he does not, he forfeits the privileges of citizenship.

In Mt 13, a series of parables is recorded which throws light on the understanding of the Kingdom. The series follows the parable of the Sower in vv. 1–23, the main point of which is to remind the disciples that their task is to preach the Word as He did, without stint and without discouragement. Not all who hear the Word will allow it to come to harvest; but the sowing cannot be entirely lost, for there will be some good ground which will yield an astonishing crop. The disciples as preachers are envoys of the Kingdom, they are representatives of its Lord and are commissioned by Him for this service. They are given insights into the Kingdom for their encouragement and understanding.

Verses 24–30 seem to point to a problem with which we are familiar today. Why should there be found in the same company people who are apparently committed to God and some who are not? Even in the Early Church there were folk who had entered under false pretences, who were there for their own selfish purposes and seemed to forget that the purpose of the Church is primarily to worship God and to embody His love to the world. We must remember the 'harvest' when the final assessment will be made. The fact that some members of the Kingdom seem unworthy must not deter the preacher from proclaiming the Kingdom. Faithfulness is the requisite for the preacher.

The parable of the mustard-seed (vv. 31-2) reminds us of the hospitality of the Kingdom. When the Kingdom first touches a man's heart, he thinks he has something for himself. But as his understanding grows, he sees he has a gift for the world, and the birds of the air do indeed find their home within the glorious concept that God is the Father of all men. Is the Jewish convert here intended to see a distinction between the burden of the Christian yearning to bring the whole world into the fold of God's love, and the narrow Judaic pride in national privilege?

In v. 33 the Kingdom is compared to leaven, and the question of influence arises. We often hear complaints that the progress of Christian faith is so slow. We sympathize with the late Archbishop William Temple when he said that 'We are the Primitive Church'. But where there is a sincere acceptance of Christ, a determination to follow Him, the influence begins; it is there in the world. The social order of the West bears testimony to the influence of Christian emphases. The concept of fair-play stems from a Christian root. The compassion that cares for the sick and instructs the ignorant likewise may be traced to the impact of Christ upon society. Nevertheless it is dangerous to set out to influence people or society, until we ourselves are in submission to Jesus. It has been said that the influence of the Gospel has been more marked in the last fifty years than in any other previous fifty years, but we do not yet see the world won for Him. We are therefore brought to our knees to pray for the coming of that Kingdom which is for ever coming when one soul turns to Christ and determines to glorify Him. The prayer 'Thy Kingdom come' must be prayed in all humility, and continually we must examine ourselves before Christ to see whether there is in us any mood, thought, attitude, desire, or ambition, which is likely to hinder its approach. But when all allowance has been made for this, the truth remains that the Kingdom is where God reigns; and is there a single part of the Universe which is outside that reign? The Kingdom in effect is here. The task of preaching is to proclaim that truth. But while the Kingdom is the object of human response it is not of human creation. It must never be identified with man's effort to build his own society. It does not mean mere good-will and kindness. It is of divine origin. It requires God to maintain it. In our thinking and preaching we must never lose sight of the emphasis of Jesus: 'Fear not, little flock; for it is your Father's good pleasure to give you the kingdom' (Lk 12^{32}).

We must see ourselves as ambassadors of the Kingdom. We are here to express the will of God and to show forth His mind. That is the comprehensive idea which will embrace every message. Now let us look at some of the great words for preaching that are to be found in the Gospels.

REPENT (*See* Mt 3$^{2, 8, 11}$, 4^{17}, 11^{20}, 12^{41})

This means far more than being sorry for wrong done. We may be sorry without hating the sin 'that made Thee mourn'. Our sinfulness springs from a wrong attitude of soul. Thought is turned inwards. We contemplate what we deem to be profitable or advantageous to ourselves. We seem to be in the centre of the universe and are distressed because all does not turn out to our convenience. It is not the wrongdoing from which we need to depart, so much as the wrong centre at which we are content to rest. Repentance means a change of heart, so that our activity is brought into line with what God wills for us. 'I delight to do thy will, O my God: yea, thy law is within my heart' (Ps 40^8).

While it is not possible to eliminate all emotion from the experience of repentance, the emotion acts only as a stimulus to the will. Our Lord Himself deprecates the attitude of those who say 'Lord, Lord, and do not the things that I say' (Lk 6^{46}). Hence John the Baptist, having administered the 'baptism of repentance', bids the baptized 'Bring forth therefore fruit worthy of repentance' (Mt 3^8).

Repentance was the object of our Lord's preaching. Unless men repented, He could get no farther with them. It is the key to the Kingdom. He cried at the outset of His ministry, 'Repent ye, for the kingdom of heaven is at hand' (Mt 4^{17}). It is as though the love and justice of God are standing at our elbow demanding a decision. We can read of the disappointment of Jesus when His presence did not have this effect in Mt 11^{20}: 'Then began he to upbraid the cities wherein most of his mighty works were done because they repented not.' It is tragically easy to remain within sound of His voice and yet to remain in much the same state as though we had not heard it. A disciple needs very much more than a light-hearted affection—as he very soon finds out. It is not until a complete dedication of the will has been made that it becomes possible to take up the Cross daily and follow Christ.

SIN, SINS (*See* Mt 3[6], 9[2, 5])

Sins are the symptoms of a fundamental state of soul whereby man is at enmity with God. The N.T. Greek word suggests failing to hit the target, 'missing the mark'. Man's intended condition is to be at peace with God, to see God as his friend and Saviour. Where God is not so seen, and man allows himself to grow into a state of alienation, the evidences are to be read in the form of sins. These are legion in numbers and types, but the underlying cause is the same. The outward act springs from the state of the heart. Mt 15[19] and Mk 7[21] show how radical our Lord's criticism of human nature was. This is worth bearing in mind when there is any tendency to portray Him as being too indulgent to man.

Mt 9[2, 5] deals with a question which is of up-to-date interest, namely the cause of physical illness. It is, of course, not to be assumed from a passage like this that all illness is a sign of sin, but it is made clear that this man's illness was. Where the mind is distraught, the conscience restless, then the body is apt to show signs of that mental condition. Again, with one of His radical insights, Jesus perceives the root of the trouble. The man needed a spiritual cure. It was a troubled soul that needed treatment, rather than a diseased body. It required Jesus to see that fact. We do not know what the sins were. Jesus does not even tell the patient what they were. There was no need to. If we were face to face with Jesus we should know very well where we were wanting, and we should not necessarily love Him for making that knowledge clear to us. It must have come as a shock to the sick man to have his condition attributed to his own wrong doing or wrong thinking.

In dealing with sin, Jesus reveals an authority which is unique among men. The Jews were shocked that He should forgive sins. This was a prerogative, they believed, of God alone. And the Jews were not wrong here. All sin, however apparently small or great its particular manifestation, is an offence against the universe and its Creator; 'Against thee, thee only, have I sinned'

(Ps 51[4]). The fact that Jesus claimed the power to forgive throws light upon the nature of His Person and implies His Deity. His forgiveness is effective because He is without sin, and because He is in perfect fellowship with the Father.

The forgiveness of Christ is real, because He has felt the impact of man's sin in His own Person. He felt the penalty of isolation from God which sin inevitably brings in its wake. The cry of dereliction from the Cross: 'My God, my God, why hast thou forsaken me?' (Mt 27[46]), is an indication of what it cost Jesus to be made aware of the power of sin. For Him there was nothing more precious than communion with the Father. Because He had also communion with man in his sin, He came to know that heartrending experience of having become a stranger from God. It is possible that here we come to the real horrifying centre of the death of Christ. If this word could be fully fathomed, we should come nearer to knowing the cost of our redemption. This was not the final word, however; it was followed by 'Father, into thy hands I commend my spirit' (Lk 23[46]). There is the final victory of His faith. In that victory we trust, for by it we also are saved. It is by that faith of His that He fortifies us. He knew the worst that the sin of man can achieve, but the love of God far outweighed all human opposition. In Him we know that the love of God is unconquerable. A man once said of a group of people at whose hands he had suffered somewhat: 'They are so ungrateful that even Jesus would turn against them.' That is not what we learn from His Cross. He will hold on to the end. Whatever our frailty, we shall not claim His help in vain. In the N.T. there are two notable sinners—Peter and Judas. The one denied Jesus, the other betrayed Him. They were both disloyal, and yet one became the Rock on which the Church was built; the other committed suicide. It is in their attitude to their sins that the two differ so remarkably. Peter was penitent. He threw himself upon the mercy of Christ. He had so learned Christ that he knew He could be depended upon. But Judas was remorseful. He could not escape from self-reproach, and had not learned that there is forgiveness. His life was wasted, not because he had sinned, but because he could not take Jesus at His word.

RIGHTEOUSNESS (See Mt 3[15], 5[6,10,20], 6[1,33], 21[32])

Essentially, it means that which makes us acceptable to God. Jesus accepted baptism at the hands of John the Baptist because

He wished to identify Himself with the cause which the Baptist represented. There are good folk who will accept the spirit but not the form. They put themselves above their Master in this respect. When, however, the word is used in the Beatitudes (Mt 5[6,10]) it seems to embrace the whole will of God. It does not signify mere human goodness, the kind which is practised by those who make no profession of faith in God or Christ. There is a great deal of such goodness about, and we should be thankful for that fact. But the Beatitude is speaking of the goodness of God for which the soul yearns, and apart from which there is no peace. 'Our hearts are restless until they find their rest in Thee.' This is in part what is meant by Christian faith out of which the Christian's good works spring. The fact that it is the thirsting and hungering which is blessed implies that the Christian has embarked upon a limitless quest. 'E'en eternity's too short to utter all Thy praise.' Hence the response to the divine righteousness can never be complete and a limit can never be set. Perhaps here we strike the meaning of Mt 5[20]: 'Except your righteousness exceed the righteousness of the scribes and Pharisees, ye shall in no wise enter into the kingdom of heaven.' There is danger when religion becomes legalistic, and we want to know how far we can go without overstepping the boundary between the lawful and the unlawful. But the Christian Faith is no minimum religion. It is a total religion. Experience teaches us that where the response to God is genuine, character develops and opportunities of service increase, as we continue our discipleship faithfully. A Christian, so long as he remains a Christian, never retires and never becomes a pensioner of the Kingdom of Heaven. But the tendency of the scribes and Pharisees was to define with too great care what was required of them. They were scrupulous as to tithes, worship, and respectability. Their deficiency seemed to occur in the lack of simple love—which is an infection caught by the true worshipper from God Himself. It is said that, when the Baron von Hugel was dying, his last words (which his niece recorded) were: 'Christianity taught us to care. Caring is the greatest thing. Caring matters most.' Caring is the righteousness of God and it is to this righteousness that every disciple of Jesus is called. We see how this cuts across the modern attitude of 'I couldn't care less'. God couldn't care more. We have in Christ and through Christ all that God has to give. If we miss that, then the rest is meaningless.

FOLLOW (*See* Mt 4[20-25], 8[1, 10, 19, 22], 9[9], 10[38], 19[21, 27], 20[34])

The word appears in all the Gospels, and indeed there can be no Gospel without it. The very record of Jesus is due to the fact that He presented men with a challenge. Most did not accept it, but even in rejecting it they learned something about themselves; and those who did accept it spent the rest of their lives learning more about God. Preaching is aimless which does not present the challenge, and a preacher has little else to do than to secure a verdict for Jesus.

Following demands an uncompromising decision. Peter saw this clearly when he said, 'Lo, we have left all and followed thee' (Mt 19[27]). At least for a time it would seem that Simon and Andrew, James and John, left their task in the world in order to learn more fully of Jesus. As far as they were concerned, they had probably met Jesus before the challenge was given. Maybe they had time to think over the implications of having a Friend so dynamic and devoted. But the day came when a decision had to be taken, if there was to be any further development and achievement. Jesus Himself is seen appealing for such a moment of decision in the life of the rich young man. There is not a Christian, rich or poor, who does not do well to ponder with earnest care the significance of Mt 19[16-30]. It is not only riches that deter a man from following Christ, though they are a potent deterrent. A man may pursue an ambition regardless of whether he must turn his back on Christ in order to achieve it. Or through the stubbornness of foolish pride, ideas and traditions may be asserted in spite of the fact that the Spirit of Christ challenges their charity and sincerity. We may be rich in popularity. Now it is not popular to be a disciple. The Christian is the target of all sorts of charges from the non-Christian and it is hard to bear them. But if men will speak evil of Christ, they will speak evil of His followers. Our wealth is the thing we live for, that which above all else seems most desirable. Christ offers Himself to us as the object of our loyalty and devotion. A child once declared that she could swim 'except for one leg'. Such a qualification meant she could not swim at all. It is possible for discipleship so to be qualified by reservations that it is not discipleship at all.

However, the invitation to follow is only the beginning of the process. When He calls us, it is from the place where He has found us. Simon and Andrew were by the shore, Matthew in the Customs house, Nathanael under the fig-tree, Paul on the road to Damascus. But He will not for ever stay where we are. He has other realms to conquer, other truths to reveal, other hopes to nourish and satisfy than those in which we have hitherto rested content. Hence the challenge is to adventure. How difficult it is to keep alert and fresh in the Christian life! It is so easy to sit back as though the best has already been. The best is yet to come. But the condition and spirit of the adventure must be grasped. Consider Mt 16²⁴⁻²⁵, where the theme, 'Take up the cross' is stated. Now to many the Cross is a symbol of sacrifice and suffering. It would be unrealistic to belittle those elements. But in its total meaning it stands for much more than that. In the experience of Christ it meant His complete offering of Himself to God for the service of God in the life of man. Think of the Cross in terms of dedication and committal. This was a point brought out in Luke's version of this passage (9²³⁻²⁴), where a significant addition is made: 'Let him take up his cross *daily*.' The Cross is part of the texture of Christian character.

Further, in order to follow we must keep Jesus in view. Our choice of a master will determine the direction of our life and the formation of our character. When Christ is our choice, there will be a great deal to be learned about Him. We are called therefore to that kind of serious discipleship which will involve continued and regular meditation upon His nature. We must submit ourselves and our thought to Him, that He may judge us and reveal where we are at fault. He is the focus of our adoration, and worship will play a tremendous and joyous part in our activity. It will be a delight to praise Him and we shall understand what the Psalmist meant when he said, 'I was glad when they said unto me, Let us go unto the house of the Lord' (Ps 122¹). Moreover, our understanding of Christ is developed as we listen to the experience of Christians more mature than ourselves. Wesley knew what he was doing when he assembled the first Methodists into classes. It does not matter what you call that particular kind of fellowship, but it is very important that you should have it. But we also keep Christ in view by obedience and the serious attempt to bring our lives into line with His teaching; to remember that we are not here merely to save our own souls, but to make known to the world that there is a Saviour. We are taught that the cup of cold water given in the name of Christ is not without its significance. When a disciple becomes idle Jesus will seem to be lost in the mist.

DISCIPLE

The function of a disciple is admirably illustrated by the contexts in which the followers of Jesus appear. (1) Mt 5[1]. 'The disciples came unto him.' They are not at first shown as rushing into activity. They have leisure to learn. They are receptive. The quietness in which we can have communion with Jesus is itself an investment. It is like banking money upon which we shall later draw. Our spiritual resources are increased through prayer and worship. Prayer is of primary value, not because it tells God that we are here, but because through it we tell ourselves that He is here and has everything under control. Beware above all things of spiritual bankruptcy. (2) Mt 8[23]. 'His disciples followed him.' The disciple is known by the direction in which he is walking. Conversion may be understood in the sense of a change of direction. Further implications of following Jesus are given in the preceding section. (3) Mt 10[24]. 'A disciple is not above his master nor a servant above his lord.' The disciple is subservient therefore to Jesus. He must not expect greater honour than his Master received. He must not complain of hardship or of lack of response. He must not shirk the Cross. Above all, he labours for the honour of his Master and is content if, after all his efforts, men are brought to think of Jesus in one way or another. It is not of success or failure of which we must first think, but of obedience. (4) Mt 11[29]. The disciple is called into an intimate fellowship with the Master. The yoke created a partnership between the animals that wore it. The yoke implied obedience and also the guidance of a masterhand. As Jesus Himself was under the guidance of God, so also will His disciples be. But the yoke settles without chafing upon the neck that accepts it and does not gird against it. The spirit of acceptance is to be 'meek and lowly in heart'. And it must be admitted that the qualities here mentioned are certainly not conspicuous today. Meekness is a kind of gentleness that springs from disciplined strength. Some strong people seem to feel that they should always be drawing attention to the fact. The mark of meekness is consideration for others. Meekness requires an inspired imagination, in order to envisage in some degree what the trials of life mean to folk; to remember that, even if we have our troubles, we are not alone in that condition. The meek man does not claim the sympathy of others, he would rather give of his own sympathy. Out of his own experience he has learnt the truth that 'It is more blessed to give than to receive'—a word that is also attributed to Jesus in Acts 20[35]. Lowliness of heart would indicate a total lack of 'thrustfulness', and a disposition not to overrate oneself. This does not mean that one must close a blind eye to merit, but must attribute it to the Giver of all merit. The word is anti-Pharisaic, and is opposed to all that savours of the pride of intellect, rank, morality, and religiousness. The lowly in heart yearn to succeed for Christ, but they do not fear to fail for Him also. There is perhaps no greater sign that a man is in partnership with Jesus than that he is prepared to risk failure. Note how the yoke is brought into connexion with 'Learn of me'. It is the kind of learning that comes from lifelong companionship. Domination, force, power are screamed at us from the house-tops. Our Lord would lead us into a new world, which is not outside this one, but within it. This learning does not come from books, nor from instructors, but from daily efforts to understand the Master who has called us to be His own. The word 'disciple' in the Greek is derived from this very word 'learn'. The disciple is not perfect, but he is on the way to being perfect, though maybe a very long way from his ultimate goal. (5) Mt 26[19]. 'And the disciples did as Jesus appointed them, and made ready the passover.' Here the note of obedience is struck. It is significant that the disciples made ready the Passover. Who paid for the bread and the wine? Could it have been Judas? Jesus seems to have been prepared to take the offerings of the least of men and to transform them into life-giving elements. In the early days of the Christian Church, the bread and the wine for the Communion were presented by the congregation to the priest. Part was used for the Sacrament and the rest used for the sustenance of the priesthood and of the poor. Today it is customary to commute that offering for a money gift. Where the offering for the poor is taken in the Communion Service, we are in effect offering resources to Christ which He will accept and return to us transfigured by His own love. There must have been a powerful significance in the fact that bread and wine, made in the home, were returned to the communicants with the words, 'This is My Body . . . This is My Blood'. If we do as He appoints, then our dedicated offering becomes the vehicle of His own communication to the world in which we have to live.

HYPOCRITES (See Mt 6[16], 15[7])

This represents all that a disciple should not be, and yet something which a disciple can so easily become. In the Greek drama the actors wore masks. These were designed partly to emphasize the features and to enlarge the voice. The mask was in keeping with the part that was being played, but it did not reveal the character of the actor himself. A hypocrite is a man who is not himself. He is playing a part. He may impose upon men, but he cannot deceive God. At the root of hypocrisy is selfishness. 'They disfigure their faces that they may be seen of men to fast.' It was then a respectable and honourable thing to be religious. It was perhaps profitable for business. Today we need to be thankful that religion and respectability are not necessarily allied, and that few people would think of performing religious duties in order to be well thought of by men. But hypocrisy can assume some subtle forms. Whenever a man enters a church or says a prayer, he is bearing witness to a certain way of life. He is acknowledging that Jesus is his Saviour and that to Him allegiance has been given. The Sunday witness is only a token witness of a loyalty that is gladly maintained in the home and place of business. The world at any rate will judge us by the outworkings of our faith. Our professions will be at a discount if our deeds are found wanting.

AUTHORITY (*See* Mt 7^{29}, 8^9, 21^{23-4}, 28^{18})

The teaching of Jesus was contrasted with the teaching of the Scribes, because the one had authority and the other had not. The function of the Scribe was to interpret the teaching of the Rabbis and to apply it to a specific instance in life, or to resolve a problem of conduct. They were experts in the appropriate 'authorities'. They were extremely knowledgeable scholars. But Jesus had this authority within Himself. He did not look up the books to find the correct or the traditional answer. He seemed to be the answer Himself. A man with a moral problem would know the course to follow when he found himself confronted with Jesus. The incident of the woman of Samaria in John 4 shows our Lord's authority at work. The woman in her questions and answers is clearly trying to dodge that challenge to her own sinfulness. Her very subtlety and ingenuity is a sign of the guilt of her conscience, awakened by her contact with Jesus. The nature of His authority is difficult to define. But it lies partly in the fact that He not only taught well, but lived well, and was Himself the best illustration of His own teaching. Word and character were perfectly linked. The Centurion in Mt 8^9 seemed to grasp this all-important fact about Jesus. In his capacity as commander of men, his word could accomplish deeds. 'I say unto this one, Go and he goeth, and to another, Come and he cometh.' This man was vested with the authority of the Emperor, and it was as though in him the Emperor himself spoke. The Roman felt that the word of Jesus was an active word, because it carried with it the whole force of His personality. We cannot but recall the activity of the Word of God as recorded in the first chapter of *Genesis:* 'God said . . . and it was so.' And we remember the passage from Isa 55[10-11]: 'For as the rain cometh down and the snow from heaven, and returneth not thither, but watereth the earth, and maketh it bring forth and bud, and giveth seed to the sower and bread to the eater; so shall my word be that goeth forth out of my mouth: it shall not return unto me void, but it shall accomplish that which I please, and it shall prosper in the thing whereto I sent it.' There was something irresistible about the authority of Jesus. As He hung on the Cross, this was said by one who was on guard there: 'Truly this was the Son of God' (Mt 27[54]). The RVmg reads: 'a Son of God.' Lk 23[47] interprets the saying as meaning 'a righteous man'. It is unlikely that the Roman soldier meant by the phrase 'Son of God' what a Christian would imply by it, but he was fully conscious that this Victim was no ordinary man. Even in death the authority was felt, bearing its weight upon a pagan life and bringing a new awareness. After the Resurrection we find it bearing down upon Peter in Jn 21[15-23]. There we read of the insistent questioning, 'Lovest thou me?' as though Peter for his own soul's sake was being compelled to discover and purify all his motives. At last he throws himself upon the knowledge which Christ has of him: 'Thou knowest that I love thee.' Does this mark the moment when our Lord's authority was fully established in the life of one who had been guilty of denial? Once before Peter had felt that authority when he cried 'Thou art the Christ' (Mk 8[29]), but to John there came a more deeply realized meaning of the Lordship of Jesus. Peter accepts the love and yields love, and becomes the shepherd of the sheep in his Master's stead.

FAITH (*See* Mt 8[10, 13, 26], 9[2, 22, 28, 29], 17[20], 21[21])

Faith, in the Gospels, is implicit trust in Jesus and in His authority. When he rebukes the lack of faith of the disciples in the midst of the storm, it is because they thought that they could really be overwhelmed, even though Jesus was with them in the boat. The promise of God has never been that those who love Him will escape all suffering and distress, but that whatever happens He is there with them, to give all the help and inspiration that is needed to wrest victory out of seeming defeat (Mt 8[13]). 'As thou hast believed, so be it done unto thee' is a reminder that without faith there is no knowledge of the active love of God. Faith is vision to make us penetrate the veil of appearances and to see the reality which is at the back of all existence. Faith is not a challenge to be unreasonable, but it is a challenge to admit that human intellect alone must not be allowed to set bounds to what is possible. Human knowledge at its best is a limited thing. The more we know, the more aware do we become of the vast fields which lie awaiting further exploration. We can never be certain that we have reached the absolute end in any realm of knowledge. The wisdom of one age is checked and corrected by that of another. Religious faith concerns contact with a Person. It is not book knowledge, though that can help. Mt 9[1-8] indicates that where there is faith there is healing. And the healing is radical. It is not the removing of symptoms but of causes. The man who was sick of the palsy must have been shocked at the diagnosis of Jesus: 'Son, thy sins be forgiven thee.' What would happen if we went to the doctor with our complaint, and found that he wanted to talk about sins? We might feel a little offended and think that he was being very personal. But where there is faith in Jesus, He will search us to the very soul. If there is peace there, then the tendency should be to physical health also. Sometimes the body is flogged to death by an imperious, haughty, greedy, jealous spirit. It is not surprising that sometimes it breaks under the intolerable weight it is asked to bear. Faith means that we shall want Him to search us to the depths. This is the word of faith that comes down to us from an age long before that of Jesus, though the words seem to take on a new meaning when we have known Jesus: 'O Lord thou hast searched me and known me. Thou knowest my downsitting and mine uprising, thou understandest my thought afar off. Thou searchest out my path and my lying down, and art acquainted with all my ways. For there is not a word in my tongue, but, lo, O Lord, thou knowest it altogether. Thou hast beset me behind and before, and laid thine hand upon me' (Ps 139).

Here are three quotations which illustrate the scope of faith and its nature:

(1) 'There is but one outer test of true faith—the incessant production of good works; there is but one inner—patience.' (Charles Williams, in his introduction to *Letters of Evelyn Underhill*.)

(2) 'Faith is always a victory, not simply a weapon which wins victory.' (Robinson: *Job and his Friends*.)

(3) 'I do not attempt, O Lord, to soar to Thy height, because I do not in any way compare my understanding with Thine; but I do desire to understand Thy truth as far as my heart believes and loves it. For I do not seek to understand in order that I may believe, but I believe in order that I may understand. For this also do I believe; that "I shall not understand unless I believe".' (Anselm.)

THE NAME (*See* Mt 10[22], 18[20], 19[29])

The awarding of a name in Biblical times was designed to express or to affect a character. Thus Jesus was so called because He should 'save his people from their sins' (Mt 1[21]). To call one's name over a place or thing would also establish ownership. When Jesus says, 'Ye shall be hated of all men for my name's sake', He means that because we are His we shall be hated. Similarly we have what is perhaps an early definition of a Christian Church in the words: 'Where two or three are gathered together in my name, there am I in the midst of them.' 'In my name' could mean because we are His, and He has called His name over us. Or it might mean 'For my sake', in the desire to realize His presence, and to give a practical expression to His will. As far as the first disciples were concerned, the will for them is proclaimed in Mt 28[19] : 'Go ye therefore, and make disciples of all the nations, baptizing them into the name of the Father and of the Son and of the Holy Ghost; teaching them to observe all things whatsoever I commanded you: and lo, I am with you alway, even unto the end of the world.' This commission has been accepted by the Church ever since, and is the inspiration of its missionary task.

DAY OF JUDGEMENT (*See* Mt 11[22, 24], 12[18, 36, 41-2], 23[33])

This is an aspect of the message which often disturbs people, and therefore is overlooked. And yet, if the coming of Christ was a serious act on God's part, it surely demands a decision on man's. The events within our life on earth are affected by our decisions, and it seems logical that when this life comes to an end there should be an opportunity to see what the eternal effects of actions have been. The Gospel does not leave us in doubt that there are eternal effects. If we are disposed to question this, then we should seriously consider the meaning of Mt 25^{31-46}. The word used for judgement is associated with our word 'criticism', which fundamentally means discernment or discrimination. The parable of the Last Judgement in Mt 25 has precisely this significance in the separating of the sheep from the goats. There is a dangerous spirit of toleration abroad, which would have us believe that there is neither good nor evil, but only a monotonous grey moral tone. The situation, however, does not seem like this to anyone who has had the tremendous privilege of knowing Jesus. It does not seem possible that any man shall 'get away with' his sin, seeing that it is an offence against God. If a man succeeds in hiding from this fact in this life, he will have to face it in an after life. 'God is not mocked. Whatsoever a man soweth that shall he also reap' (Gal 6^7).

THE END OF THE WORLD (See Mt $13^{40, 49}$, 24^3, 28^{20})

The RVmg reads 'the consummation of the age'—a phrase that again reminds us of the essential seriousness of life. There is an easy-going interpretation of life that would lead us to suppose that, just as an evolutionary process is discernible in the realm of nature, a similar process may be seen in the moral world. But recent events have shown that modern man has a wonderful capacity for reverting to barbarism in the midst of his boasted civilization. This age to which we belong is not an immortal one. It seems to be a probationary one. Man has a responsibility for his actions, and by that responsibility he will be judged. When all allowances are made for environment, heredity and the host of influences good and bad that are brought to bear upon us throughout our life, there still remains the element of choice. Some would say that we cannot even help our choices, that they are already determined for us by what has happened before. Such an interpretation does not, however, seem to fit the facts. We act as though we were free and not irrevocably bound to our destiny. Our attitude to others implies that we regard them as being free, and our opinion of them is based on the assumption that they can help being what they are. There is no escaping that this is the Bible outlook. If it is true that man cannot help being what he is, then the work of the prophets and the coming of Jesus are made nonsensical. A glance at the passages cited above will show that the future life is definitely determined by decisions taken here and now. The determinative factor is repentance followed by decision.

The question of heaven and hell arises in this connexion. An excellent modern treatment of the subject is *The Great Divorce*, by C. S. Lewis. The book will be found to contain first-rate material for sermons on the subject, as well as for meditation. We must be wary of too materialistic an interpretation of the after-life. We shall not experience it in the flesh, but the language in which we try to express our understanding of the future is the language which belongs to earthly human existence. At the best we can suggest only analogies, not actualities. This is what the N.T. tries to do. Some are a little distressed because heaven is sometimes described in terms of harps, golden pavements, and crowns. But these are only images which are intended to suggest perfect harmony, infinite preciousness, and victory over evil. If the images are a stumbling-block, change them, but keep the ideas. For surely heaven can have no meaning apart from harmony— primarily harmony with God. All the discord of life arises from being out of tune with God. The discords with our fellows are subsidiary to that. Think of this harmony in terms of the reconciliation which Jesus effected for us. It will then seem to be precious gold indeed, and the fact that the crown of victory over all sin has been placed on our heads by His hands should be the cause of abundant rejoicing. But hell seems to be a corollary of heaven. How long can a man resist the grace of God? That is a grave theological problem. God will never force a man to love Him; if He did, love would lose its significance. Then presumably some men may assert their 'independence' of God indefinitely. C. S. Lewis suggests that those who will not accept the love of God will find heaven intolerable. The spirit of resistance to God, out of which men make their individual hells, will of itself exclude from the enjoyment of heaven. Our future destiny is not a matter which God decides by an irrevocable fiat; it is decided by our own determination. It is asserted of Judas that 'he went to his own place'. He went whither he was fitted. A man who is inured to living in the darkness will find the light of day unbearable, and in an agony he will seek to hide himself from it. The joy of heaven lies in the discovery that we have God for company for ever. The real pain of hell lies in the knowledge that a man has only himself for company. For a state like this, the lake of brimstone, weeping and gnashing of teeth, seem to be very mild metaphors.

RANSOM (*See* Mt 20[28])

This is the only occurrence of this word in the N.T., apart from the parallel passage in Mk 10[45]. To Jewish ears there would be nothing strange in the word. The natural association would be with the Temple sacrifices. The sacrifice was a means of approaching God, and expressed the desire to establish right relations with Him. Nevertheless, there was no propitiation for deliberate sin or sins committed 'with a high hand', but for sins of unconscious omission which had largely to do with ritual uncleanness. The meaning at the heart of this word is probably reconciliation, and it would be that suggestion which would be conveyed to the original hearers.

But the actual Greek word used in the text describes ransom-money that secured the freedom of slaves. In the early Christian centuries, there was great controversy concerning the person to whom the ransom was paid. Some said that Christ handed Himself over to the Devil, in order that he might let the sinners that he held in thrall go free. The Devil, having agreed to the bargain, was thwarted because God intervened and raised Christ from the dead and thus cheated him of his prey. The picture seems crude, and is a sad warning as to what may happen when we allow a mere metaphor to be treated as though it were literal truth. The word appears to be used by Jesus in order to drive home the facts that through Him we are brought into a state of peace with God, and obtain freedom from all that unfits us for His worship. As to how this happens we must appeal to experience. Everyone knows that he is unable to fit himself for communion with God. We cannot cleanse ourselves. Even if it were possible to do so for the future, what shall be done about the past? We cannot rid ourselves of all its influence merely by determining to do so. But we have the assurance of Christ that, if we trust in Him, the past is forgiven and the future assured. Peace with God is obtained through Him, and we are endowed with His strong love which fortifies us against evil. Christ died to sin; sin no longer had dominion over Him. He was perfect in His Manhood and there was no bar to His approach to God. By faith in Him we are brought to God, not by merit of our own. We are strengthened against sin, because we are enabled to recognize it in the light of His wise presence. Discrimination is a Christian gift and is developed as the relationship with Christ develops. Many people fall into sin because they do not recognize its presence, nature, or effects. But more is required than the recognition of sin, if it is to be overcome. We can see and still fall, simply because we have not settled our priorities. We are given 'the expulsive power of a new affection' in Christ. Paul, remembering out of his own experience what his love for Christ meant in practical living, was able to write these sound words of advice: 'Whatsoever things are true, honourable, just, lovely, of good report; if there be any virtue and if there be any praise, think on these things' (Phil 4⁸). In Christ all these noble qualities are summed up, and to think of Him is to lose the thoughts that are likely to lead to sin.

LOST (See Lk 15)

Luke has a special concern for the sinner, and Lk 15 contains much material which is found in none of the other Gospels, and deserves separate consideration. The preacher will find here abundant material for evangelical appeal; it will always be relevant to the human situation.

Among the Jews a man might be regarded as being 'lost' because he had wilfully behaved in ways unbecoming to a Jew. 'Publicans and sinners' were regarded as being lost. They had not lived up to the dignity of their nationhood and religion. Allowances do not seem to have been made for environment, heredity, and other influences. Our Lord was very critical of the loveless attitude which some Pharisees assumed towards their sinful brethren. In the sight of God, it would seem that no amount of 'religious' activity can compensate for a lack of charity. Paul placed charity, or love, foremost among the three supreme Christian virtues (1 Cor 13). So, in dealing with sin in others, we need to show mercy, even while we display a fearless understanding. The human heart is desperately wicked, but we too have a human heart, and even if it be true that we have more virtue than others, that is all due to the operation of Christ upon us. In preaching we do not declare human merit; it is not to human perfection that we desire to draw attention. We are at best only heralds, calling attention to what God has done in Christ.

But a Jew might also regard as 'lost' the people who belonged to other nations. It is difficult for us to realize the contempt with which the Jew might regard the Samaritan. They were near neighbours, but of different origins, and no love was lost between the two parties (see relevant paragraphs in AOT and ANT). The antipathy between Jew and Samaritan was of long standing.

By the time of Jesus it was well established as traditional. It had become almost instinctive and the justification for it was never examined. Jesus, however, was not the victim of irrational prejudice. His inclination was to estimate the Samaritans by what He knew of them. On this basis they compared very favourably with the Jews. We call one of His parables 'The Good Samaritan', not always realizing how very novel it is to attach such an adjective to such a noun. On the showing of Jesus the Samaritan of the story displayed a finer sense of humanity than the Jews who passed by on the other side. Jesus was attacking foolish national prejudice in His story, and would surely remind us today to be on guard against those irrational prejudices that we assimilate almost without knowing how. It is surprising how our theoretical knowledge about any nation receives a rude shock when we happen to meet an actual citizen. It is a moot point how far nations actually have general characteristics. It is certain that our judgement of individuals can be gravely prejudiced because we will not see them as individuals, but only as members of a particular nation. In the Gospel there is no room for prejudice of that kind. God is the God of all men and His Son is the Saviour of all. How characteristic and fitting it is that Luke, who was a companion of Paul, should emphasize this aspect of the teaching of Jesus. Read what Paul writes about our Lord's attitude to racial conflict and enmity in Eph 2$^{13-18}$.

Nothing can be lost unless it has first belonged. It may seem to many a man that he has lost track of God; but God has not lost track of him. The Church will always have this mission to those who have not yet realized that they 'belong'. The parables of Lk 15 are parables of coming back home. Home awakens a nostalgia in many hearts, from the schoolboy to the exile. It is said that among some members of the British Commonwealth, it is the custom to refer to England as 'home', though they have never been there. But their ancestors were born there. The Church has today a mission to many whose ancestors acknowledged that they were children of God, but whose descendants have become careless of the fact. There must be many to whom the Gospel will be preached, who will not be so far from home that they will not listen to the call to come back. But there will be others who will be so far off that they will not know that there is any other place than the 'far country'. For them the kindness and the yearning love of God will have to be established afresh. And when we speak to them it must be as brother to brother. Moreover, the company into which they are invited must give them all or more than they were seeking elsewhere. Full weight must be given to any criticism of the Church as being cold, unfriendly, or clannish. A community of Christ which has these characteristics is not likely to make much headway with the mission on which we are sent to the 'lost'. Lk 15 suggests three necessary attitudes to the lost. They are not mutually exclusive, but should exist together in harmony. First there is the compassionate search of the shepherd for the lost sheep. The capacity to care will carry through any task of redemption, whatever the weariness and cost to body, mind, and spirit. Not many have awakened to the compassion which will drive a man to prayer on behalf of a lost soul, as well as to the most costing forms of self-denial. Secondly, there is the diligence of search for the lost coin. No method needs to be justified, if it results in the bringing of any individual into the orbit of the Christian family. But it is not becoming that the entrenched members of that family should greet such methods with uncom-prehending criticism, simply because it was not the method which brought *them* into the Kingdom. The true seeker needs to be experimental, but he must never let experiment blind him to his aim—which is the finding and the rescuing of the lost. Finally, there is the welcome of the Father to the returned son. How unfeigned was that reception. How readily the Prodigal was made to feel that the home was really his, and that he truly belonged there. There was nothing wrong with the Father's welcome, but a deep shadow was thrown over the homecoming by the grudging attitude of the elder brother. It is easy enough to sympathize with him. After all, he had stayed at home. Yet it is a strange thing that it did not seem to have occurred to him that there could be no greater privilege than being with the Father. He wanted to bring up the whole past and keep it ever fresh in the family circle. If only he had known that the past was fresh enough in the mind of the younger brother; that it seemed all the more terrible in view of the kindly welcome that greeted him on his return. May God forgive any member of His Church who becomes so staid and proper that there is no good-will for one who returns from the far country, and no zeal in the welcome that makes the far-traveller know that he is wanted.

THE GOSPEL OF JOHN

It is proposed to devote part of this section to the affirmations which our Lord made concerning Himself, but first, attention will be drawn to some of the key words upon which John places special stress.

THE WORLD (See Jn 1⁹, ²⁹, 3¹⁶, ¹⁷, 9³⁹, 14¹⁹⁻³⁰, 16³³)

The world looms large in *John*. The Greek word is *kosmos* and occurs only 14 times in the Synoptics, and 46 times in Paul; but in John's Gospel 80 times, and in the First Epistle 22 times.

For the Jew the world was involved in the Fall and thus could not be perfect. But there must have been something very precious about it, if Christ could die for it (Jn 3¹⁶). Yet it was the very nature of that fallen world which compassed the death of Jesus.

Jn 14¹⁷. The world cannot receive the Spirit of Truth. It is not comfortable to be known through and through and to be searched as the Spirit searches. Every bad tradition and unexamined prejudice, and all personal infallibility, cause blindness to the Spirit. One must be humble before God if the vision of the Truth is to be granted.

Jn 7⁷. The world is wilfully hostile. It hates Christ. To be sure, men unthinkingly pay certain tributes to Him, but when it is clearly understood that He reads us like a book, can plumb the deepest secrets, and when He shows that not one is righteous and that no one is as good as he thinks he is, then human self-respect is in revolt. Men will sometimes accept an adviser, leader, friend, without complaint. There is no damage to pride in that. It is a *Saviour* that men will not have, for that means the admission of defects that have been covered up, and, above all, the confession that no man can save himself by his own efforts.

If only the Christian would keep off this point, he would be well thought of. Even when the Master is hated, there still might be esteem for the servant (Jn 7⁷). This seems to have been temporarily true for the first disciples. But later, when they were fully committed to their Lord, the opposition increased and they drew the world's animosity upon themselves (Jn 15¹⁹, 17¹⁴). Jesus does not leave us in any illusion as to what we may expect from the world.

Jn 16³. The world does not know Christ. Knowledge means surrender, committal. If you try to keep Christ at arm's length while you inspect Him, He turns into a phantom. The world cannot commit itself, because its self is already committed to things seen and handled. But the world will betray our trust even when it appears to be giving us what we want.

A newly-married couple moved their wedding gifts into their

new home. A letter arrived for them containing two tickets for a play they had longed to see, but there was no indication who had sent them. The night of the performance arrived, the couple left for the theatre, wishing they could thank their benefactor. The evening was enjoyable and they wondered still who their unknown friend could be. On opening the door of their home they found that the place had been ransacked and the best of their property removed. And on the table lay a note saying: 'Now you know.' The world ever takes away more than it gives, hence the wisdom of 1 Jn 2[15].

Dr W. F. Howard has defined the world as 'The mass of mankind mobilized in defiance of the divine purpose'. Conflict with the world is lifelong, if only because every Christian has something of the world within himself. These words of Cardinal Newman will make one ask to what extent we have vanquished the world. 'Are we tempted to neglect the worship of God for some temporal object ? This is of the world and not to be admitted. Are we ridiculed for our conscientious conduct ? This again is a trial of the world, and to be withstood. Are we tempted to give too much time to our recreations: to be idling when we should be working; reading or talking when we should be busy in our temporal calling; hoping for impossibilities, or fancying ourselves in some different state of life from our own; over-anxious of the good opinion of others; bent upon getting the credit of industry, honesty, and prudence ? All these are temptations of this world. Are we discontented with our lot, or are we over-attached to it, and fretful and despairing when God recalls the good He has given ? This is to be worldly-minded.'

Jn 16[33]. But we are not alone in the world, nor do we fight in our own strength. Jesus knows the world for what it is. He has been tempted in all things like as we are, yet without sin (Heb 4[15]). He shows up the world in its true colours and He was never taken in by it. That is why He could say to His followers: 'In the world ye have tribulation, but be of good cheer, I have overcome the world.' In fact the victory over the world has been won; it remains for the disciples to realize it.

LOVE (*See* Jn 3[19, 35], 14[15-30], 15[9-18], 17[23-26], 21[7, 16])

The Gospel of John might be called the Gospel of Love; yet it would perhaps be misleading to do so, for there are many possible interpretations of 'love', ranging from the grossest forms of self-indulgence to the most heroic forms of self-sacrifice. Broadly speaking, there are two main forms of love:

(1) *Eros*. This form of 'love' is represented by the Greek god whose statue stands in Piccadilly Circus. He represents the desire to possess. This may result in the unloveliest demonstrations of possessiveness, which in common speech may stand for 'love'. Or it may be shown in the love of honour and distinction and power: a desire to exalt oneself in order to exercise authority over others.

The direction of *eros* is ever upwards, striving for more, self being always at the centre of activity and its prime motive. Closely related to it is what Paul calls 'lust'—though that also is an unfortunate word, for the root idea of the original Greek word is that of self-aggrandisement. There was once a popular advertisement, showing a little boy in a bath-tub, struggling to reach a piece of soap which was on the floor, just out of his range. The caption was: 'He won't be happy till he gets it.' That is suggestive of self-seeking love; though it is often found that, even when we do 'get it', we are still not happy! The possession of one thing only leads to the desire for another. There are forms of love which, on the surface, seem to be disinterested, but which in fact are forms of selfishness. It was once said of a woman: 'She lives for others, and you can tell the "others" by the hunted look in their eyes.' That is perhaps a hard saying, but it does remind us that it is not the highest kind of love which seeks to dominate and control, and which results in making the recipient afraid or resentful.

(2) *Agape*. What a contrast to *eros*-love is that new form of 'love' which we find in the N.T. In order to describe it, Jesus brought back into circulation an old and rarely used Greek noun, *agape*. It was the nearest thing to being a new word to describe a new quality. It is inadequate to translate it as 'love'. The AV sometimes renders it as 'charity', but that is misleading. The real connotation is that of caring, of self-giving to the uttermost.

God's nature is *agape* (1 Jn 4[8, 16]). Then whatever we can learn about God will illuminate the meaning of this word. The love of God was in operation long before men discovered it (1 Jn 4[10]). For God, love consists not in getting good, but in doing and giving love, and His children take after Him. Bishop Anders Nygren, in his famous study of *Agape and Eros*, says: '*Agape* sets its mark on everything in Christianity. Without it nothing that is Christian would be Christian. *Agape* is Christianity's own original conception.'

Moreover, Christian love is not kindled by the attractiveness, nor killed by the unattractiveness, of its object. In the course of his duties, a minister once visited a slum home where there were six young children. As he was leaving, one of the older children brought the youngest to him and said: 'Mister, it's her birthday today. Give her a kiss.' The little one was grubby, her face unwashed, and her nose dirty. Relating the incident to a member of the congregation afterwards he asked: 'What would you have done?' The reply came readily: 'I should have said, "Ask Mummy to wash your face and wipe your nose, and then I will kiss you".' Now God is holy. Between us and Him there is a great gulf fixed. But He has bridged it and offered His compassionate love to all without reserve. He has not waited until we were ready for Him. He did not give us His love because we deserved it, for 'while we were yet sinners Christ died for us'.

Christian love creates value in the one loved. It is now no longer possible to despise any man since every man is 'the brother for whom Christ died'. How quickly human dignity can be lost when there is none to care; how quickly it can be attained when it is realized that one is the object of God's vital concern. God Himself initiates fellowship with Himself. There is no way from man's side for man to come to God. The implications of the coming of God to man are set out in the wonderful message of Jn 3[16].

This love is not of human origin; it is a divine gift. It inspires adoration and awakens the spirit of receptiveness. Because all love is received, all pride in works is eradicated, for works are the result of the overflow of God's love in our own life. Christian love does not mean the death of self, but of selfishness; not the death of self-hood, but of self-centredness.

Finally, here are three pertinent quotations of passages that appear in the biography of Florence Allshorn by J. H. Oldham:

(1) Quoted from the Russian novelist, Dostoevsky: 'Jesus died because of love, but what do you and I know about it? We who prattle of love, blind as to what it is, reducing it to some small humdrum notion of being kind. To suppose that it is a quality which we can call up and use, when and as we like between the rising up of the sun and its going down, and then to talk from this common habit of mind about the love of Jesus, or the love of God, or any such love, is an offence, almost a blasphemy.'

(2) Quoted from Nietzsche, the German philosopher: 'And this hypocrisy found I worst among them, that even they that say

they have the virtue of love, feign that virtue . . . it is mediocrity though it be called love, and ye shall perish of your many petty virtues. Too much yielding to yourselves, that is your soil. But for love to grow tall like a tree, it must wind hard roots round hard rocks. O that ye would renounce half-willing.'

(3) 'The love of Jesus does not start with the romantic love of the poets, but with the very unpoetical neighbour. There was a difference between the thing we had known as friendship and this all-embracing friendliness which Christ epitomized in His own life.'

THE WRATH OF GOD (See Jn 3³⁶)

It may seem strange that, in a passage which speaks so tellingly of the love of God, there should come also this reminder of the wrath. Wrath and love are two sides of the same coin; wrath is the negative side of love. Paul has more to say about the wrath of God in Rom 2⁵* and in Eph 5⁵⁻⁶, and full weight must be given to the fact that it is those who have spoken most plainly about the *love* who have paused to consider the *wrath*. The love of God is not indulgent, and God has too much respect for His creation to pretend that we are children who need to be humoured, pacified, and spoiled. The wrath is not doled out arbitrarily, but is actually the way in which God is experienced when He is refused or disobeyed. Transgress the laws of good health and you receive what you deserve and ought to have expected. Jesus came on earth that we might come to know God as love. But if we ignore His witness, transgress His word, it will not be surprising if we find that life is a disappointing affair, and is very apt to betray our hopes. God's wrath must not be confused with the impetuous anger that disfigures human relationships. It is part of the logic of man's spiritual being. If there were no wrath, we might begin to doubt whether the love were serious. Make no doubt, God hates all sin, wherever it may be found and in whatsoever form. Since this is true, what can we suppose His attitude is, when men deliberately toy with thoughts and deeds that He has shown to be inimical to His Will and Kingdom? Does He look on indulgently and say 'Boys will be boys', or does He lead us to believe that all will come out right in the end? Is it not rather the truth that sin is a disease to be dealt with here and now, lest it extend its malicious influence and bring about widespread disaster? It is at our

* See ANT, para. 451.

peril that we ignore the warning of 2 Cor 6[2]: 'Now is the acceptable time; behold now is the day of salvation.' To turn our minds upon the wrath of God will help us to remember what an urgent thing preaching is, and how great is our responsibility to our hearers.

ETERNAL LIFE (*See* Jn 3, 4, 5 and 6)

Some are frightened at the prospect, because they think of eternal life in terms of endless time. If that were the correct interpretation, we should do well to be intimidated. But look for a moment at some of our earthly experiences. When we have been intensely occupied, or when we have been enjoying perfectly congenial company, the clock has ticked away without our noticing it. It is only when we are bored, unoccupied, or giving but grudging attention to the work in hand that time hangs heavily and the moments pass with leaden step. Now John interprets eternal life as personal contact; it is 'to know thee, the only true God and him whom thou didst send, even Jesus Christ' (Jn 17[3]). This life partakes of the qualities of the eternal world. They are made known to us in the midst of our mortality that we too may become immortal. These qualities are obedience to a heavenly Father, generous outpouring of love towards Him and His creatures, and the realization that we are created to glorify Him and not ourselves. Where these attitudes are realized, eternity has begun. We do not need to wait for an indefinite future in order to experience it. It may begin any time when a man chooses. The common criticism of the Church and its teaching is that all the good things are postponed until after death. We are familiar with the cheap jibe of promising 'pie in the sky when we die', which seems to be repeated in a more cynical form in Rupert Brooke's poem, *Heaven*. But this mockery by-passes the real Christian teaching that the joy of fellowship with God may be known *now*. When the preacher goes out with the Word, his offer is a present offer. Heaven is made real to us before we come thither. Life hereafter brings to us an intensification and consummation of an experience that has already begun.

OUR LORD'S AFFIRMATIONS ABOUT HIMSELF

(1) *I am the Bread of Life* (Jn 6[35, 51])

This occurs in the discourse attached to the story of the feeding of the multitude. John has no account of the Last Supper, but his teaching and exposition of the meaning of the event are partly given in this chapter. It is quite clear that he has in mind the first Holy Communion. The bread is the staple diet of life. It becomes assimilated to the body, supplying it with nourishment and sustenance. It is necessary for existence. There is nothing spectacular or sensational about it. It is commonplace and belongs to the home. Part of Jesus' teaching surely is that the life of Christian faith is meant to be associated with man's ordinary needs. He requires faith as he requires food. Both in their own way supply him with elements that he vitally needs. Withhold food and he dies. Withhold the ministries of Christ and the soul dies. It would be a rash man who would try to define the soul. But it may be thought of perhaps as that part of our make-up which is capable of apprehending God and of responding to Him. This capacity is part of man's essential being. It is not peculiar to some and withheld from others. By the exercise of this faculty man becomes fully man, for it is this faculty which ultimately distinguishes him from the beasts of the field.

The bread of the miracle is amply sufficient for all needs. The multitude is satisfied. In the Sacrament of the Holy Communion we realize to the full the truth of the words:

> *Thou, O Christ art all I want,*
> *More than all in Thee I find.*

He gives Himself to us as strength in weakness, health in sickness, guidance in perplexity, salvation in sin. This affirmation reminds us of the Necessity of Christ.

(2) *I am the Light of the World* (Jn 8[12], 9[5])

John treats the miracles of Jesus as acted parables. Thus in Jn 9 he makes the healing of the blind man an occasion for dealing with our Lord as the bringer of light. He is the Light of the world because he removes spiritual blindness. The most serious blindness is that which causes oblivion to the work of Christ. This blindness is obvious in those who are afar off, but it is not unknown in those who are nigh. The Pharisees, with all their religious tradition, with their very determined efforts to meet what they thought were the divine requirements, nevertheless could not perceive in Jesus the activity of the very God to whom they were offering their worship. Pharisaical faults are faults of the religious, and may easily develop in the community which claims to belong to Christ. Within the Church we can become blind to the power of

Christ and indifferent to His true work. We can value its fellowship above Christ's saving power from sin. We can use it as an
outlet for our talents, instead of as an opportunity for worshipping
the living God. When Elisha wished his servant to perceive the
fact of the activity of God, he prayed 'Open his eyes that he may
see' (2 Kings 6[17]). That should be the daily prayer of every
Christian. Blindness is the affliction most to be feared in the
Christian life.

Christ as light means that in His presence we are able to discern
truth from falsehood. In false light, even tawdry things look
splendid. Stage clothes are very impressive in strong artificial
light, but bring them to the light of day and how shabby they
appear. They are made to look well under artificial conditions and
they do well there. But the Christian is meant to do well in real
life, and we need to bring our words, thoughts, and deeds into
the true light, that their artificiality may be seen and purged, and
the qualities of sincerity and truth encouraged.

If there were no light in the world, there would be no colour
either. Imagine what life would be, if all around were coloured
grey. Someone who was making a great struggle of the Christian
life admitted that, when she saw the good time being enjoyed by
the girls in the office who were not Christians, she found herself
envying them. Evidently something had gone gravely wrong with
her knowledge of Christ, whose intention was to bring His joy
and the life abundant to men. It may well be that some reject the
call to Christ because they think of it in terms of giving up, rather
than of receiving. This is a good reason why, in all our advocacy
of Christ, we need to be positive, and to make quite clear that the
Christian life begins with the acceptance of an offer of abundant
life.

(3) *I am the Door of the Sheep* (Jn 10[7, 9])

When the sheep were in the fold, the shepherd lay across the
opening, as though he were the door. No intruder could thus
enter without disturbing him. While the sheep slept he watched.
Christ as the door acts as the guardian of His disciples. When we
pray, we do not need to call God's attention to ourselves. To
listen to some prayers you might think that God knew very little,
and that everything must be mentioned in case He should forget.
Not a very worthy conception of prayer! We pray to remind ourselves that He is in charge, that He is in control of the traffic of
life and that we can afford to trust Him. It is not necessary for us

to do His work for Him. Jesus discouraged lengthy prayers. Is it possible that some long prayers may be symptoms of a shaky confidence in the power of God?

But the shepherd as the door is the only way into the fold. If a man would enter the Kingdom of God, he can come only through Christ. There is no other way. It is possible to approach God through other ways than Christ. Philosophy and the various world religions throw some light upon the divine Being. So much so that there are times when we are impressed by the similarity between them and Christian teaching. Of all the religious teachers, Jesus stands alone only in the emphasis which He placed upon God as *Father*. 'No man cometh unto the Father, but by me.' In Jesus alone do we see that caring, self-giving, holy Fatherhood which constitutes the Kingdom. When the preacher goes out, he has a unique thing to say, and he can be sure that no one but the Christian can say it. Perhaps, if it be said often enough and graphically enough, it will be at last believed, to the comfort of many souls.

(4) *I am the Good Shepherd* (Jn 10[11])

A good pen is a pen that is well suited for the job of writing. The good shepherd is well fitted for the task of looking after sheep.

(*a*) The good shepherd leads. In the West the shepherd drives. The dictators have taken their cue from him. In the East the shepherd leads. He is the first to encounter the danger and to give warning of it. The disciple will know that Jesus has met the hazards of life and negotiated them on our behalf. Jesus had first-hand experience of all that would arrest our progress and He may be trusted to see us through.

(*b*) The shepherd protects. 'Thy rod and thy staff they comfort me.' The rod repelled the wild beast that would carry off a member of the flock, the staff with its crook rescued the sheep which had fallen into perilous places. The shepherd's life was shared with his flock. His well-being could not be separated from theirs.

(*c*) The shepherd lays down his life, if need be. The hireling is there only to fleece the sheep; the shepherd is there for the sake of the sheep and to give them of his own joy and life. He will not desert them in their time of need. Even if they need his life for their saving, they shall have it.

(5) *I am the Resurrection and the Life* (Jn 11[25], 5[24])

Where Jesus is, death is conquered. When we have faith in Him, death no longer has dominion over us. It dominates neither by its fear nor by its power. The Christian does not fear death, because it brings him into a richer experience of the Lord who has been his delight in the time of his life upon earth. Neither has death power to bring him to an end. Already the Christian has become what he is by reason of the fact that Christ lives and was raised for ever from the thraldom of death by an act of God. The witness of the Church, the progress of the Gospel, the experiences of individuals, the testimonies of changed lives, are all evidences that Christ lives, and that the record of His resurrection is authentic. What we know of Christ now fortifies us and guarantees the future to us.

(6) *I am the Way, the Truth, and the Life* (Jn 14[6])

The way is meant to be followed, the truth to be believed and the life to be lived. For following, the will must be dedicated; for believing, the mind must be dedicated; and for living, the whole personality must be dedicated. The claim of Jesus upon mankind is a totalitarian claim, and He will be satisfied with nothing less than the whole. In John's Gospel there are more than twenty references to the need to 'abide' in Christ. This means that we cannot afford to permit Him to be a casual visitor. He must be treated as a resident. The door must be opened so that He may come in and stay with us. You cannot be a Christian worthy of the name unless your roots go down very deep. You must, therefore, give yourself time to grow. The condition of growth is that complete surrender implied in this affirmation of our Lord.

(7) *I am the True Vine* (Jn 15[1])

This, coupled with the discourse of Chapter 6, completes the teaching on the sacrament of the Holy Communion. Here is emphasized the New Israel, established by the death and resurrection of Jesus. The Vine was the national emblem of Israel (cf. Jer 2[21], Isa 5[1-7]), but in Jesus there arises a new unity. All in communion with Him receive His love, as the branches receive the sap through the main stem. The branch does not yield fruit of itself. The fruit becomes possible only because it belongs to the fellowship of the vine. It is thus a fellowship of sharing.

But it is also a fellowship of discipline. If anything interrupts the flow of the sap, the branch is removed and burnt. And even the branches which are bearing are likely to develop suckers that will drain away the life into unprofitable directions. Hence there has to be used the pruning knife, that all dangerous growth may be removed. No Christian can afford to be complacent. He needs continually to look to himself, lest he should be encouraging interests and occupations that will lessen his love for God and his sense of indebtedness to the Christian society in the Church. It is in this chapter that the word 'abide' is used again and again. We ought to be detached from many things, but there can be no detachment from Jesus without death.

Thus ends a survey of some of the great words for preaching from the Gospels. But many more remain. The preacher's resources are inexhaustible, and he will always find joy and strength in exploring them.

3. An Outline of Church History

By the Rev. NORMAN P. GOLDHAWK, M.A.

IT is obvious that, in attempting to recount the history of Christianity during the course of its 1900 years, much more will have to be omitted than can be included. We shall try to sketch an outline which may help the student to understand in some measure the main course of this long story, and within which he can insert the details of some of the more significant parts. Even this limited objective will be well worth while if it helps to make clearer the broad sweep of events, for although history does not allow us to forecast the future, yet the vitality of the Church and its capacity for adaptability and recovery amid its varied fortunes is impressive and gives grounds for confidence in regard to its future. In this edition of the *Preacher's Handbook* our task is to take the story roughly down to what is known as the high Middle Ages. We shall not burden the student with more names than are absolutely essential. We shall attempt to record the Church's relationship to some of the situations in which it found itself, its victories and its defeats, but we shall not attempt to sit in judgement upon its life and doctrine. We must accept it as a factor in history. The Church as we see it and can describe it is the earthen vessel, rooted in the divine will, which in spite of its faults contains and makes available the treasure of the Gospel. We today are part of its ongoing life. To try to understand sympathetically this institution, as it has appeared and acted in the situations in which it has found itself in the past, is an essential requirement of the student, particularly when those situations seem strange to him.

It is vastly significant that it was within the Roman Empire the Church was born. At that time the Empire was a great concourse of some eighty-five million people living within the 6,000 miles of frontiers which stretched from the Atlantic to the River Euphrates and from the English Channel to the African desert. The power of the Roman Republic had been extending in the centuries before Christ, until in the middle of the century before our era social and civil war broke out. Finally Octavian became supreme and in 27 BC a new system was inaugurated with him as Emperor. Although nominally responsible to the Senate, he was in fact a dictator controlling the machinery of State. Under the imperial government, internal peace and security were enjoyed for many years by the inhabitants of the provinces and most of them had cause to be grateful to the Roman administration. During the first century AD, England and part of Scotland were annexed, but the most northerly conquests were later abandoned and the Wall of Hadrian, which stretched from the Tyne to the Solway, became the recognized frontier. The Empire was indeed a sort of league of nations, within which a traveller could have gone without let or hindrance, from the Cheviots or the Rhine in the north, some 2,000 miles to Mount Atlas or the deserts of Egypt in the south, or the 3,000 miles from the Atlantic in the west to the Euphrates in the east. The Romans were great administrators, engineers, and builders, and the Roman peace made possible the development of a high civilization. In this connexion it is important to remember that Rome took over the conquests of the great Macedonian soldier and ruler, Alexander, who before his death in 323 BC had planted centres of Greek civilization far and wide in the east. It has been said that this Hellenism meant fusion of races, unity of language, union of cities in a great monarchy, and religious toleration and comprehension. This was the cultural heritage which the Romans took over from the Greeks: Greek philosophy was widely studied and Greek customs observed over a large area. The Greek language could be understood nearly everywhere. It can be said that the characteristic features of the time were Roman discipline and Greek culture.

The area covered by the Roman Empire became the principal territory through which Christianity spread during its early years. It is one of the most significant facts of history that, within five centuries of its birth, Christianity won the professed allegiance of the vast majority of the population of the Roman Empire as well as the support of the Roman State. Perhaps even more significant is it that, although large areas of the Roman Empire were subsequently lost to Christianity, the Christian religion never died out completely within its borders. The Empire (a map can be found at the back of many Bibles) included much of the territory we know now as Western Europe. As we shall see, most of this was later overrun by invading barbarians. In the resulting confusion it is hardly true to say that the Roman Empire was overthrown: in the words of a modern historian, it rather took the barbarians into itself. They were captivated by the idea of the Empire and were soon deeply influenced by its language, customs, and laws. Above all, they were converted, however rudimentarily, to its religion, Christianity. That fact has had far-reaching consequences. Modern history, from AD 1500, has seen the geographical expansion of the peoples of this area, one effect of which was that by the middle of the eighteenth century Christian communities were to be found on all five continents and on many of the islands on the fringe of those continents. This world-wide spread of Christianity has continued to our own day, so that its professed adherents are now more numerous than those of any other faith and spread over a much wider part of the earth. In one way or other this has been largely due to those nations which have entered into the inheritance of the Graeco-Roman world. On the whole, there has been no corresponding expansion of Christianity amongst those peoples which possessed a relatively high culture untouched by Graeco-Roman civilization. The Roman Empire, of course, embraced only a minority of the world's population. Contemporary with it were the Persian Empire, the great cultural area of India, and the huge expanse of China. From the first, Christianity spread throughout the Roman Empire to an extent greatly in excess of that beyond the Roman borders, and it must be said that in spite of devoted missionary enterprise the numbers of Christians in such areas as India and China have remained until now relatively small. It must, therefore, be concluded that in many ways Rome provided the outward conditions which facilitated the growth of the Church. One need only mention such factors as the unity of the Empire, the means of easy communication which were used by the early missionaries, the cities in which they delivered their message and worked, and the widely understood language in which the Christian Scriptures were written. In spite of undoubted contradictions between the spirit of the Gospel and that of the Roman world, it must nevertheless be recognized that to a certain extent Christianity was woven into the pattern of Western civilization. This has not been an unmixed blessing to the Church and its Gospel, yet it has been partly instrumental in the modern world-wide expansion of Christianity.

But this is to anticipate a very great deal, and humanly speaking the eventual victory of the Church within the Roman Empire must have seemed at the first extremely unlikely. The Church began from Jerusalem of all places, on the very eastern edge of the Empire, and it sprang from a people who could never be easily accommodated within the Empire. It very soon broke through the confines of Syrian Judaism and by AD 50–60 was spreading rapidly around the Eastern Mediterranean. It quickly became evident that the Jews as a whole would not accept Christianity, with the result that the Church had to move out entirely into the non-Jewish world of the Empire. This overcoming of the barriers of Judaism, and adaptation of itself to the Gentile environment, must have been one of the severest crises through which the Church ever passed. Nevertheless, the Jewish background and heritage of the Church meant that certain fundamental convictions were bequeathed to the Church which were basic to its attitude. They may be summarized as follows.

1. There is only one God, the Creator of all things, and He has a righteous Will. The Church soon entered a world which accepted the existence of many different gods, many of whom had little or no connexion with moral behaviour. This contemporary polytheism was a direct challenge to Jews and Christians.

2. Since will is expressed in action and actions are done in time, the time-process had a meaning for Jews and Christians which it did not have for most other people in the Empire. The Hebraic-Christian conviction was that what we know as history is the realm in which God's purpose is being worked out, and it is moving toward a goal, the consummation of God's Kingdom in righteousness.

3. The out-working of this purpose implies the existence of a divine community, the People of God. The Church thought of itself as the *New* Israel.

4. The Old Testament was regarded as the Scriptures of the early Church. Its obvious Jewish characteristics presented many problems, both of acceptance and interpretation, yet in spite of tendencies to the contrary, the Church held on to it as a sacred book. It was not long, of course, before Christians began to use in addition their own body of writings which we know as the New Testament.

1. *THE FIRST THREE CENTURIES*

It must not be imagined that the Christian Church won the allegiance of the Roman State without a severe struggle. In so far as we can give titles to different periods in the history of the Church, it would not be an exaggeration to call the first three centuries the *Martyr Period*. Jesus had clearly warned His disciples that they would experience persecution, but generally

Rome was tolerant of all sorts of local religious worship. We must try to understand why the little body of Christians incurred official hostility, and to do so it is necessary to have some picture of religious conditions within the Empire. There were, of course, many religions to be found, but Roman authority interfered with them as little as possible, and took action against them only when they were held to imperil public order or decency. The Romans themselves were not a very religious people, although much given to superstition, and official Roman religion was in the main a matter of the due performance of traditional rites and ceremonies. All who served the State in any official capacity were expected to honour the gods who protected the city and gave victory to the Roman armies. In addition, each family had its private gods who looked after the special concerns of the household. In the rest of the cities of the Empire, many other gods were worshipped and often the cults were maintained by the civic authorities. Performance of religious duties was bound up with patriotism and social well-being. Quite apart from whether folk really believed in the gods, the traditional rites were good for the welfare of society and to neglect them was to be guilty of anti-social behaviour. In particular this applied to the so-called worship of the Emperor. This came originally from the east, where great rulers were thought of as divine. The feeling was transferred to the Roman Emperor in the west, although it would appear that not all the early Emperors were particularly enamoured of the idea. Yet they saw its practical value. Devotion to the genius of the Emperor was a useful bond of union which provided a focal point for the different peoples of the Empire. How far people really believed in the cult we need not stop to discuss, but those of us who have lived in a country with a totalitarian dictatorship can appreciate the attraction of the idea, and it does often seem to be the case that when vital belief in the true God is absent, some human substitute has to be found. Suffice it to say that the cult of the Emperor became a convenient way of testing a person's loyalty to the State, and it probably involved no more than burning incense before the Emperor's statue.

There were other religions which were becoming generally popular by the time of the Christian era. We know them now under the general title of Mystery Religions. Coming originally from the East, their origins are obscure and lie far back beyond the reach of history: basically all were concerned in some way with a belief in the relationship between human life and the annual dying and rising again of Nature. By secret rites of initiation and other ceremonies people were admitted to their closed fellowships and united with the god, and this purported to release them from destiny and give them the promise of immortality. Since these cults disappeared after a few centuries of our era, our knowledge of them is imperfect. We know enough, however, to realize that for three centuries at least they were serious rivals of Christianity, and the fact that they had ceremonies which bore some resemblance to the Christian sacraments and that they used language akin in some ways to Christian modes of expression, only underlines this rivalry. Most people in Britain are familiar with Mithraism through the excavations on a bombed site in the City of London. Mithras was an old Aryan god coming from India and Persia, identified in some way with the Unconquerable Sun. The cult was introduced into the West during the first century AD and spread rapidly, particularly among the army. But, apart from other differences, Christianity possessed one decisive advantage over these Mysteries—they told their myths of the gods, but the Church could point to One who lived in history and who 'suffered under Pontius Pilate'.

It ought to be added that many of the educated classes were sceptical about contemporary religion and sought help from philosophy, which was yet more akin to the search for a way of salvation than the name suggests to us. When Christianity moved into the Gentile world, it had to accommodate its message in some degree to these people, whose intellectual background was Greek rather than Hebraic. This accommodation is the enduring task of every evangelist, who must try to speak to people in terms they can at least understand. The risk that the content of the message will be changed is always present, yet there is no escaping the task or the challenge (the 'communication' of the Gospel is a basic requirement of the Church today). It was in such an environment that the Church had to work out the statement of its theology, and it had to be done for the most part in Greek and Latin terms. Obviously the intellectual atmosphere influenced the expression of the Gospel to some extent (as it does today) and there was always the threat that foreign elements would be too greatly intruded. One of the greatest dangers of the contemporary philosophy was that most systems were based on a dualism which regarded matter as evil and the spirit only as good. Under many different guises this influence threatened Christian thought and practice, and its challenge can be seen already in the New Testament. Obviously it removes the 'spiritual' or 'divine' so far from the 'material' or 'human' that the very central truth of Christianity, the Incarnation, is threatened, for human experience, on these terms, could not be ascribed to One who was God. Extreme expressions of this type of thought are usually classed together under the general name of Gnosticism, and thinkers who tried to expound the Christian Faith under its influence constituted a real danger to the Church in the second century.

One fact about this profusion of religious belief and practice must be borne in mind. The many cults were not mutually exclusive; none had a 'jealous' God. The gods were many; therefore without any sense of incongruity a person could join in the traditional rites of his city, whatever his private views might be, and even although he might belong to one of the Mystery sects. The one exception to this general attitude of mutual tolerance, based as it was upon polytheism, were the Jews. Even though they were not generally popular, they were granted a special privilege in the Empire. They were exempted from the Imperial cult.

For a time the Christians sheltered under Jewish protection, since those authorities who took any notice of them regarded them as a Jewish sect. Obviously their situation was precarious from the beginning and sooner or later it would become clear to non-Christians. Already in the New Testament we find Christians in trouble, but the early opposition to the Church came not from the Roman authorities, but either from Jews, who through jealousy stirred up the Gentile populations against the Christian missionaries (Acts 13^{50}, 14$^{2, 19}$; cf. 17$^{5-7}$, 1 Thess 2$^{3-6}$), or from people whose financial interests were threatened by the Christian preaching (Acts 16^{19}, 19^{25}). But it was not long before it was realized that Christians were different from Jews, and in Roman eyes this meant that they stepped outside the security normally granted to Jews: on their own they had to justify their position, as it were. It was not long before the young Church felt the heavy hand of Rome.

The first direct attack upon Christians from the Roman government took place during the reign of the Emperor Nero. In AD 64 a great fire destroyed most of the city and rumour suggested that Nero was responsible. Probably through Jewish influences in the imperial household Nero arrested some Christians as the people responsible. Fifty years later the Roman historian, Tacitus, described the events thus:

> So in order to suppress the rumour Nero made into scapegoats

and subjected to exquisite punishments persons detested for their outrageous practices and known to the populace as Christians. Christus, from whom the name took its origin, was executed in the reign of Tiberius by the procurator Pontius Pilate. Checked for a time, the pernicious superstition broke out afresh, not only in Judea, where the trouble started, but even in the City, where all that is vile and shameful flows in from every quarter and is welcomed with enthusiasm. Those therefore who openly admitted to being Christians were first arrested, and on their information a large crowd was convicted, not so much on the charge of arson as for hatred of the human race. Their execution was made an occasion for cruel mockery: some were sent to their death covered with the skins of wild beasts for dogs to tear, some fastened to crosses, some set up to be burned as torches and to serve, when daylight failed, for nocturnal illumination.

We cannot be absolutely sure of the procedure taken against the Christians: it looks as if the charge of arson was dropped and that of hatred of the human race substituted. Probably the authorities inquired into the nature of Christianity and came to the conclusion that it was a threat to the safety of the State. It is obvious that the Christians were generally unpopular and so regarded as the sort of people who might perpetrate attacks upon public safety and order, and it is instructive to ask what it was about them which could have given rise to such ideas—ideas which go contrary to what we might have expected. Yet it is not hard to imagine how pagan neighbours soon realized that Christians were different from themselves, a fact which often gives rise to feelings of suspicion or hostility. No doubt Christians were disliked because they claimed alone to have the truth; their religious scruples made them seem unsociable, since most social occasions would begin with some idolatrous act and Christians accordingly tended to keep themselves apart; they were considered to threaten certain vested interests, while their hopes of the speedy return of Christ and their devotion to His Kingdom raised serious doubts in many minds about their loyalty to the Empire. We know from some of the early Christian writings that Christians were suspected of practices which indicate the queer notions many people must have entertained about the Church (a state of affairs not entirely confined to the first centuries!). Christians were held by many to be atheists (a religion without images, etc., might easily seem to be no religion at all), sorcerers (a popular charge when others broke down, and the miracles of Christ and the apostles could always be cited to substantiate it), cannibals (due no doubt to misconceptions about the language used at the Lord's Supper). Christians had also to defend themselves against accusations of sexual impurity, in which many non-Christians were no doubt attributing to Christians their own misdemeanours; yet there were antinomian excesses among certain Christians from an early date, and the custom of holding love-feasts in the Church might have given false impressions to outsiders (one second-century Christian writer says concerning the 'holy Kiss' that Christians have a word which says, 'If anyone kiss a second time, because it has given him pleasure, he sins!'). Nevertheless the final charge against the Christians was that they were a danger to the State and that the profession of Christianity was tantamount to an attack upon the Roman way of life. Christians were anarchists, because they refused to acknowledge the total claims of the State in matters of faith, and the cult of the Emperor's divinity was the outward expression of this. For the Christians, Jesus, not Caesar, was Lord. It is a disputed historical point whether a special law was in fact promulgated under Nero making the profession of the Christian faith illegal; nevertheless from that time onwards for nearly 250 years Christians were always more or less in danger. During this whole period persecution was sporadic and it is mistaken to imagine that Christians were always being attacked. There were fairly lengthy periods in which the Church in certain areas was able to settle down to a comfortable existence, and some Christian writers complain of the consequent decline in the quality of Christian living. In spite of what we have said about the withdrawal of Christians from certain aspects of civic and social life, it must not be concluded that this was by any means complete or intentional. Certain features of pagan life were avoided, yet Christians are soon found in the Imperial Palace and the Senate and among the philosophers in the Forum. Indeed, the great apologist Tertullian wrote at the end of the second century to pagans: 'We others, Christians, do not live apart from this world; we, like you, frequent the forum, the baths, the workshops, the shops, the markets, the public places; we follow the profession of sailor, soldier, planter, merchant, we put at your service our labour and our industry.' Yet the constant threat of persecution and the hostility of many of the populace imposed a need for restraint on the part of Christians, and this applied to a certain extent to their worship. Private houses were used for this for a long time, but by the third century public churches were coming into use. In certain cities, catacombs or underground cemeteries were used in times of danger as places for worship; they had the advantage that tombs were protected from violation by Roman law, but they cannot really have provided accommodation for secret meetings.

During the first two centuries in particular, the worst outrages against Christians were often perpetrated by mob passion and it is not certain that any of the persecutions were in this period Empire-wide. A great many Christians suffered, but many did not. They were presumably always in danger, since their legal status was at best precarious and a local or provincial official might at almost any time proceed against them. 'Their peril was further accentuated by a procedure which gave their possessions to those who brought a successful accusation against them. Confiscation of goods, imprisonment, and torture might overtake them at any time, followed by hard labour in the mines, or by execution,' yet 'it may well have been that, compared with the total number of Christians, the martyrs were very few' (K. S. Latourette: *A History of Christianity*, p. 86). Records of some of these martyrdoms have come down to us, in some cases reports of eyewitnesses. It will be readily understood how highly these were valued by the Church, for the martyr was looked upon as the true follower of Christ who was led as a lamb to the slaughter. If some of these surviving accounts seem to have been over-elaborated and if certain of the early Christians appear to have expressed an unnatural desire for a martyr's death, this too we can understand. The martyr was *the* public witness to Christ. The preacher will find plenty of illustrations from those early days, and if he turns to such a book as H. B. Workman's *Persecution in the Early Church* he will not be able to read unmoved the chapter on 'The Experiences of the Persecuted', nor easily forget such a witness as that of the aged Christian bishop, Polycarp, who lost his life in the middle of the second century, and who, when bidden to acknowledge Caesar as Lord and blaspheme Christ, gave his immortal reply: 'Eighty and six years have I served Christ and He has never done me wrong. How can I blaspheme my King, who saved me?'

During this period the Church grew apace. The third century saw long periods of peace, broken only by short and severe outbreaks of more highly organized persecution than in the first days. Events were clearly moving towards a final crisis: what should the religion of the Empire be? The last attack on the Church of any real significance began in AD 303. Imperial edicts ordered the cessation of Christian worship, the destruction of Church buildings, the burning of Christian sacred books, the arrest of all the clergy; finally, all Christians were commanded to sacrifice to the pagan idols or suffer for it. Here was the most frightful assault yet made on the Church—the decisive clash between pagan Rome and Christianity. Christian victims were tortured and killed everywhere, although the attacks were severest in the eastern portion of the Empire. It was at this period that a layman of the Roman city of Verulam in Britain, named Alban, is reputed to have been martyred on the hill where the great abbey now stands: he is the first Christian in Britain whose name is recorded. In the end even the pagans began to feel sympathy for the persecuted Christians, but in the east the persecutions raged until AD 311, when toleration was finally proclaimed.

This last and fiercest persecution coincided with a crisis in the government of the Empire, during which several men strove for mastery. There eventually emerged to power a leader who was to change the whole situation, so far as the Christians were concerned. The Roman legions at York proclaimed Constantine emperor in 306; by 312 he had made himself supreme in the western portion of the Empire and in the following year he joined with the eastern Emperor in proclaiming toleration for the Church alongside other religious cults. The proclamation contained the significant words: 'We judge it consonant to right reason that no man should be denied leave of attaching himself to the rites of the Christians, or to whatever other religion his mind direct him. . . . Accordingly the open and free exercise of their respective religions is granted to all others as well as to Christians; for it befits the well-ordered state and tranquillity of our times that each individual be allowed according to his own choice to worship the Divinity.' Certainly this statement marks a great advance in man's religious history, although it was not until many centuries later that liberty of conscience and worship were established (in some areas at least). Yet it has been said that it substituted for the old Roman notion that a man's religion is the State's affair, the doctrine of the rights of the individual conscience. Furthermore, property was restored to the Christians, who were thus granted equal rights with pagans. But something else which greatly affected the position of the Church had occurred: Constantine had become a Christian or had at least befriended the Church. Before one of his battles in 312, he had been thinking about the failure of the heathen gods to help those rulers who worshipped them, and he prayed for guidance to the God of his father, a man not unfavourable to Christianity. Just after noon he saw in the sky a Cross of light above the sun, bearing the inscription: 'In this conquer.' The following night Christ appeared to him in a dream, carrying the same sign of the Cross, commanding him to use it as his standard of victory. Henceforth the new ensign went before Constantine's armies. By 324 he was supreme and sole emperor, and a new era was introduced. The martyr period of the Church was ended, a Christian Emperor was at the head of the government, and the Church had won the struggle for survival and recognition, and all within the comparatively short period of less than three centuries. Such a result would have appeared most unlikely when the first missionaries went forth, or Christian tradesmen and slaves took with them the knowledge of Christ.

It must not, of course, be imagined that all the inhabitants of the Empire were now Christians; nor, in spite of the endurance of many under the fierce onslaughts of persecution, must it be thought that all professing Christians were of a high quality. During the intervals of peace between the attacks on the Church the standard of life of many Christians sank low, and by no means all withstood the test of persecution without denying their faith. Undoubtedly there were many lives gloriously transformed by the Gospel, but it is neither helpful nor truthful to entertain idealized pictures of what the Church was like in past ages. As to the extent of the Church, it has been suggested that at the time of Constantine's conversion it embraced about ten per cent of the Empire's population. There was a higher proportion of Christians in the eastern part of the Empire, but the Church was quite strong in Spain, Gaul (France), Italy, and North Africa. It was concentrated almost entirely in the towns; the country districts were barely touched.

Why did Christianity gain the victory over rival faiths? Many reasons have been suggested. Thus we can point to the action of Constantine, the felt need for a universal religious faith, the apologetics of martyrdom and charity, and the organization of the Church—no other rival faith possessed so powerful and coherent a structure.* Yet these reasons are not sufficient in themselves

---

* The growth of the Church's organization and ministry is a complicated and controversial subject, which cannot be gone into at any length in this chapter. On the ministry, see further *ACD*, pp. 169 ff. The development of the Church's organization was most probably a natural reaction to the circumstances in which the Church found itself. At first there was probably no rigid uniformity of organization in the various local churches, although it is clear that there were officers with specialized functions within the congregations. By the end of the second century the

to account for the Church's success. The point has been expressed in the following way: 'The more one examines into the various factors which seem to account for the extraordinary victory of Christianity the more one is driven to search for a cause which underlies them. It is clear that at the very beginning of Christianity there must have occurred a vast release of energy, unequalled in the history of the race. . . . That burst of energy was ascribed by the early disciples to the founder of their faith. Something happened to the men who associated with Jesus. In his contact with them, in his crucifixion and in their assurance of his resurrection and of the continued living presence with his disciples of his spirit, is to be found the major cause of the success of Christianity. That experience and that assurance were transmitted to succeeding generations' (K. S. Latourette: *History of the Expansion of Christianity*, I.167 f). Of course, other factors must not be ignored, and in spite of the opposition of the Roman Empire in many ways, it must be acknowledged that it provided the necessary conditions for the spread of the Christian faith. In the end we are driven back to the total condition of things as they

---

'clergy' had become a separate order from the 'laity', and the various officials are known by well-established names, which however may not carry precisely the same meanings as in the New Testament or in later times. The chief minister in any place was called a bishop, and he was assisted by presbyters (i.e. elders or 'priests'), and deacons, as well as by a number of subordinate officers. At first the bishop was a minister of a local congregation, but later his parish grew into a diocese, of which he was the administrator, while the presbyters served the separate congregations. From the first, Christians had a strong sense of belonging to one body; with the growth of the Church this had to find expression in a unity of organization, especially as various diverging or 'heretical' versions of the faith soon made their appearance. This urgent need drove the Church to stress the supreme authority of the apostolic writings we know as the New Testament; to look increasingly to the succession of bishops in the great apostolic churches, particularly at Rome (where both Peter and Paul lost their lives during the Neronian persecution), as guaranteeing the apostolic faith; and to use short statements of Christian belief, i.e. creeds, especially for the training of candidates for admission to the Church. The word 'catholic' as applied to the Church soon came to mean, not merely *universal*, but also *orthodox*, and was used to denote the central tradition or party within the Church as distinct from the 'heretics'. Of the worship of the Church, space only allows it to be pointed out that from the beginning Sunday was regarded as the great weekly festival of the resurrection, and the main Sunday service centred around the reading and exposition of Scripture and the celebration of the Lord's Supper or Eucharist (i.e. Thanksgiving); while baptism was universally observed as the rite of admission into the Church.

were at the time, which is perhaps only another way of referring to the Providence of God. With Constantine, the Church enters upon a new era, but the message which comes to us from this first period of the Church's history is that Christ is worth living *and dying* for. And certainly, as Tertullian wrote, the blood of Christians was seed!

2. *AFTER CONSTANTINE*

The Church had survived the fires of persecution, but in another sense its real difficulties were now to begin. We enter the period of the Church's growing power and authority, when rulers were Christians, and ecclesiastics came to hold important places in the life of society. The Church obviously now enjoyed great advantages—a Christian Emperor clearly made the profession of Christianity advantageous in many ways and the Church grew numerically at a high rate. It is easy for the student to be disappointed with events subsequent to Constantine, yet it must be remembered that Christian leaders were faced with new difficulties and new temptations. It is an error to imagine that conditions could have been changed rapidly. At least one new problem arose which has never been finally settled, namely, the relations of the Church to a State which is in name and intention Christian. Such a situation is hardly contemplated at all in the New Testament (which is but one more indication that Christians constantly need to use their intelligence in the application of their faith to changing circumstances). Clearly the Church and the State (or civil authority, to be more accurate) were now to be interrelated in a new way. How is a Christian ruler to act, particularly when many of his subjects are not Christians ? Is the Church to be a branch of the civil service, or the State an executive of the Church ? Within these extremes there are many possible variations of opinion and practice.

During the fourth century the Emperors exercised great influence over the affairs of the Church, continuing thereby their traditional role in the State. The Church had now ample opportunity for proclaiming its message and it is possible to trace an increasing Christian influence in some aspects of secular legislation. On the other hand, it cannot be denied that great numbers of people found it convenient to adopt Christianity, and Church leaders with the secular arm behind them found it easy to persecute either pagans or those Christians whose opinions they considered erroneous. The history of the Church during the fourth century is both complicated and important. Some decisive theological definitions were agreed upon. Constantine soon discovered that the unity of the Church was threatened by a doctrinal dispute concerning the status of Jesus Christ. Associated with the teaching of a presbyter named Arius, Arianism placed Jesus Christ in a subordinate position to the Father. The Emperor may not have realized all that was at stake in this controversy, but his calling together the first general or ecumenical Council of the Church at Nicaea in 325 led to the assertion in a creedal formula that the Son is of one substance with the Father. More than fifty years of further controversy and troubled relationships within the Church were necessary before the implications of the dispute were fully recognized by the Church as a whole, and what we know as 'The Nicene Creed' is associated with the second general council held at Constantinople in 381. In this creed, which is the one we recite during the Communion Service, the Holy Spirit is also affirmed to be a divine Person, and the doctrine of the Trinity thus formally stated. The reigning Emperor, Theodosius I, proclaimed this the official religion of the Empire to the exclusion of all others. It is easy to feel impatient with the prolonged and often embittered discussions and events of the fourth and fifth centuries, but it must be remembered that the central doctrines of the Christian Faith were being thought out as well as fought out. The great protagonist of the Nicene position, Athanasius, knew very well that, if Arianism were correct, then to have dealings with Christ or the Holy Spirit is no guarantee of being brought into certain relationship with God Himself, and so the basis of man's salvation is threatened. Similarly the Council of Chalcedon in 451 defined what is known as the orthodox doctrine of the Person of Christ, who was stated to be at once fully human and fully divine, one Person made known in two natures. During this same period when the Church and the State became so closely interrelated we also find, as if in protest against this new-found security and well-being, the beginnings of a movement away from the world which we know as monasticism. So far-reaching did this become that we shall devote a special section to it at the end of this chapter. Nor must it be overlooked that, on and beyond the borders of the Empire, the missionary spirit was taking the faith to some of those barbarian peoples which were soon to overrun great areas within the Empire, as well as to other places much farther east.

One further event from Constantine's reign was to influence future history to a high degree. This was the removal of his headquarters to Byzantium on the Bosporus, and the building of a new city, a new Christian Rome—Constantinople. It was to become the centre of the eastern portion of the Empire, which thus began to lose its unity and cohesion. After Constantine it is common to find the Empire divided between an eastern and a western Emperor, as well as a growing tension between the eastern and western parts of the Church.

The ecclesiastical events and doctrinal decisions of the century and a half after Constantine helped to prepare the Church for the unexpected political developments which took place during the fifth century. To most inhabitants of the western part of the Empire at the beginning of that century, life must have seemed secure enough. They shared in a common culture, and Latin was by now the language they used, Greek being confined to parts of the eastern Empire. Of course, the west had long carefully guarded the frontiers on the Rhine and Danube, but in 406 these defences suddenly gave way and wild Germanic tribes poured in. Rome was sacked by the Goths in 410, the year 476 saw the last Roman Emperor in the west, and by the end of that century all the western half of the Empire had fallen to the barbarians, who set up their own kingdoms. Yet most of them were deeply attracted to the idea of the Roman Empire and regarded themselves as upholding and continuing its tradition, and many of the invading peoples had at least some acquaintance with and allegiance to Christianity, albeit in its Arian form (a tribute to some great missionaries). Others were pagans. The Romans lost all control of England, for instance, early in the fifth century, and the eastern part of the country fell under the pagan domination of the invading Jutes, Angles, and Saxons. The Christian Church there was destroyed and a form of heathenism substituted, but it continued in the west of the island among the old Celtic inhabitants.

In the chaos caused by the collapse of the Roman system in the west, the Church was the one thing which survived, and it is remarkable how soon the invading peoples adopted the orthodox type of Christian belief which had its western centre in the Roman Church and its bishop. The end of the Empire in the west meant that in a real sense the bishop of Rome, whom we will now call by his usual title of Pope (which simply means 'father' and which was applied as well to the bishops of certain other leading cities in the early Church), inherited the position of the Emperors. The Church outlasted the old Empire and became the centre of unity between the old Roman inhabitants and the Teutonic invaders. This was the Church which, a few generations before, the Roman State had tried to exterminate, and which was to accomplish what the Roman legions had failed to do! For this reason the Church becomes one of the main themes in the history of succeeding centuries. On the other hand, the eastern Empire went on with the Emperor in Constantinople, the imperial power extending over Church and State. For centuries Constantinople was the first Christian city of the world and retained its Christian tradition unbroken until it fell to the Turks in 1453.

The years between the fifth and tenth centuries are sometimes known as the Dark Ages: life was certainly often crude, rough, and marked by ignorance and superstition. Compared with the first 500 years Christianity suffered great reverses and indeed larger losses than at any period in its history. To conclude, however, that all was darkness would be absurd. Some great Christians lived, pioneered on behalf of the Gospel, wrote or suffered. Significant things were happening. The Christian nations of Western Europe were coming to birth. Referring to the fact that Christianity survived, Prof. John Foster has written: 'This surviving Christianity was itself shut in by ignorance and violence; and yet, because it was Christianity, it pointed beyond such limitations. The local church or monastery might be at the mercy of the feudal lord, but what happened in church was not local but universal' (*Beginning From Jerusalem*, p. 36). Let us look at some of the features of the period.

(a) A missionary movement was taking place. Ireland was to play a leading part in this, and the story of the introduction of Christianity there is noteworthy. A native of Roman Britain named Patrick was taken captive by raiders at the beginning of the fifth century and carried to Ireland. He had been brought up a Christian, but found himself now a slave, tending flocks. After at least six years he escaped into Gaul, where he was apparently trained in a monastery in the faith which had begun to deepen within him while in Ireland. He eventually returned to his family in Britain, but in his dreams he seemed to hear the voice of the Irish calling him back. 'Holy youth, come and walk among us once more.' In response to this call, Patrick went back to the land where he had been a slave and in some way was consecrated a bishop. For thirty years he laboured as a missionary in the island and many were brought into the Faith. The planting of Christianity among the Irish was soon to have important results elsewhere, for from the Irish monasteries many were to carry the light of the Gospel far and wide. We are naturally most interested in the conversion of the pagan inhabitants of Britain to Christianity. The missionaries came from two centres, Ireland and Rome, and it is not amiss to see it as a Christian pincer movement. In one of the Irish monasteries Columba was educated. In 562 or 563, in the full vigour of middle life, he left Ireland with twelve companions and landed on the island of Iona, off the west coast of Scotland. There he built a monastery after the Irish fashion— a church and refectory of wood, a number of beehive huts, and a surrounding wall. The little group worked as farmers and fishermen, reading and copying books, keeping up the daily round of prayer and praise. Moreover, they made the island a base from which further missionary journeys were made to the mainland of Scotland and the islands of the Hebrides. In 635 Aidan, coming from Iona, built a monastery on Lindisfarne, an island off the coast of Northumberland which can be reached on foot from the mainland at low water. From this centre missions went to many parts of England, which was converted in the main by these Celtic missions from the north; but this Celtic Christianity was soon linked up with the main stream of the Faith which issued from Rome, for significant events had been taking place in the south-eastern corner of England. Gregory, who became Pope in 590, had conceived a desire to send a Christian mission to England, inspired, according to the well-known story, by the sight of Anglian boys in a Roman slave-market. In 596 he despatched a party, led by the monk Augustine, on a missionary expedition to Britain. On the way the missionaries heard such terrible tales of the savage characters of the British that they returned to Rome. Urged on once again by the Pope, they landed in Kent in 597 and were favourably received by Ethelbert, King of Kent, whose wife Bertha, the daughter of a Frankish king, was already a Christian. King Ethelbert soon accepted the Christian faith and was baptized, and the mission spread through Kent, Augustine being appointed bishop with his headquarters at Canterbury. In 664 the Celtic and Roman streams of Christianity were fused into one at the Synod of Whitby, and the English Church was brought into line with the ecclesiastical practice of Rome and into closer association with the Church in the rest of northern Europe.

As a result, within less than a hundred years after the arrival of Augustine in England, English missionaries in their turn were going to the Continent and were largely responsible for planting Christianity in the heathen borderlands of the Franks in the territory we know as Holland and Germany. Willibrord, with a party of monks from Ripon, was the great missionary to Holland: after labouring for fifty years he saw the Church firmly established in the Netherlands. During his last years he had as companion the young English monk from Exeter and Winchester, Winfrith, better known as St Boniface, who became the great apostle to Germany. Among the heathen of Hesse and Thuringia he laboured mightily and with considerable success. The strategy of these missionaries was to plant monasteries in the territories which had been evangelized, and Boniface left a series of these communities beyond the Rhine, the most famous being at Fulda. Wherever he went he bequeathed a reverence for the papacy to the new Church in Germany, and it has been pointed out that this monk was in fact a maker of history, far greater than the able Popes whose authority he used and extended. We can see the unity of the Western Church, centred in Rome, becoming effective and real through Boniface. This great missionary met his death in 754, when with a band of his converts he was slain by heathen attackers. In his old age, having retired from the Archbishopric of Mainz, he had gone to the scene of his early missionary labours among the Frisians, and it was there that he was cut down with a sword, 'enjoining non-resistance on those about him. . . . Humble, a man of prayer, self-sacrificing, courageous, steeped in the Scriptures, a born leader of men, affectionate, a superb organizer and administrator, he was at once a great Christian, a great missionary, and a great bishop. The Church in Germany owed him an incalculable debt. By the end of the eighth century the remainder of the pagan Frisians, for whom Boniface had given his life, had accepted Christian baptism' (K. S. Latourette: *A History of Christianity*, p. 349). The further conversion of the Germanic people known as the Saxons was carried out by the great king of the Franks, Charlemagne, unfortunately largely by force. We are going to hear of him again below, but it can be said at this point that one of the things he did was to promote the advancement of education and learning in the Church of his dominions, and in pursuance of this aim drew to his court scholars from other regions, especially England. These came from monasteries which were centres of learning. Before Charlemagne's time, a monastery in Jarrow had been the scene of the education and life-work of the great scholar known as the Venerable Bede (673-735), whose best-known book is the *Ecclesiastical History of the English People*. The most distinguished of Charlemagne's scholars was the Englishman Alcuin, born about the time of Bede's death, and educated at York. For a time Alcuin was head of Charlemagne's school at Aachen, and it is encouraging to notice that he protested against his master's forceful 'conversion' of the Saxons, saying that adults ought not to be baptized before they had been properly instructed.

So, during what must be regarded as dark and in many ways barbarous years, the light of the Gospel was being spread abroad. The peoples of what came later to be known as Western Europe were being evangelized (one can hardly say converted). This usually took place by mass movements of whole tribes or peoples following the example of their leaders. Yet before this happened there were missionary pioneers who, with a minority of converts, often lost their lives before the leaders embraced the faith. Nevertheless, Christianity was usually adopted as the religion of a whole community, and it is not surprising if the Christian understanding and level of attainment of the majority were not very high, although there were always individuals and groups who richly adorned the Gospel by their lives and characters.

(*b*) In the eighth century the Popes found an ally in the Franks, a people already Christian, who supported the Papacy against the barbarian Lombards, then conquering North Italy. The Franks under Pippin invaded Italy (754-5) and forced the Lombard king to surrender to the Pope certain of their conquests. Thus began the 'States of the Church', signs of the temporal sovereignty of the Papacy, which marked the Pope a territorial as well as a spiritual ruler. One of Pippin's sons, Charles, eventually emerged as sole ruler of the Franks. He is best known as Charlemagne (which means Charles the Great) and by the time of his death in 814 ruled over what we know as France, Belgium, Holland, nearly half of Germany and Austria-Hungary, more than half of Italy, and a part of N.E. Spain. In Rome on Christmas Day, AD 800, Charles was suddenly and apparently unexpectedly crowned by the Pope as 'Emperor of the Romans'. The precise significance of this action is a matter of debate, but it inaugurated the Holy Roman Empire in the west, a Germanic Empire in close association with the Papacy. Once more it was felt there was a successor to the Roman Emperors in the west, and henceforth an Empire in the west which was not a mere appendage to the east. After Charlemagne's death his domain suffered many disasters and losses, but the west was now working out its own fate. Underlying the creation of the western Emperor by the Pope is the further question as to whether the Pope as representing the spiritual power is supreme over the Emperor as representing the civil power. Tensions between the two authorities were bound to arise.

(c) Beginning in the seventh century, Christianity suffered enormous territorial and numerical losses through the rise of Islam in Arabia. Mohammed died in 632 and by then the Arabs had begun to sweep across Palestine, Syria, and Egypt. The hosts of Allah went on through North Africa and Spain, and were only stopped in the heart of France in 732 by the Franks and driven back to the Pyrenees. Constantinople itself nearly became a Moslem city and Asia Minor was overrun, until the eastern Emperor, Leo the Isaurian, restored Roman supremacy there. Although Christianity was subjugated in the lands overrun, in North Africa it was annihilated and Latin civilization disappeared from the territory. In Syria, Palestine, and Egypt, Christian minorities survived and are still to be found. But no European Christian nation conquered by Islam was converted to the new faith. In Spain the Visigoth kingdom was destroyed and the Christians driven into the north-west corner; not until the fifteenth century was the whole peninsula restored to the Church.

(d) Throughout the ninth century Western Europe received its last barbarian invasions at the hands of Scandinavian warriors, Vikings and Normans. The Danes harried England, the Normans ravaged France, the Hungarians harassed Germany. The evil effects upon the Church can be easily imagined, but it is remarkable how rapidly the invading peoples were assimilated and converted to Christianity. From the chaos of the ninth and tenth centuries the modern Western European nations as we know them gradually arose. Out of Charlemagne's Empire there developed an eastern and a western section, France and Germany. By the end of the tenth century, Germany had become the most powerful country in Europe, ruled over by the Emperor. Through some of these Germanic Emperors the Papacy was helped and revived in the eleventh century. If conditions round about AD 1000 seemed bad, better things were in store. At least the growing administrative power of the Papacy gave a degree of unity to western Christendom which contrasted with increasing schisms in the east. Soon a new stage of culture was to emerge in the west, in which an effort was to be made to mould all life by the Christian spirit and which was to be more successful than anything achieved before the break-up of the old Roman Empire and the barbarian invasions.

3. AD 950-1350

By a very rough division of time, these four centuries form a period in which Christianity seemed to receive a new surge of life. The completion of the 'conversion' of Northern Europe between 950 and 1000—Denmark, Norway, Sweden, the beginnings of Russian Christianity, Poland, Hungary, and Bohemia—heralded the birth of a new civilization. Early in the eleventh century, 'Nestorian' Christianity began to spread into Central Asia, Southern India, and China (where it had been before, but had disappeared after AD 900). Such an outburst of fresh vitality is difficult to explain, although it would seem to have been the pattern of Christian history until now. As a rough generalization it would appear that Christian institutions, as well as Christianity viewed as one great movement, are subject to periods of expanding vitality followed by the gradual loss of energy and effectiveness, which are succeeded in turn by fresh outbursts of new forms of life. At any rate, in the period now under review and so far as the west was concerned, the invasions were over and accordingly the possibilities of more settled life were stronger.

Attention must at the outset be drawn to one tragic event. This was the final break between the Western Church with its centre in Rome and the Eastern Church—that part of the Christian world which fell under the jurisdiction of Constantinople. Although there had been difficulties between Roman and Byzantine (Eastern) Christianity before, the two centres nevertheless had regarded themselves as part of the one Church. Yet the break which took place in 1054 was but the culmination of growing cultural, political, and theological differences. Ever since that date the Roman and Eastern Orthodox Churches have been out of communion with each other, and the effects of this division are obvious to this day in the cultural rifts which tend to separate Eastern and Western Europe.

The period after AD 1000 was to see many of the Church's institutions revived and reformed. This was true in particular of monasticism and, as we have indicated, of the Papacy itself. From now on there were some great Popes, who, being powerful men, could not tolerate with complacency the control of the Papacy by the Emperors. Their aim was to make the spiritual power supreme, with the secular authority co-operating. Clashes were inevitable. The greatest of the early medieval Popes was Hildebrand, who reigned as Pope Gregory VII (1073–85). He asserted in the strongest terms the supremacy of the spiritual power, independent of all secular authority. His 'ideal was of a world united under the spiritual rule of the occupants of the chair of St Peter. This has never been realized, though the grandeur of its conception is undeniable. It is entirely a Roman view of supremacy' (F. J. Foakes-Jackson). Impelled by this spirit, the Papacy attained from *c*. 1150–1250 the summit of its power in Western Europe, and under Pope Innocent III (1198–1216) its greatest splendour.

One expression of this Western European vitality is seen in the Crusades, those religious wars undertaken ostensibly to capture and defend Jerusalem (and ultimately Constantinople) from the Seljuk Turks, a westward-moving Mohammedan people from Central Asia. The motives behind the Crusades were very varied, but the religious impulse was dominant. Urged on by the Roman pontiffs, great numbers of people from Europe set off to defend Christ's honour against the followers of the Prophet. Following the First Crusade in 1095 there were nearly 200 years of military action. A great many crusaders never reached the Holy Land. The most pathetic incident was that of the Children's Crusade, in which a great crowd of youths set out in response to emotional appeals, only to finish as slaves in Egypt. The most scandalous event was the diversion of the Fourth Crusade from its original objective into an attack upon Constantinople, as a result of which the rift between the Eastern and Western Churches was widened. The Crusades failed to capture permanently the Holy Places for Christians, yet they had other important consequences. They were a sign that Western Europe was emerging out of its isolation; contact was made with the learning, culture, and generally higher civilization of the East, and trade was expanded, bringing new wealth to the rising cities of Europe. The most questionable part of the whole movement was the growth of the tradition of a holy war which might be waged against any considered to be enemies of the Faith.

The twelfth and thirteenth centuries, often called the High Middle Ages, saw the climax of western medieval civilization, a civilization largely created by the Church. Over-arching an expanding society was the papal monarchy, a highly centralized and many-sided government which was a development of the idea that the bishop of Rome was intended to be supreme in the

Church. The Church's teaching was the recognized background of all existence; it set before men the realities of hell, purgatory, or heaven after this life, but in their preparation for the next world guided them and helped them, above all by the seven sacraments. So far as worship was concerned, the Mass (derived from the Lord's Supper) was the central service; in relation to practical life it was the Church's penitential system which was most influential. To be deprived of the Church's administrations was generally feared, and in extreme cases the Pope might impose an interdict upon a whole district or nation as a disciplinary measure, whereby the normal services of the Church were drastically curtailed. During the twelfth century, heresy called forth a form of discipline known as the Inquisition, which in some cases employed torture or took the extreme measure of condemning the unrepentant heretic to death.

The Church played a leading part in the spheres of education and learning. The thirteenth century saw the great theological and philosophical synthesis of St Thomas Aquinas, who made full use of the many works of Aristotle which had only shortly before become available through contact with Moslem scholars. St Thomas's work marks the climax of the intellectual movement known as scholasticism. Similar activity was to be found in the study of law, and the twelfth century saw the rise of universities. The great medieval cathedrals and churches are familiar to all: the best craftsmanship and artistic skill went into their building and adornment, for they were to be Christ's abode, and nearly all members of the community contributed in some way to their construction.

Opinions about life in the Middle Ages vary greatly. If it is unwise to entertain too rosy ideas, as some do, it is equally perverse to regard the era of the Church's power as all superstitious, ignorant, or corrupt. Sins there were in plenty and obvious shortcomings, yet it must be remembered that the Church was dealing with the children of whole peoples which had rapidly accepted Christianity after the periods of barbarian invasions. Great problems and difficulties faced the Church and it is not surprising that the Faith itself was often perverted in the event. In various ways it happens thus in every age. Man's attempts to promote the good are themselves tainted with sin, while the evil in the world is but the opportunity for further expressions of the good. The High Middle Ages were followed by a period in which many of the great features of that particular civilization were to decay and become corrupt. While it is true that Christianity did permeate and influence the culture and life of the Middle Ages to a great degree, yet that same culture and life are judged by Christianity at all points. The Kingdom of God is not yet consummated in this world, and although it may not be identified wiih any particular culture it can influence every age. The Church throughout its long history is the company of those who have been engaged in the high endeavour of bringing the principles of that Kingdom to bear upon the life of their day.

4. *MONASTICISM*

This remarkable movement stretches from the fourth century through the history of the Church. Like many other features in Christian history it showed great spiritual power, followed often by periods of stagnation and degeneration, which in turn gave rise on occasions to fresh outbursts of vitality. Its importance for 1,000 years as a missionary weapon cannot be overestimated, even if it was never by intention consciously such. The so-called mass-conversions of the peoples of Europe meant that at first few people had much understanding of the Faith, but when they learned more about it, it was in the main the monks who taught them. Accordingly they came to regard the monk as the ideal type of Christian, and Christianity itself as a religion of which monasticism was the best and highest expression. Moreover, monasticism gave many great leaders and reformers to the Church itself, and during the whole of the medieval period all churchmen came under its influence in one way or another. Into part of its heritage we have all entered.

In itself monasticism is not a specifically Christian phenomenon, and indeed at the first gave expression to ideas which were in some ways contrary to the Gospel. The early ascetics who retired into the Egyptian deserts went, not as missionaries, but to flee from the world in order to save themselves. There is no doubt also that these men regarded the body, and therefore matter, as in some sense inherently evil, a view which we noted owed much to non-Christian sources, but which has always influenced Christians to some extent. Nevertheless there is, of course, an essential element of self-denial in Christian teaching, and the Christian life is one of discipline of body and mind. Perhaps the deepest motive behind the monk's leaving the world was a search after a higher type of perfection by renouncing everything for Christ's sake and by devoting himself to a life of prayer and worship.

It is significant that the movement developed at the time when the Church had won its right to exist and the persecutions were over. The ascetics who went into the Egyptian deserts gradually formed groups of hermits, from which a more developed type of community life was evolved, with its own buildings, rules, etc. The movement spread widely during the fourth and fifth centuries both among men, most of whom were laymen, and among women. In the hands of certain great leaders it was adapted to particular needs and fashioned into an instrument which could be used for the Church's purposes. There is only space to draw attention to a few of the landmarks in the long story, which the student will find fascinating and instructive if he turns to such a book as H. B. Workman's *The Evolution of the Monastic Ideal*. At the end of the fourth century Basil of Caesarea established a well-organized monastic community which served to some extent those outside it, and his *Rules* became influential in later developments. Because of his great gifts Basil was not allowed to spend all his time in monastic retirement, but was drawn into the life of the Church in the world as a bishop: in this he was the prototype of many great monks who came to play leading parts in the general affairs of the Church, although preferring the monastic life. This characteristic can be seen in the man who must be accounted one of the very greatest and most influential figures in the whole history of the Church, St Augustine of Hippo (354–430), the 'doctor of grace'. Augustine's *Confessions* is one of the most moving and revealing autobiographies ever written, describing his spiritual struggles and final conversion. Contemporary with Augustine were Ambrose, Martin of Tours and Jerome, each of whom will repay study. Of the highest importance to monasticism was the influence of Benedict (480–542), an Italian, whose *Rule* became the standard for nearly all monasteries in the West: it is said that at one time there were 15,000 Benedictine monasteries in Western Europe, at their best centres of work, worship, and learning, which made them for centuries the bulwark and rampart not only of the Church but also of society; 'schools for the Service of God' which became at the same time schools for the service of man.

During the centuries many new monastic movements sprang up, usually seeking to return to the stricter ways of former days, and in many a dark hour a fresh reforming impulse was imparted to the Church at large. A great figure in the twelfth century was the abbot of the Cistercian monastery at Clairvaux, whom we know as St Bernard. Highly influential in the life of the whole Western Church of his time, we know him as the author (or teacher of the authors) of those hymns which breathe devotion to the name of Jesus and which we still love to sing in their English versions (*see MHB* 106–9). Again, the thirteenth century produced a movement in the monastic tradition, yet with novel features. The members of these Orders were called friars (brothers) to distinguish them from ordinary monks, and since cities were now rising again after their disappearance with the decline of the Empire, and the older monasteries were mainly in rural places, the friars directed their efforts in the main to these new centres of population. They combined the monastic life and its ideals of poverty, chastity, and obedience, with preaching to those outside their fellowship, thus carrying a stage farther a feature already found among certain monks. The friars or mendicant Orders became great missionaries in all parts of the world. The two best-known Orders which arose at this time were associated with the men we know as St Francis of Assisi (Franciscans or Grey Friars) and St Dominic (Dominicans or Preachers or Black Friars). These Orders also became devoted to learning and produced many famous scholars, the intellectual leaders of Europe. The friars soon made the discovery that to preach to people, many of whom in their new urban surroundings were caught up in a ferment of unbelief, the evangelist must study deeply.

NOTE

Preachers who want further information about some of the characters or subjects mentioned in this chapter may consult a good book of reference in a library, e.g. *The Encyclopaedia Britannica* or *The Encyclopaedia of Religion and Ethics*. There are, of course, a great number of Church Histories. Very useful for the preacher or teacher are two simple but well-written accounts:

R. Bainton: *The Church of Our Fathers* (S.C.M.).

V. E. Walker: *A First Church History* (S.C.M.).

For a much greater detailed and most readable and brilliant survey of the whole history of the Church in one volume, see:

K. S. Latourette: *A History of Christianity* (Eyre & S.).

In using illustrations from Church History, the preacher should take every care to get his facts as accurate as he can, and also try to see the character or incident in the setting of its particular historical situation.

4. The Missionary Obligation of the Church

By the Rev. N. ALLEN BIRTWHISTLE, M.A., B.SC.

IN 1953 Methodism set up a Commission with the following terms of reference: *The Conference, recognizing the profound changes now taking place in the political, social, and economic structure of the nations, and their influence upon the moral and religious outlook of mankind, appoints a Commission to consider the effect of these changes upon the missionary work of the Church, and in particular the presentation of the missionary obligation in its new setting to the Church at home.* The Report of that Commission was presented to the Conference in 1955 and it contains much that every preacher needs to know; much that every evangelist can use. It forms the basis of the main ideas developed in this chapter and it is to this document that the page references are related.

1. ON THE MOVE WITH THE GOSPEL

We are part of something that never stands still. From the start, movement, haste, and urgency have been the daily bread of God's messengers (*Report*, pp. 81 ff). The men sent out with the Good News of what God has done for man were told not to linger where they were not well received, but to shake off the dust of such places from their feet and press on to where people would listen (Lk 9[5]).

Wesley in England and Asbury in America believed that the preacher must truly be on the move, breaking new ground, entering new territory. In 1774 Wesley wrote, after a visit to Glasgow: 'How is it that there is no increase in this society? It is exceeding easy to answer. One preacher stays here two or three months at a time, preaching on Sunday mornings and three or four evenings a week. Could a preacher preserve either bodily health or spiritual life with this exercise? And if he is but half alive, what will the people be?' Asbury had not been in America a fortnight before men were trying to peg him down in the towns. But he had no intention of settling. He had heard the call of the wild. He saw that the plan that had carried the message throughout England was the way to keep in touch with the outposts, as the tide of

British penetration rolled westward. And the most important part of that plan was a ministry on the move.

It must always be so with any missionary enterprise. In our own day 'Mr Wesley's travelling preachers' are still breaking new ground, still on the move with the Gospel. Men like Ephraim Alphonse, evangelizing the Valiente Indians of Central America in the *Silver Jubilee*, the launch presented by J.M.A. collectors in Britain, are to be found in all parts of the overseas Church. The equipment is modern. A mobile cinema van that is also a travelling bookshop or operating theatre, has replaced the eighteenth-century horse. But the motive and the message are the same. Men need to be saved. We have the words of eternal life. What are we waiting for?

As the Church today goes out to break new ground, the boundaries that are crossed are not always geographical: new areas of life, new realms of thought are penetrated (*Report*, p. 77). Men like Michael Scott and Trevor Huddleston, in their fight against colour discrimination, are the Wilberforces of our day, claiming new territory for God. The Church in Ceylon works in a confined space as far as acres are concerned, but it is on the move against nationalism and racial exclusiveness. And it is the whole Church, Ceylonese members and ministers as well as missionaries from Britain, that is in action (*Report*, pp. 76 f).

In this changing pattern of equipment and conditions there are many elements that are new, compared with those of the early days of the missionary enterprise; new, indeed, compared with the situation only a few years ago. It was because of these rapid and revolutionary changes, in the world which we are called to evangelize and in the Church overseas which is now the missionary to the people, that the Conference Commission was asked to consider the missionary task in our time.

In the panels round the gallery at Wesley's Chapel, City Road, London, are carved two ancient symbols; one is Christian, the other comes from more ancient religions. A snake, with its tail in its own mouth, symbolizes eternity—the circle that goes on and on without end. It also represents the serpent lifted up in the wilderness and the healing power of God (Num 21[9]; Jn 3[14]). Within each circle, repeated all the way round the church, is a dove carrying in its mouth a spray of leaves. That reminds us of the story of Noah, and the message of hope (Gen 8[11]). It recalls, too, the New Testament symbol of the Holy Spirit and the descent of the Dove at the Baptism of Jesus (Mk 1[10]). It was that same

Spirit that drove Him into the wilderness to face the call of God and in the power of that Spirit He entered upon His ministry. All these thoughts are entwined in the symbolism of the snake surrounding the dove. Here, at the heart of Methodism, is a reminder of the eternal message of hope in the deliverance that God will bring to man in his need, a pictorial representation of the perpetual compulsion of the Holy Spirit to go out with the healing Gospel to men dying in darkness.

2. GOD'S CHANGING WORLD

What is the link between the Gospel we preach and the culture and conditions of the people we evangelize? It may be that by examining that question for the overseas Church we shall throw light on our task at home (*Report*, p. 22).

It has long been known that if Asia, static for so many centuries that her people became a by-word for fatalism and apathy, were to awaken, vast energies would be released. 'When China is moved', said Napoleon, 'it will change the face of the globe.' Lenin, surveying an even wider field, predicted that the future history of mankind would 'be determined by the fact that Russia, India, and China represent a crushing majority of the population of the globe.'

In our day and age all this is coming true. Professor Latourette, an American, has described Asia as the New World and America as the Old. Once it was Asia that stood still, generation after generation reproducing the same pattern of life, while Europe and America experimented with new forms of government, mercantile method, and social structure. Now it is America that seems to cling to the past, holding to known ways, conservative of its gains, its glories, and its ghosts, while others take the lead in the adventure of life. Asia has struck camp (*Report*, p. 25). Millions of her people have pulled up their tent poles and are on the march. They do not know where they are going, nor do they very much care. That is part of the exhilaration of being on the road. At least they know the evils they have left behind—poverty, sickness, oppression, ignorance, and fear. They believe that if only they could train more and more scientists, and grasp more firmly the political power over their own people, they could move right away from these ancient torments. But we who have seen what science and politics together can do without Christ know where all this is likely to lead. There are few more powerful arguments for the continued world-mission of the Church than the dangers that lie ahead of these marching people, if they are denied the guidance, let alone the regenerating force, of Him who is the Way, the Truth, and the Life.

(a) Eternal Change

In the realm of mind and spirit, whatever may be true of matter, change is the opposite of decay. Perhaps one of the most important insights of the Missionary Commission Report is to be found in its restatement of the Christian paradox that the eternal changes (*Report*, p. 11).

The change is not one of essential nature, but of mode of expression. Jesus Christ is the same yesterday, today, and for ever (Heb 13[8]), but the universe hangs together in Him (Col 1[17]) and men of every generation find Him their contemporary and the answer to their changing need (Phil 4[19]). He claimed that He had not come to destroy the Law (Mt 5[17]), yet, when He thought of the ferment of new ideas that He brought to act on the ancient religion of His people, He said that it was no use putting new wine into old bottles (Mt 9[17]). Indeed, so great is the change that comes into the life of a man when he is in Christ, that Paul says that it is as if there had been a new creation (2 Cor 5[17]).

We are liable to fall into thinking that it is the material world of things we touch and hear and see that changes, the world manifest to our reason and senses only that alters, while the eternal stands still. This Greek idea does not do justice to the facts. It is He who sits on the eternal throne who says: 'Behold, I make all things new' (Rev 21[5]). The Bible is more up-to-date than the morning newspaper. That is why Nazi jailers threw the Bibles of their Norwegian captives into the prison corridors and swept them away to be burnt. The truths of the old Book came too near home for them. The eternal truth of God is ever presenting itself in new and vigorous forms, while the transient withers and decays.

There is an inspired illustration of this truth in Stanley's book on Westminster Abbey. In the early Middle Ages the altar stood at the extreme eastern end of the church, in keeping with the simple, uncomplicated views of the period. With the thirteenth century came a new veneration of local saints and the Virgin Mary. The architectural effect on the Abbey was seen in the lengthening of the east end to make a Lady Chapel for the worship of the Virgin and the building of a shrine for the tomb of Edward the Confessor. This brought the high altar more into the middle of the building.

In the fifteenth century, divisions arose everywhere in Christendom. Towards the end of the previous century there had been the Great Schism. Two Popes, one in Italy, the other in France, each claimed to be the one and only head of the Church on earth and each had followers in every European country. At the same time the Renaissance was gaining momentum and the shadow of the Reformation lay ahead. It was the beginning of the modern world. It was then that men began to think as we think. The foundations of our present science and philosophy were being laid and the process did not go forward easily. Right through society ran the division between old and new. In the process a new form of division arose: nations as we now know them came into being, with national languages and literatures. These divisions in the minds of men were reflected in the architecture of the Abbey. A screen was built to shut off the altar from the east end.

At the Reformation and during the Commonwealth a wooden movable table, which stood in the body of the church, replaced the massive stone altar. When Laud triumphed at the Restoration, back went the altar to its present place and in subsequent years the theological and artistic tastes of each succeeding generation have been revealed by its furnishings. Yet all this time the monuments on the tombs have stayed still. One has lost a finger here, another a nose there, but as they have decayed they have not moved. It is the living thing that has been on the move, accommodating itself to every change of thought, but remaining essentially the same.

From the memoirs of Churchill comes a hint as to how the missionary Church must be ready to change, while keeping its essential nature, if it is to cope with each succeeding age and bring to each new generation the Word of Life in words that can be understood. He tells how between the wars, though Germany was forbidden an army, the military spirit and tradition were fostered and a large general staff maintained. Under pretence of getting together as Departments of Reconstruction, Research, and Culture, plain-clothes officers continued their training and their plans. The biographer of Seekt, the creator and sustainer of this army, in a most revealing phrase says: '*Although the form had to be broken, the content was saved !*'

(b) What must Remain?

What is it that must endure in Christendom if it is to remain Christian? In spite of the changes of the centuries and of the differing conditions of the nations that accept the Faith, some kernel must remain constant in the life of the Church. What is it? (*Report*, p. 38).

Stanley's illustration from Westminster Abbey and Churchill's reference to Seekt point back to Biblical ideas. It is the teaching of the Old Testament that the material world is not permanent, but that the Creator of the universe is eternal. The grass withers, but the word of our God shall stand for ever (Isa 40[8]). James uses this quotation as a reminder to the rich man that he and his property are as ephemeral as the flower of grass that blooms only for a few hours (Jas 1[11]); it is the man who endures temptation who shall receive the crown of everlasting life—the evergreen laurel wreath, we might be tempted to say, in contrast with the quickly fading grass (Jas 1[12]). The writer to the Hebrews brings his Epistle to a climax at this point. What is the scene, the setting, of our approach to God, he asks. It is no longer a mountain that can be marked on a map or a city set on a hill. It is the celestial mountain, the heavenly Jerusalem, the city of the living God (Heb 12[18 f]) says the writer, echoing the reply of Jesus to the Samaritan woman at the well (Jn 4[20-4]); God is spirit. The time is coming when men shall neither go up to this mountain nor to Jerusalem to worship, but shall worship in spirit and in truth wherever they may be. Just as, when God spoke to Moses, the mountain shook and those who tried to excuse themselves had no escape when He uttered His warnings, so, once again, He will speak. It will be once only, and this time He will shake all creation. The created universe will be removed. Only the things which cannot be shaken will stand firm. The Kingdom we have inherited belongs to this order of things that cannot be shaken (Heb 12[25-8]. The writer to the Hebrews goes on to utter words that again recall Jn 4[24]. In view of all this, he says, let us worship God as He would have us worship Him, in awe and reverence.) The Old Testament basis for this passage may perhaps be found in Ps 102[25-7], where the Psalmist says that God laid the foundation of the earth and flung out the heavens; they will perish, but He will endure.

It is in line with our modern scientific, social, and philosophical thinking that we should emphasize the aspect of energy rather than of shape, of meaning rather than of form and order. Lord

Hailsham, writing of the totalitarian menace to democracy, said: 'Believers in freedom can reply that the very strength of their institutions lies in their continued ability to evolve and give place to new forms under the pressure of changing events.'

It is this doctrine of inner energy as the last significance of things that makes the poetry and painting of William Blake (1757–1827) so acceptable today. In many ways he was a century and a half in advance of his time. The discoveries of Freud and Jung are there in his works. His belief in the creative power of inner conflict is in his well-known poem *Jerusalem*. He had a great admiration for Wesley and for all whose vision drove them to reform the evils of the day. It was for this reason that at first he welcomed the French Revolution and in the hopeful mood which that event induced he wrote the happy, lyrical *Songs of Innocence*, which include the lines:

> *For Mercy has a human heart,*
> *Pity a human face.*

But when the Terror came, when Napoleon was turning the new Republic into an Empire, and England was at war with France, he was sadly disillusioned and wrote, in *Songs of Experience*,

> *Cruelty has a human heart,*
> *And Jealousy a human face.*

Blake was influenced by Swedenborg's philosophy, and in these two quotations we see his strong belief in the two contrary states of the human soul, the balance of good and evil. For him, poetry and art were not to be dismissed as trivial, they were profound prophecy. Always he looked not *with* his eyes but *through* them to the world of eternity. It is this that gives his engravings their peculiar power. It was his delight 'to see a world in a grain of sand', to look beyond matter to the eternal form. The call of Jesus to His disciples to leave all and follow Him was the kind of challenge that stirred him deeply. He believed that prophecy did not come without trouble. It was as though the message of God were written in invisible ink which only became apparent when held to the fire of God's love.

We now know that Blake was right in regarding energy, not matter, as the ultimate reality in the universe. That is what the scientists are saying today. In the giant convulsions of the atomic bomb, matter is converted into an easily recognizable form of energy. Static ideas are not in line with this conception of the universe. Wordsworth and Matthew Arnold and the other admirers of the starry heavens, Blake would have said, were worshipping at the shrine of death, as do those who admire perfect poise and serenity in the individual. How right William Temple was when he claimed that only a better dialectic could drive out dialectical materialism, and that the better dialectic was Christian Theology. The word dialectic comes from two Greek words *dia*, between, and *legō*, to speak. It means a conversation or discussion, with emphasis on the clash of opposite opinions. Two truths that appear to be incompatible may be seen to be reconcilable when viewed from a higher vantage point, or seen as parts of a larger whole. In the interplay of contraries that we call life there is the force of creative contradiction. 'The immortal dies.' 'The invisible appears in sight,' says Wesley with good New Testament authority (Col 1[15]. An *image* is, by definition, something that can be seen).

Blake is at once ancient and modern, orthodox and progressive, in that he not only bore witness to the existence of the eternal world, but to the possibility of each man attaining it here in the present life. His teaching has been summarized as: 'Eternity on this side of the grave.' The words recall those of Harnack: 'The Christian religion is something simple and sublime, it means one thing and one thing only: Eternal life in the midst of time, by the strength and under the eyes of God.' Though Christ's Kingdom is not of this world it is offered to those who are still in it (Jn 18[36]; Mk 1[14¹]; Lk 17[21]). It is one of those things that cannot be shaken, but it is offered to those who must continue to live among things that will pass away. In the 'creatures of bread and wine' (belonging to this world which, in the language of Heb 12, can be shaken, as did also the changing altars and communion tables of the Abbey in Stanley's parable) are offered eternal life through the death of the immortal Son of God. His words give eternal life (Jn 6[68]) and the word of our God shall stand for ever.

When we ask of the Methodist Church what is transient and what is eternal, we find unexpected help from legal quarters. The British Methodist Church, in the eyes of the law of our land, is an unincorporated association, completely mutable as to form but immutable as to doctrine. In legal fact, then, we could retain all those outward forms which we think are the signs of Methodism—church buildings of a certain architectural standard, correctly attired ministers, pipe organs, choir outings, class meetings, Quarterly Meetings, and the rest of our church courts—but if we cease to preach 'our doctrines' we are no longer the Methodist Church (*Report*, p. 38). Here, with a vengeance, is the doctrine of the inner energy of the eternal Word.

What *must* remain, is not our private opinion on some matter of public interest, or our personal interpretation of Scripture, but the Living Word, active still in His Church, revealed once and for all in Jesus Christ who is the same yesterday, today, and for ever (Heb 13[8]).

(c) Mobility

Rigidity of method spells death for any religious community. It is peculiarly lethal for a missionary society, at home or abroad, which must be free to follow the impulse of the Holy Spirit while remaining disciplined in its structure and obedient to the Laws of God (*Report*, p. 74).

From two directions comes the demand for mobility: from inside, through the concept of energy and the inspiration of the Holy Spirit; and from outside, since we are living in a changing world where volcanic forces are at work altering the very structure, the political, social, and economic order of the countries we serve —including our own. The mobility we seek is not that of anarchy, but of well-directed attack; the swift deployment of our forces in the places where they are needed most. It is not for the Church to be rooted, chained, incapable of reaching dying souls with the Word of Life. It is not for us to be so inflexible in our programme, policy, and plans that we cannot see the signs of our times and grasp the opportunities that God presents. It is no part of our calling to punt quietly into a backwater and grow barnacles.

The Apostles took literally our Lord's command to shake off the dust of unresponsive places and push on to pastures new (Mk 6[11]). Paul and Barnabas at Antioch offered Christ in the synagogue. The next week almost the whole city came to hear them and the Jews in a spirit of nationalism attacked the speakers. Trenchantly, Paul and Barnabas replied to those who had abused them: 'We regarded it as our duty to bring God's message to you first of all, but since you reject it and so make it clear that you are not fit for eternal life—see, we now turn to the Gentiles' (Acts 13[46]). Subsequently, when the Gentiles received the message with joy, the Jews worked up a persecution against the Apostles and made it impossible for them to stay; so they shook off the dust from their feet in protest and went to Iconium (Acts 13[51]). A similar pattern of events developed at Corinth. Once again, Paul, when he found that he was making no headway with the Jews, announced: 'From now on, with a clear conscience I devote myself to the Gentiles' (Acts 18⁶). In these two incidents we see the early Church mobile enough to switch from one method of approach to another, when rejected by the Jews.

Jesus calls us to be fishers of men. Fishers are of two temperaments. There are those who erect a comfortable seat and then surround themselves with luncheon-baskets and reading-matter, as well as the equipment of their pursuit. They are the kind who cover their faces with their hats after throwing in the line, and sleep right through success and failure. The other sort are constantly on the move. A swiftly-running stream suits them best. If there is no bite soon after they have cast, they are away to try elsewhere.

It is a matter of *time*. At the very beginning, just after the first Easter and the first Whitsuntide, it seemed as though history were finished; time had given place to eternity. So in a way it had. Heaven had begun below. But as day followed day, year followed year, and the Final Consummation of all things did not take place, the Church and time had to come to terms with each other. It became clear that, although God through Christ offers eternal life here and now, we have to go on living in this world where time is all too short. The complete acceptance of time came when the Emperor Constantine carried Rome over to the new Way. Then ordinary life, and marriage, and intellect, were accepted too. As is the way of the Church, it had taken a long time to hear what God had been saying. At last men knew what God meant when He said in the vision to Peter: 'It is not for you to call profane what God has cleansed' (Acts 10¹⁵).

'Nothing is more precious than time,' wrote the author of the *Cloud of Unknowing*. 'There is no other institution which suffers from time so much as religion,' wrote Charles Williams. These two statements by English mystics contain the whole of the problem. In the first place, time brings its urgency because, if we do not reach the men of our generation with the Gospel, no one will. God's everlasting years are not at our disposal for proclaiming the Good News to those who are alive in the world with us now. In this sense, time is not on our side. Nor is it on our side when we remember what Charles Williams is saying: in the very moment when it seems possible that a whole generation may have learnt what the Christian religion is all about, death takes both learners and learning, and the task has to be begun again.

It is not only a matter of time. It is also a matter of *space*. We are not called to dig in, to put our roots down. Here we have no abiding city (Heb 13¹⁴). It is only the fool who is lulled by the false sense of security that comes from successful business, increasing turnover and extended premises (Lk 12¹³⁻²⁴). The Christian is to be more like the raven, with no permanent base (Lk 12²⁴)—that is to say, no permanent base in this material world. How can there be such a permanent base in a world which is to pass away? (Heb 12²⁶⁻⁷). We need a permanent base, and indeed we have one which has true foundations because its architect and builder is God (Heb 11¹⁰,¹⁶). We have an everlasting city, but it is not here: we move towards the city that is one day to be (Heb 13¹⁴). This is our answer to those who, because of war or rumours of war or fear of atomic weapons, have suddenly realized, what all along was true, that the so-called securities of this world are not secure at all. The only city that remaineth is the City of God. The citizens of that City, while they are on this earth, are pilgrims. They are permanently on the move. Nightly they pitch their moving tent a day's march nearer home.

Christian mobility is a matter of space, because from the start the Church has taken on the whole world as the arena of its conflict with evil. Just as it had to move forward in time, so the Gospel had to move forward to the conquest of all lands. Again, as in the reconciliation with time, there were tensions. That which had been superbly right in the intimate family relationship of Jesus and His disciples had to be made to stretch out over the whole family of God. How could it work? How could that, 'I, if I be lifted up from the earth, will draw all men unto myself' (Jn 12³²) apply to vicious Greece and Rome, to savage Europe and Africa, to China and India and the remote islands of the sea? Yet it was not long before a Christian in Rome, seeing British slaves for sale, said of their children, 'These are not Angles but angels!' and planned to send men to them with the Word.

In a broken way, imperfectly and incompletely, the reconciliation with space is taking place and we are moving to the End when the redeemed family will be complete. For though we are pilgrims, we are not exiles from the Eternal City, or aliens in the commonwealth of God. We are fellow citizens of the saints, members of God's household (Eph 2¹⁹), always at home.

It is true, then, that we are mobile, part of something that never stands still. We are on the move with the Gospel and we are going in a direction that God has willed. The symbols of the serpent and the dove in Wesley's chapel have a double significance. The snake, the circle, is partly pagan in origin.* The dove is derived from the Old and New Testaments (Gen 8[11], Mk 1[10]). We do not move in circles, wearily and for ever going the round of reincarnation, history repeating itself and for all its labour returning to the same spot. We go straight forward as the dove bearing glad news. We go out as citizens of a heavenly country, and it often seems as though we are aliens among our own people. We go in the solemn knowledge that every moment of time must be answered for in eternity. 'Remember,' said Jesus, 'I am sending you out to be like sheep among wolves. Be as wary as serpents and yet as innocent as doves' (Mt 10[16]).

3. GOD'S FINAL WORD

The Bible is first and foremost a message about God (*Report*, p. 15 f). It tells us about the loving, personal, holy God, who created the universe, who is active in history, and who, in Jesus Christ His Son, personally took action for the redemption of the world. It is that kind of God with whom we have to do. We affirm that in Christ God spoke His final word about His own character and His intentions (Heb 1[1-2]).

(a) What hath God wrought!

The early Methodist missionaries, like all the other pioneers of the modern missionary movement, were men of the Book. Not only their sermons but their speech, their letters, and their journals betrayed a close knowledge of the Scriptures that came from long and loving study and meditation. Two passages, one from the Old Testament, the other from the New, appear time after time, either directly or by implication, in what they wrote. When we come to look at the second great message of the Bible, what it tells us about the people of God, we shall examine more closely the New Testament passage (2 Cor 5[14-15]). Here we are primarily concerned with what the Bible says about God, and it is the Old Testament passage (Num 23[19-23]) that is of interest. The theme of these verses is that God is at work in His world. The link between the two passages is that both assert God to be active in and through His people.

Man does not take the centre of the stage in history. Whatever

* Though, as we have seen, it also refers to Num 21[9] and Jn 3[14].

we may read in the newspapers, the most important events today are not those that men have caused: they are the things that God is doing in His world. That has always been true. God has always been active in our affairs. God came into our world in human form (Phil 2⁸) with grace and in judgement (Jn 1¹⁴, 3¹⁹) when Jesus was born. God, in Jesus Christ, came to do for man what man could not do for himself. He came to redeem us from ourselves, to set us free from our sins, our weakness, and our pride. He came to take away false securities and to guide our feet into the way of peace (Lk 1⁷⁹). As Irenaeus said in the second century: 'In His infinite love He became what we are, in order to raise us to what He Himself is. It is in this sense that Christ has redeemed us by His own blood and that He has given His soul for our soul, His flesh for our flesh. Since His glorious ascension, He works powerfully upon the Church; He communicates to it His spirit; He guides and sustains it by His life. For us He suffered, for us He rose again.'

When we look in this way at Bethlehem and Calvary and the Empty Tomb and the spirit-filled disciples at Pentecost, it is clear that God has done something that need not be done again. The revelation is final. Much good there may be in other religions and in political or other panaceas for improving man's lot, but nowhere else is found this direct Act of God. Christ is the Way, the Truth, and the Life (Jn 14⁶). It may be that in some countries Christianity would have more appeal if missionaries and national preachers could say that Christianity is a way, an aspect of truth, one kind of good life. But we cannot take that position without betraying our heritage. In the light of what has already been said in this chapter about eternal change and what must remain, it is of value to know what some thoughtful Asians and Africans are saying about the presentation of the Gospel to their people. This will be considered more fully later, but here it is worth recalling what Professor K. A. Busia, Head of the Sociology Department of the University of Achimota, said at a Conference held by the Christian Council of the Gold Coast on *The Christian Faith and African Culture*:

'The African peoples' interpretation of the universe must be appreciated if Christianity is to become meaningful within their culture, and until Christianity has come to grips with this problem, not only in Africa, but in other non-European countries, Christianity will remain an alien and superficial addition to more hospitable creeds.'

God has spoken once and for all in Christ (*Report*, p. 17). The revelation is final, not in the sense that we know all there is to know about God, but that the direction of human history is now known. The revelation is final, not because Church order and forms of worship have received their ultimate shape—sovereign life is ever expressing itself in new forms—but because the nature of the Church is now known; we know in whom we have believed (2 Tim 1[12]) and whom we worship (Jn 4[22]).

What hath God wrought ! (Num 23[23]) was the text of John Wesley's sermon at the first Methodist Conference, as it was also at the opening of the Chapel in City Road. How much more appropriate would he consider the text to be, if he could now survey what has sprung from those beginnings. The first Conference, small as it was, for him was the fulfilment of a cherished dream. When it came to the time for the opening of the Chapel in City Road, the concern of many was no longer lest the mob should disturb the services by their violent opposition, but that 'the multitudes, crowding from all parts, would have occasioned much disturbance' in their desire to be present. But 'all was quietness, decency, and order'—so much had the Spirit of God done in the hearts of men since Wesley began his mission.

In 1885, a hundred and forty-one years after the first Methodist Conference, Thomas Birch Freeman, one of the early pioneers of the modern missionary movement, preached the sermon at the Jubilee celebrations of Gold Coast Methodism. Beneath the pulpit and around it were buried men and women who had died while serving with him in the early years. Some of them had lived but a few days or weeks in what were then lethal conditions for Europeans on the Coast. But their sacrifice had now borne fruit. It was because the church had had to be enlarged to accommodate its steadily increasing congregation that the pulpit now stood among the graves of the pioneers. As Freeman contrasted the heathenism and cruelty of the past with the present conditions of the people, his hearers began to realize what a change Christianity had made in so short a time in their own country. In the great meetings held in every circuit, worship passed into testimony and one member after another rose to say what God had done in their lives and what they would give in token of their gratitude for His blessings.

Still the same story continues. In the last report by the Africa Secretary of the Methodist Missionary Society on his visit to Kenya and the Rhodesias, he heads the chapter on Southern

Rhodesia: *What hath God wrought!*, and tells of how wide self-supporting circuits with a keen evangelistic spirit, regular leader-training classes, and a well-run Bible School, a vigorous Women's Fellowship, character-training through Christian education and fine Youth work, have developed in the brief sixty years that Methodism has been serving there. The God who saves is still at work.

(b) How shall we Escape?

We began the discussion of the theme *On the move with the Gospel* by saying that urgency is a permanent part of the Christian mission. We have seen that time brings part of this urgency, since only we can witness to the men of this generation. It is because of what God has done that we say the time is short (*Report*, p. 80). He has gained so great a victory for us men and for our salvation that we must ask ourselves why we delay in telling the message. It must not be said of us, 'this day is a day of good tidings, and we hold our peace' (2 Kings 7⁹). The Bible meaning of time has little to do with our idea of moments ticking away on a clock, of days torn off a calendar. 'Time', in the minds of the ancient Hebrews, was connected with what happened in it—just as to a child who asks rather saucily, 'What time is it?' instead of saying 'Five to ten', we might reply: 'Time you knew your manners!' They spoke of the 'month of flowers' or the 'month of ripening ears'. It was no use going out with seed to sow in the month of ripening ears, any more than it was right to go out with a sickle when the corn was green. But the day came in the spiritual life of the people when *the time*, the time of harvest, the time when history came to its ripening, had arrived. God stepped in with His justice and salvation to set the people free from their oppressors. In fact the prophets spoke of two such times. One, for them, was in the past: it was when God had brought His people out of slavery into the Promised Land, when they who had been no people were made a nation. The other was in the future when He should remake His people—for again they were in bondage, though now it was to their sins (Hos 1⁹, 2²³). This 'time' was inaugurated when Jesus came (Rom 9²⁴ᶠ; 1 Pet 2¹⁰). It is with us still. Now is the day of salvation, for us as for the people who heard Jesus preach (2 Cor 6²), and now the day of salvation is for all men, Gentiles as well as Jews (Rom 9²⁴). It is still God's harvest time. The field is the whole world. We must put in the sickle *now*.

There are other reasons why it is urgent that we should proclaim the Good News. The world's population is increasing at such a rate that, if we go on like this, in fifty years it will have doubled its present figure and the greatest increases are in the non-Christian areas (*Report*, p. 79). But all these urgencies are summed up in the one idea of Jesus as the Final Word of God. In Christ God has shown us Himself (*Report*, p. 82). Through Christ God has spoken what He has to say to us. What more can He do for us? He has come and lived among us and died for us. In that sense He has said His last word to us and He has no greater powers to call upon to save us from our sins. How shall we escape if we neglect so great a salvation? (Heb 2[3]). There is nothing more that God can do for us.

4. *GOD'S CHOSEN WAY*

The Bible is first and foremost a message about God, but it is also a message about the people of God who are the Church.

What sort of people are the people of God? The first thing to be said about them is that they are a *redemptive people*. What God is doing in His world today He is doing through His Church. The writer of *Hebrews*, having asked what excuse we can possibly have if we pay no heed to the message of salvation, points out that this message, in the first instance, was given to us by Jesus Christ Himself, then guaranteed to us by those who had heard it from His own lips (Heb 2[3]). So from the start the people of God were a *committed people*, not of this world. While in this world they are guided in their thinking and in their acting by the eternal and unchanging Rule of God—the Kingdom that has been revealed in Christ. They are committed to show forth the excellencies of God (2 Cor 5[14-15]). That is God's chosen way of making Himself known.

(a) *Making Many Rich*

The people of God are here to tell others about the One who has bought them and called them out of darkness into His marvellous light (1 Cor 6[20]; 1 Pet 2[9]) (*Report*, p. 18). We are to proclaim Him by preaching and by teaching, by consecrated thought, by the personal quality of our lives which we call holiness—integrity in the sight of God—by a fellowship which reflects the very meaning of our faith. In all this we are to challenge the age in which we live. That challenge may be accepted or, for whatever reason, it may be rejected. Acceptance of the revolutionary Christian Gospel leads to revival, rejection to rebellion. An example of its acceptance is seen in the Indian legislation against caste inequalities. No more revolutionary act has been seen in modern times than that of the Hindu state writing into its constitution the assertion that men of all castes have equal political and social rights. The origin of this act is in Christian teaching on equality and, perhaps even more, in the Christian practice which springs from that teaching, as in works of mercy and healing to those who had been regarded as outcastes, less than human and untouchable.

Perhaps the most inspired item in the programme arranged for the Queen when she visited Nigeria was when she went to the leprosy settlement at Oji River. In that one act she brought new grace, new dignity, new status to men and women who in heathenism are regarded as having lost all human standing and rights. Cursed by the gods, they are thought to be cursed not only now but in eternity. Let no one help those whom the gods have cursed. It was to these rejected people, whom missionaries have long succoured, that the Queen went, so removing the stigma which had lain upon them in the eyes of some of their own people.

There could be no better parable of what the New Testament means by the power of Christians, themselves poor as this world counts riches, to make others wealthy in the treasures that belong to the spirit (2 Cor 6^{10}).

The passage 2 Cor 6$^{1-10}$, in which the expression 'as poor, yet making many rich' is found, is closely tied to that which we have already noted as being much in the minds of early missionaries, 2 Cor 5$^{14-15}$. It begins by reminding us that we are workers together with God, and then recalls the closing verses of the previous chapter, where God's messengers are spoken of as ambassadors on behalf of Christ. An ambassador has a delicate task. He has to make a good impression and must always keep a balance, for instance between consideration for the other country's point of view and firmness in maintaining the position to which his own country is committed. This is the theme of the ten verses under review. The quotation from Isa 49^8 takes up the point that we made above: *Now* is the day of salvation. God's peace offer had better be accepted now, for who can tell whether the guilty world will be given another chance? (2 Cor 6^2).

The following verses (2 Cor 6$^{3-9}$) are a vivid description of what the Christian ambassador should be like, the difficulties he will meet, and the resources that are behind him. It seems as though he has an impossible task, but it is those resources that make it possible, not his own strength. As in John Dryden's time, he belongs to a Church 'still doomed to death, yet fated not to die' (2 Cor 6⁹). How true this has been in our own lifetime in Russia and in China.

Then, in verse 10, Paul reminds us that in a world that is bored by the pursuit of rather feeble and forced gaiety, we are looked upon as kill-joys, though in point of fact our lives have the poise that comes from being centred on God, not on ourselves, and in this we are fulfilling the conditions for true and lasting happiness. They call us beggars, whenever we remind men of their obligation to return to God a part of His gifts to them so that His work may go forward, and so that they may be enriched by sharing with Him in His redemptive work. They call us money-grubbers because they do not know the value of what we give. 'If you are expecting silver or gold', said Peter to the beggar at the Beautiful Gate of the Temple, 'you are going to be disappointed, for I have neither. But what I have I will certainly give you. In the name of Jesus Christ of Nazareth, get up and walk!' (Acts 3⁶). Like the visit of Queen Elizabeth to the lepers of Oji River, this again is a parable on the physical level of what Paul meant when he described us 'as poor, yet making many rich' (2 Cor 6¹⁰). In the feverish markets of the world where shoddy goods are eagerly sought, we stand, unnoticed, offering the pearl of great price. 'Disinherited, yet the world is ours,' says Paul (2 Cor 6¹⁰). We possess the secret of life, of eternal life, yet the great majority, intent on the things that will pass away, go past as if we were a sideshow.

Yet there are those who hear and who receive the alms that God offers. Talk to the Fijian people, once cannibal, now Christian; or to the Doms, once a criminal tribe in North India, now respected members of society; or to those who, having wandered as far away as Mau Mau, have heard the Redeemer's welcome voice and have come home again; these and all like them will tell of the riches that have come to them from God through those whom this world calls poor. And it all started with One who, though He was rich, yet for our sakes became poor, that we through His poverty might become rich (2 Cor 8⁹). We are back to Irenaeus again: 'In His infinite love He became what we are, in order to raise us up to what He is.'

(b) Bringing Men Home

'God setteth the solitary in families,' reads the Authorized Version at Ps 68[6], but Moffatt gives the verse more life with his translation, 'God who brings the lonely home'. Home is the place where we are understood; where the intimacy is so great that every mood and motive comes under the devastating scrutiny of those we love, where our faults and failings are known and in the complete understanding of love creatively forgiven. If one member of the home suffers, then all suffer; if one member is glad, then all are glad (cf. 1 Cor 12[12-27]).

The binding force in home life is our mother tongue. There is no true intimacy, no complete knowledge of each other, no real understanding, where people do not speak the same language. Here we meet the great paradox of our age. The Church today can use more powerful and immediate means of communication than ever before. Yet it is harder than ever to speak the same language as 'the outsider'. This is a problem not confined to the Church. It is met by all who try to get men and women to think seriously. The Workers' Educational Association knows the difficulty. 'Like the Churches we are constantly discussing the situation of apathy which confronts us today, though we haven't any answer to it.' Politicians and revolutionaries know it. Overseas missionaries know it. The great problem for them, as it is for us, is whether the Church is to be more the home of the people than any other place on earth, or whether it is to be an alien intrusion (cf. Ps 23[6]) (*Report*, p. 37).

The Tower of Babel has again become the symbol of our age. Daily, higher, and more powerful masts thrust their way up to the sky and broadcast messages in every tongue. The strangeness and obscurity of these languages are not the only obstacle to catching their meaning, when the Governments of the people for whom they are intended spend vast sums on the 'hospitable' custom of jamming programmes. All this in an age which has done more than any other to facilitate communication. Appropriately enough, in view of what was to come, the first edition of *The New York Times*, in 1851, carried an exciting scoop. News, rushed by steamboat and train, was in print not much more than a fortnight after the recorded events took place. Now we seem to be present at the moment when news is being made. But we have not attained greater understanding between the nations for all our brilliant inventions. Babel cannot produce unity by some spontaneous, inevitable process of its own. Babel must be reversed by Pentecost before there can be harmony (Gen 11$^{1-9}$; Acts 2$^{1-11}$).

But Pentecost has taken place. It is a false comparison to set the task of the Church in communicating the Gospel alongside that of a politician wanting to be heard about his party's plans. It is true that we must come as close as we can to people, at home and abroad; we must listen, as well as speak, so that when we talk we reach them. We must try to discover not only their language, but what lies behind their words; what goes on in their minds and hearts. In each generation we must restate, reinterpret the eternal Word. But when we have done all that we can in this way, we have hardly begun to 'communicate the Gospel'. That is not our work, but God's. We do not build the bridge into a man's soul. That is done by the Holy Spirit. Our business is to proclaim the Gospel in every way that is open to us, as clearly and as faithfully as we can, honestly covering the whole range of life. The Holy Spirit will then carry our message across the bridges that He Himself has built.

It is God, not we, who brings the lonely home. That must be so when we remember what 'home' is. To come home is to re-enter Eternity. It is Paradise regained. The way back is the way to Eternity and it lies through the reintegration of our being and through reconciliation with God and man. According to the Bible, salvation is the harmony that God restores when He makes us at one with Himself, with our neighbours and in ourselves. This is a cosmic task that God will accomplish. His word calls the universe to return to its home in Eternity. 'He that dwelleth in the secret place of the Most High shall abide under the shadow of the Almighty' (Ps 91^1).

Reintegration of our being means becoming ourselves. It means losing the self that we are not; removing the mask that we wear before men, losing the pretences we try to keep up even in the presence of God. The Prodigal began to return home when he came to himself (Lk 15^{17}). This is the rebirth that Jesus spoke about (Jn 3^8). When He called on His disciples to leave all and follow Him (Lk 5^{11}), or to sell all that they had to buy the pearl of great price (Mt 13$^{45\,f}$), He meant that they had to abandon their old selves; give up all that had seemed good and dear, every cherished belief and tradition, to set out with Him on an unknown way. If we cling to this world, if there is no real change of heart that goes deeper than a code of morals, if there is no insight and no vision, even the very existence of the unseen eternal world will be unsuspected. Where there is no vision the people perish (Prov 29[18]). When we sacrifice our selfhood, we discover our true Self and there is ecstasy in self-annihilation. The condition for remaining alive is this willingness to be reborn. This is not the weary return of the circle to the same place that we call reincarnation. It is a transformation into spirit that is brought about by the consuming fire of God. It is not a timid clinging to truths that once had power to set us free, but the advance to ever newer truths that God is waiting to reveal through Christ; so that the soul, like a butterfly emerging from a chrysalis, has new freedom and new power. Even in Eternity, life is not static but dynamic. So the way back home is not the way back to the self-same spot that we have left, but to some place much farther on the pilgrimage.

'God setteth the solitary in families,' says the Psalmist, 'He bringeth out the prisoner into prosperity' (Ps 68[6]). The prison is our body, the senses being its windows. 'Just as one can do without windows by walking out through the door, so the mystic "steps into Eternity" at will.' But it is an *inward* freedom that Christ gives. The Kingdom of Heaven is within you (Lk 17[21]). The pilgrimage is inwards. It is away from things, 'for a man's life consisteth not in the abundance of the things that he possesseth' (Lk 12[15]); it is also away from the view of God as one who is afar off (Jn 17[21]). We are 'home' if we are pruned, fruit-bearing branches of the Eternal Vine (Jn 15[1-11]).

(c) For All the World

When Paul said that Christ died for all (2 Cor 5[14]) he meant for *all* (*Report*, p. 19).

The theme of the New Testament is that life and history are moving towards the final fulfilment of God's intention to bring all things back home to Himself. It has always been a central belief of Methodism that this means we are free to offer Christ to every man on earth. The Commission seized on this as a vital part of 'our doctrines'. 'No narrowing of the task; no exclusion of anyone, however unprivileged or however rich as this world counts its riches, can be squared with Wesley's view of the world as his parish'. Theologians say that we preach universal grace. Charles Wesley in a verse that repeats the words 'for all' in opposition to those who would narrow down the grace of God, insists:

For all my Lord was crucified,
For all, for all my Saviour died.

In these words the Commission's Report states our world charter. From time to time men talk of groups of people as beyond the Gospel. They talked like that about those who had taken Mau Mau oaths. To all such, our reply is that all men can be saved because God wills it (1 Tim 2⁴).

The first church to die out was the first church of all, the one at Jerusalem. It died because it wanted to save its way of life. Rooted in Jewish ways, it was not able to be on the move with the Gospel. It crossed no national frontiers. The Apostle Paul, with his uncomfortable manner of mixing with Gentiles and bringing them home to God, was not welcomed there (Acts 15). Yet he knew that he had been entrusted with a task that would break the old mould, and bring the Church out of prison into the freedom of the whole world. 'There is one God,' he says, 'and one bridge between God and men, who is a man like us—Christ Jesus who gave Himself a ransom for all. At the appointed time He bore His witness, and of that witness I am the chosen herald, a messenger sent to be a true and faithful teacher of the Gentiles' (1 Tim 2⁵⁻⁷).

In the same way, other churches have vanished because they did not live on the frontier where there is no retreat and no false peace. In the rough places there is only struggle, riot, danger; but new life is emerging there. No new upsurge of life comes to the people who try to keep the vision to themselves. Islam wiped out the great North African church because it confined itself to the tiny Roman ruling group. The church that gave us teachers and thinkers like Cyprian, Tertullian, and Augustine did not reach out to the Berbers who in their little villages were the vast majority of the people. Because they were conquered peasants, no services were held in their mother tongue. They were the common folk, so no word of hope was offered to them. Thus, when Islam removed their Roman rulers, the light of the North African church was put out. For long centuries the people were to be Muslims.

The church that refuses to reach out will pass out.

5. THE PARADOX OF LOVE

We do not seek paradoxes, but when we begin to see what God is doing in His world and what He would have us do along with

Him, paradoxes are forced upon us. We have seen the paradox of time and eternity: we are to offer eternal life here and now to people who have still to go on living in the midst of time. We have to plan for eternity, and work, for the night is coming. We have seen the paradox that we who are poor are to make many rich.

Deeper than these, lies the tension within love itself, for it is love that brings us both passion and peace. We are called to lay all on the altar, and to rest in the Lord. In one sense the mission-ary work of the Church goes from crisis to crisis. It is always urgent, though it is never desperate. The difficulty is not to be too human in our concern for the Cause. Even in times of man-power shortage or financial stress, we must not talk as though we had no faith. It is well enough for us to put our human heads together and to hold meetings, but we must not think that we are doing God's work in our own strength. In many ways the Chris-tian is like the artist, seeing not with his eyes, but through them to the greater reality beyond the surface. There has never been an artist who more consistently believed and practised that than William Blake. Once a young artist who relied on him for help and advice found that for two weeks his inspiration had been dead. So he went to see Blake and found him at tea with his wife. When the young man told of his distress, he was astonished to hear Blake say to his wife, 'It is just so with us, is it not, for weeks together when the visions forsake us? What do we do then, Kate?' 'We kneel down and pray, Mr Blake.'

At Blantyre, where David Livingstone was born, is a very moving memorial to one who, if ever any man did, kept on the move with the Gospel in spite of pain and opposition and distress. A simple cross, made from the wood of the tree which grew where his heart was buried in Africa, is flanked by two quotations. One is from his own pen: *The love of Christ compels me.* The other is from a New Testament passage we have already mentioned (2 Cor 5[14]): *The love of Christ constraineth us.* Both reflect valid Christian experiences, but experiences that are widely different. Every prophet, every preacher, every man sent from God, knows the power of the Spirit that can drive a man into the desert to face his God and to hear His call to a life's work (Mk 1[12]). Every missionary knows that he has been compelled by love to make his choice—and both parts of that paradox are real and true. But this experience, reflected in the words of Livingstone, was not in the mind of Paul when he said, 'The love of Christ constraineth us' (*Report*, p. 84).

The word *constrain* does not mean propel, but control. The idea is that of restraint, of being kept in, prevented from straying to any object or for any purpose, however wholesome, if it be not the will of God. This, too, is the common experience of those who hear God's call. They know that they can no longer live unto themselves, but unto Him who died for them and rose again (2 Cor 5[15]). This is the experience which the Bible calls salvation; being set in a large place, being delivered from the desire to wander away from Home. It is the experience of the Prodigal coming to himself, and of the Saint—the man who is being saved and who is well away on the inner pilgrimage.

We are indeed a part of something that never stands still. We are members of the company who are compelled to be on the move with the Gospel, and constrained never to go away from Home.

PART THREE

Commentaries for Preachers

---

1. On Isaiah 40-55

By the Rev. GARFIELD WADE, M.A.

INTRODUCTION

THE author of these sixteen chapters is usually called 'Second-Isaiah', to distinguish him from those who wrote Isa 1-39 ('First Isaiah', or Isaiah himself) and Isa 56-66 ('Third Isaiah'). We know next to nothing about the personal life of Second-Isaiah, and yet he is without doubt the greatest of all the Jewish prophets. The circumstances in which he delivered his message fall into two main divisions:

1. *One set of circumstances relate to Isa 40-48.* In 597 BC, the Babylonians, in their conquest of the surrounding nations, had attacked Jerusalem and carried off many of the Jews into exile. Ten years later (587 BC), a second attack resulted in the complete destruction of Jerusalem, and a further deportation of Jews into Babylon. Yet a third deportation in 581 resulted in some 4,600 persons ultimately finding themselves in Babylon. There they and their children remained until those who were still alive were released by Cyrus the Persian.

Cyrus had begun to rise to power in 558 BC, and, after startling victories against the allies of Babylon, he finally defeated the Babylonians themselves and entered their city in triumph in 539 BC. It is as Cyrus is advancing victoriously on Babylon that our prophet speaks the message of Isa 40-48 to the Jews, and in the name of God foretells their release from captivity.

2. *Another set of circumstances relates to Isa 49-55.* As far as we can judge, this part of the prophecy was written between the Fall of Babylon and the actual release of the Jews in 538 BC. There would naturally be an interval of some months between the final

conquest by Cyrus and the publication of his edict conferring freedom on the Jewish people, and the situation to be inferred from Isa 49–55 fits these circumstances. The prophet speaks no more of the coming of Cyrus, or the political situation, or the Fall of Babylon. These events are behind him. But he is still prophesying the emancipation of his people, and all he says is meant to prepare for the restored Israel that is to be. We find in these chapters many and urgent appeals addressed to the people for a new way of life, in order that the future Jerusalem may be more glorious than it has ever been in time past.

What the Prophet said

1. *About his People.* They are God's people. They have suffered terribly, but God has all along had them in mind and now at last, as proof of His care, the exile is ending. God will not only deliver Israel; He will exalt it among the nations, and heathen peoples will one day be subject to it. But before this reversal of fortune can take place, there must be an inward and spiritual transformation of the national character, so that Israel can be used by God for His purpose among the nations.

2. *About God.* The OT teaching about God is nowhere loftier and nobler than it is in Isa 40–55. God is set forth as the One who is beyond all comparison. He is the Creator and Sustainer of all things, by the side of whom everything and everybody else is completely insignificant. He is the God of all the earth, He is the only God, the Controller of nations and the Lord of all history.

Yet at the same time He is a gracious God who deals tenderly with His children. Second-Isaiah has much to say of God's grace and mercy, because to him they are the outcome of God's righteousness. This is difficult for us to understand, because we normally think of righteousness as the method by which men are rewarded according to their deserts. Righteousness to us is strict justice, 'an eye for an eye'; but to the prophet the righteousness of God is to be found in the harmony which exists between His promises and His deeds, between His words and His acts. Whatever God says, He fulfils, and He can be relied on to fulfil it because He is completely righteousness. Now God's promises, His words and all He says regarding His people, are concerned with their welfare. Since His people are lost to Him, He desires above all else to save them. In other words, God's purpose towards Israel is a saving purpose. Isa 40–55 is noted for its many references to God's righteousness and His salvation, it being taken for granted that they are one and the same. This saving purpose of God is the grand theme of all history. Martin Büber has called Second-Isaiah 'the originator of a theology of world-history', and from all we know of the prophet we can estimate him as Israel's profoundest thinker.

3. *About the Servant.* This is the title which the prophet uses, in the main body of his work, to describe Israel personified (*see* 41^{8f}, 43^{8-13}, $43^{14}-44^5$, $44^{6-8, \, 21-3}$, $44^{24}-45^{13}$, 48). He employs the term with the thought that Israel is called to be God's messenger, to offer His salvation to all nations.

But in the four Servant Poems (42^{1-4}, 49^{1-6}, 50^{4-9}, and $52^{13}-53^{12}$) the term Servant is used anonymously (49^3 is an exception, though the original MS reading is in doubt here). Various explanations have been offered as to the identity of the Servant in these songs. Some scholars believe the term to be a collective one, and hold that a Remnant of Israel or the Ideal Israel is intended. Others hold that the Servant is an individual (and there are strong grounds for this view), and identify him with Hezekiah, Zerubbabel, Jeremiah, or Isaiah himself. But an even stronger case has been made out by those who hold to a development of this idea, and think that the prophet had in mind a Messianic figure still to come. Most scholars would hold that Second-Isaiah was not directly foretelling the coming of Christ, but someone necessarily unknown who would actualize the Servant ideal.

What is beyond all doubt is that our Lord Himself interpreted Messiahship along the lines of the Suffering Servant depicted in these songs (*see* Index of *ANT*). When the close resemblances (in spite of some differences) between Isa 53, for instance, and our Lord's own Person and Work are fully considered, it seems reasonable to suppose that OT prophecy is here at its most wonderful.

Commentaries for Further Study

The Book of Isaiah (40–66). George Adam Smith (H. & S.).
Isaiah 40–66. J. Skinner (C.U.P.).
Isaiah 40–66. W. L. Wardle, in Peake's Commentary.
Isaiah 40–55. Christopher R. North (Torch Comms, S.C.M.).

COMMENTARY

40$^{1-2}$. GOD SPEAKS COMFORTABLY

The prophet declares his message in a situation strangely like our own. So many of his people had grown weary with waiting. They had known nothing from childhood but captivity, and they yearned for Jerusalem. As Cyrus advanced on Babylon, they must have asked themselves what new hardship awaited them and—more to the point—what was God doing about it all? Could He in fact do anything or were the heathen gods stronger than He?

Thinking people today sometimes wonder if God is big enough for an age of nuclear fission. To many it seems that the more science advances, the less room there is for God. Are men stronger than God and are they able to determine their own destiny apart from Him?

The Christian preacher has no room for doubt; like Isaiah, he begins his message with Almighty God. He must say to most people, using the title of J. B. Phillip's book, *Your God is too Small*. Whilst the scientific humanist urges men to action in an effort to save themselves, the Christian first points to God who is active within history, a God indeed to whom all history belongs. History is 'His story', it is not merely the sum total of man's activities. The whole message of the Old Testament is that God is the Living God, and its record is the account of what God has done, is doing, and is about to do within history, to save men. To the Old Testament writers, God's Righteousness was no mere attribute—it was the way in which He acted, and the New Testament shows the climax of God's saving activity in the Cross which is His Righteousness—'being justified freely by his grace through the redemption that is in Christ Jesus, whom God set forth to be a propitiation through faith by his blood, to shew his righteousness' (Rom. 3$^{24-5}$).

We begin our message to men today, as Isaiah of Babylon began it—with God and His offer of forgiveness. And this is what men need more than they need anything else. We sometimes think they need more to be challenged if they are to come home to God, but Christianity is an offer before it is a challenge. Dr Jowett at the end of his day said, 'If I had my time over again, I would preach more comfort', and he meant that what men need is not scolding, but strength, for there is true strength in the comfort of God. Comfort is not a weak word to be despised. It is derived from two

Latin words meaning 'with strength', and, when we offer men
the forgiveness of God for their sins, we are bringing them into a
situation where, if only they will keep with God, they will ultimately have all the strength of God Himself, both for their own
lives and the life of the world in which they live. In the words of
a modern writer: 'The concern of God is not to fill people with a
sense of guilt, but to use the feeling of guilt as a door of understanding to open new opportunities for living. So guilt leads to
confession and confession leads to freedom and freedom leads to
new life and God is at work in each step of the way.'

40^{3-5}. MAKE WAY FOR GOD

Isaiah daringly declares that God will go before His people on
their triumphant return to Jerusalem. They are obsessed by the
difficulties—not only the physical difficulties, but the spiritual and
political obstacles that seem to stand in the way. What reason is
there to think that Cyrus will be more favourable to God's people
than the tyrants who have previously oppressed them? But Isaiah
knows that God's glory is about to be revealed and nothing and
no one shall stand in His way. All the mountains shall be brought
down and all the valleys shall be filled in and the way made easy.

Can we, God's modern prophets, be as daring with regard to
the almost insuperable difficulties of our time? We can, if we
know who God is. If we have the Bible view of God, we shall not
hesitate to say that God is going before His people, and the vast
political and international problems of our day will be made into
a highway that will lead to God's Kingdom.

But men must co-operate and make way for God. The sooner
they do so, the quicker shall we find deliverance from the evils
that spoil our life. Our trouble is that we will insist on trying to
do the job ourselves and in our own way. We do not realize our
sinful nature and therefore we do not see that all our efforts have
the seeds of destruction within themselves.

Today, perhaps as never before, we are called to make a highway for our God, through colour prejudice, through the colossal
barriers between East and West, through appalling differences of
living standards in which so many people have more than they
need, whilst half the world's population is hungry. God can overcome all these, if only He is given a chance.

Of course, we ourselves may not see the promised deliverance
in the way we expect it, but it is our high privilege to join in

making a road for God. John the Baptist did not see the fulfilment
of his task. These words of Isaiah are applied to him: 'The voice
of one crying in the wilderness, Make ye ready the way of the
Lord, make his paths straight' (Mk 1³). But from his prison cell
John sent messengers to Jesus, 'Art thou he that cometh, or
look we for another?' and Jesus sent word back that all was well;
'The blind receive their sight, and the lame walk, the lepers are
cleansed ... and the poor have good tidings preached unto them'
(Mt 11³, ⁵).

> We shall not travel by the road we make.
> 'Ere day by day the sound of many feet
> Is heard upon the stones that now we break,
> We shall be come to where the cross-roads meet.
>
> For us the heat by day, the cold by night,
> The inch-slow progress and the heavy load,
> And death at last to close the long, grim fight
> With man and beast and stone: for them—the road.
>
> And yet the road is ours as never theirs;
> Is not one thing on us alone bestowed?
> For us the master-joy, oh pioneers—
> We shall not travel, but we make the road.
>
> (V. H. Friedlaender.)

40⁶⁻⁸. TIME AND ETERNITY

The hot wind of the desert—the Sirocco—quickly substitutes
death for life, and man's life when viewed in the light of eternity
is as short as that of desert grass. The prophet seeks to impress
this on his people, for they are pessimistic because of the might of
Babylon. Everything about that mighty Empire, its pageantry,
its worship, its architecture, its commerce, seemed so abiding,
whereas the Jewish religion and its God seemed so small and
insignificant. But Isaiah knows that Babylon could quickly be laid
waste by the winds of history, and he therefore asks why his
people should be so despondent? True, they themselves are only
short-lived and, after thirty-eight years of exile, most of their
strong men had perished; but their God is an Eternal God whose
word stands for ever and therefore, if their trust is in Him, they
are in a very different situation from the Babylonians.

Our life is indeed short—'As for man, his days are as grass: as a flower of the field so he flourisheth' (Ps 103¹⁵)—but time is only relative. We know from our own experience how time can drag and how time can fly. Some people have to kill time, others are killed by it. Everything depends upon the quality of our living. If we are living in God, in whom time passes into eternity, then we too can be above time and it has no power over us.

Let us present to our people, who are often depressed by the shortness of our earthly day, this fact that time, like everything else, can be redeemed, for in the midst of our transient world we have an abiding God. He is, in the words of James (1¹⁷) One 'with whom can be no variation, neither shadow that is cast by turning'. Too many people are at the mercy of time. Someone has said, 'All of us are always going to do better tomorrow and we would too, if only we started today'. The Christian has started today and he alone knows that the only time worth having is 'time for amendment of life', to which God has joined 'the grace and comfort of the Holy Spirit'. Resting in God as he does, the Christian enjoys eternal life here and now, and therefore he is not depressed by the apparent abiding nature of evil. His God is in history, but He is at the same time above it and He lifts His people above it too. So the believer lives both in time and eternity and the shortness of life holds no terrors for him.

40⁹⁻¹¹. GOD THE SHEPHERD

What a contrast the journey back home is to be from that which Israel took when first the nation was deported to Babylon! Then it was the forced march at the pace of the conqueror, with the spear and the lash for the weakling. Now it is to be a walk in which even the children and the infirm can take pleasure, because they are being guided gently home by One who is their Shepherd.

The term shepherd was greatly loved by the Jews and it was the figure of speech which was always applied to the Israelitish king. He was conceived of as guiding and caring for the nation, and in process of time the title was given to God Himself. The 23rd Psalm is the classic example and none of the names ascribed to God has meant more to people in all the history of religion.

It is worth pointing out that the analogy between shepherd and sheep as it relates to God and men cannot be pressed too far. Even as long ago as Ezekiel's day, this fact was realized—'Ye my sheep, the shepherd of my pasture are *men*' (Ezek 34³¹)—and as men our relation to God is a nobler one and a more responsible one than that of sheep to shepherd. Yet it is the fact that we can become so irresponsible which gives the title of shepherd, as applied to God, such a wealth of meaning. For it is when we think of ourselves as sinners that we are able to see ourselves as sheep. 'I have gone astray like a lost sheep' (Ps 119[176])—how true that is! A sheep strays from the fold without meaning to, and that is how most of us go astray. We do not intend to get lost, but again and again we find ourselves away from God. Then it is that God our Shepherd seeks us out and it is significant that Jesus saw His own work primarily as that of shepherding. He saw the whole race of men as sheep without a Shepherd, and, when He applied to Himself the title of Good Shepherd, He described a great deal of His divine task—seeking and saving that which is lost.

Dr Russell Maltby once put Christ's work as Shepherd in these moving words:

Where are you going, Shepherd? To find My sheep.
How far will you go? As far as My sheep.
How far may that be? To the world's end.
How long will you seek it? Until I find it.
When you find it, will it come to you? No, it will fly from Me.
Where will it go, then? To the rocks and the sand.
When will it stop? When it can run no more.
What will you do, then? Carry it home.

40[12–17, 21–7]. GOD HAS 'WHAT IT TAKES'

The prophet has to deal with the defeatism which is sapping the spiritual strength of his people and leading them to complain: 'My way is hid from the Lord and my judgement is passed over from my God' (v. 27b). The years of captivity had begun to tell, and Isaiah of Babylon did not see around him folk who were ready for the march through the desert; much less could he imagine them capable of fulfilling the great missionary role to which God was calling them.

What is the antidote then to physical and spiritual fatigue? It is not a call to greater effort that Isaiah makes, but a call to look up and behold God who is the Lord of creation and the Lord of history. When the great Jowett of Balliol was near the end of his days, he wrote to an aged friend: 'Judging from my own experience I should say that the greatest difficulty was to get above moods of mind which vary from day to day and really arise from physical causes. When we feel ourselves weakest, it is a new strength to think of the unchangeableness of God.'

That is Isaiah's belief. He bids men look up and behold first their God who is the Lord of creation (*vv.* 12–17). God did not require any assistance when He made the world and the universe of which it is a part. Why, then, should the Jews lose heart and suppose that God is no longer able to carry out His purposes? He does not need anyone to uphold Him, and that ought to be obvious from contemplation of the universe which is God's handiwork.

It is not fashionable in our time to remember God the Creator, but it would be none the less salutary for people who have little faith in God, to do so. We speak of Nature, or Mother Nature, or the Laws of Nature, and ignore the God who has made all things. We bow God out of His universe by supposing that Nature somehow made itself. But Nature is a sacrament of God, and if so to the Hebrews with their limited knowledge, how much more to us who know ourselves to be living in an almost limitless universe? We should know ourselves to be children of a God whose power is infinite.

This confidence should be increased when we remember that our God is also the Lord of history! The power of the mightiest tyrant is feeble in the extreme compared with the sovereignty of God.

Professor Farmer tells of a man of weak mind who regularly posted himself at the crossroads in one of Glasgow's busiest areas, where he solemnly directed an enormous flow of traffic. But all the time the traffic signals were flashing forth their messages and the traffic proceeded smoothly without him. We often feel like that with regard to God, that we are called on to direct the affairs of the universe, but all the time it is fulfilling His will because He is in control. 'Lift up your eyes on high' is the only adequate message for the defeatism of our day.

40$^{18-20}$. THE IDOL FACTORY

The Babylonians were idol worshippers on a vast scale and they attributed their national might and power to the work of their gods. Inevitably the Jews had been greatly impressed by these heathen deities. They could not help contrasting their own weakness with the strength of their conquerors, and the sight of the countless idols and the vast system of worship that had grown around them made their own religion, centred as it was in an unseen God, seem very feeble.

But that which attracted them produced nothing but fury and scorn in the prophet, and he employs all the sarcasm and the irony of which he is capable in denouncing idolatry (cf. also 44^{9-20}; 46^{6-8}). His whole point is that God is the Incomparable God and any attempt to represent Him in wood and stone is the utmost folly and wholly dangerous.

It may seem a far cry from the pathetic attempts of heathen peoples making their own gods, to our modern age which supposes itself to be rid of superstition and to have what it delights to call a scientific attitude to life; but the prophet's message has a greater relevance to our times than is at first apparent. Dr Fosdick has a sermon which he entitles, *On Worshipping the Things we Manufacture*, and in it he tells of a man who had been to an Exhibition and had there prayed to a dynamo. He had, he said, nothing else left to worship and the dynamo had emerged as the last word in the modern world with power to do magical things. 'Why,' he wrote in a letter to a friend, 'why shouldn't the dynamo be worthy of worship?'

The majority of men today have come to believe that power resides in material things and few would subscribe to the belief that the greatest power is spiritual. So long as this situation continues, we must join with the prophet in denouncing idolatry.

Many, too, of those who have escaped the crude forms of modern idol worship are still bound by their own conception of God, which is only a subtler type of idolatry after all. It is God's revelation of Himself which is all-important, not our ideas about Him. We must point men to Christ who is 'the image of the invisible God' (Col 1^{15}), and ask them to accept only Him.

40^{28-31}. THE STRENGTH WHICH GOD SUPPLIES

The name of George Adam Smith will long be linked with this passage. It was he who pointed out, what is not at first sight so obvious, that Isaiah is here describing three results of life with God which are actually in an ascending order. Smith wrote: 'Put forth wings—run—walk. Is the order correct? . . . and is not the next stage, a cynic might ask, standing still? On the contrary, it is a natural and true climax, rising from the easier to the more difficult, from the ideal to the real, from dream to duty, from what can only be the rare occasions of life to what must be life's usual and abiding experience.' He then went on to show that history would actually follow this course as Israel returned from the Exile—first the wonderful hope of the prospect, then the preparation and 'the first rush at the Return', but after that, 'the long tramp, day after day, with the slow caravan, at the pace of its most heavily laden beasts of burden, when they shall walk and not faint, should indeed seem to them the sweetest part of their God's promise'.

It is undoubtedly a great experience to mount up with wings as eagles, and the moment of vision, when we see something of God's plan for us, clear and unmistakable, is precious indeed. There is something ecstatic about such experiences which come to us all in greater or less degree. Then, with the ideal before us in all its splendour, we know and are sure. Such insights are a necessary part of the Christian life. As it has been put: 'You must have your castles in the air, before you can put them on the ground.'

But it is a greater thing to run and not be weary. Once the vision has gone, how satisfying to be able to fulfil it! To tackle the really big things in life and to be made really adequate for them—the responsible post, the important piece of Christian service—this is much more wonderful than the moment of the vision splendid.

Yet to walk and not faint is the greatest thing of all! To be able to meet the ordinary demands of life and to go on meeting them day after day unfailingly, this is what we would all covet for ourselves. What a large part of the success of the Church depends on the faithful plodder who keeps at his work and does his job faithfully! How much we owe, for instance, not only to the saints and the princes of the Church, but to ordinary men and women of every Christian community whose chief characteristic is that they never tire of doing the spade-work of the Kingdom.

Well, this threefold strengthening is God's reward to those who wait on Him. 'Waiting on the Lord', may not be an exercise which commends itself to the people of our time, but it holds the secret of all true strength. Through prayer and communion with God, through our worship of Him in a spirit of confident expectancy that God will answer our needs, is to be found the only power that is really worth having.

41^{1-7}. NOT EVEN POWER POLITICS ARE APART FROM GOD

God calls the nations to examine the situation which has arisen. They are all afraid of Cyrus, whose meteoric rise to power has so suddenly upset the political scene. His conquests have been so startling and so swift that it was as if, in his advances, his feet had never touched ground! 'He pursued them and passed safely; even by the way that he had not gone with his feet' (v. 3).

The whole heathen world had been thrown into a ferment. Herodotus, the historian, gives a graphic picture of the way in which the heathen kings feverishly consulted their oracles and propitiated their gods in the hope that Cyrus might in some way be thwarted. George Adam Smith quotes some telling passages and writes: 'The oracles in doubt and ambiguous; the priests, the idol-manufacturers and the crowd of artisans, who worked in every city at the furniture of the temple, in a state of unexampled activity, with bustle perhaps most like the bustle of our government dockyards on the eve of war; hammering new idols together, preparing costly oblations, overhauling the whole religious "ordnance" that the gods might be propitiated and the stars secured to fight in their courses against the Persian; rival politicians practising conciliation and bolstering up one another with costly presents to stand against this strange and fatal force which indifferently threatened them all' (p. 116).

But Isaiah of Babylon claims Cyrus for God! And this in spite of the fact that Cyrus was a devotee of the heathen deities Bel and Nebo! The whole point is that God uses all men for the fulfilment of His purposes, and the very appearance of Cyrus in the affairs of men is proof positive that God presides over the destinies of the nations.

Perhaps no age more than our own has been upset by the conquests of tyrants, and men's lives today are too often fear-ridden by whoever may appear to dominate power politics. Isaiah's message is greatly needed in our time. The Hitlers and Stalins of this world are part of God's judgement upon its sins, and the man of God need never fear that things are getting out of hand, for everything is in the hands of God. As in Isaiah's day, so in ours, God says: 'Who hath wrought and done it, calling the generations from the beginning? I the Lord, the first, and with the last, I am he' (v. 4).

42$^{1-4}$. THE SERVICE GOD REQUIRES

This is the first of the Servant passages, in which it would seem that the Servant refers not to Israel but to an individual, and quite clearly that individual is not Cyrus. The prophet has shown how God uses Cyrus in judgement, but now God turns to some other for the salvation of His people.

This passage was undoubtedly in our Lord's mind at His baptism. Mk 1^{11} joins together two Old Testament quotations— Ps 2^7, 'Thou art my son', and the first verse of this Servant poem. We shall see, with regard to the remaining Servant passages, that it was the unique work of Jesus to identify Messiahship with Isaiah's Suffering Servant and to carry out the redeeming work of both in His own life and death.

How closely Jesus adhered to Isaiah's conception of the Redeemer! Here is the only kind of service which God can use to save:

(1) It is self-effacing. There is none of the noisy propaganda so much to the fore in our modern world. 'What you are shouts so loudly, I can't hear what you say', holds a lesson which many of our generation would do well to heed. The true servant of God does not draw attention to himself, but he makes himself known as God Himself does in a 'still small voice' and by the un-advertised quality of his life.

(2) It is tender. The true servant of God knows what it is to have a giant's strength and use it like a child. He does not break the bruised reed in impatience and despair, for he knows that no one is so spoiled by sin that he cannot be redeemed. Neither does he quench the smoking flax, for he believes that the first dim signs of goodness can always be fanned into a flame.

(3) It is righteous. God's servant, for all his meekness, is never afraid of the truth and condemns sin and unrighteousness wherever he finds it. It is one of the striking characteristics of Jesus that He stood unflinchingly against all forms of privilege and oppression—'he shall bring forth judgement unto truth' (v. 3) might be taken as one aspect of our Lord's dealings with those who perverted justice and held down the truth about God.

(4) It is enduring. The Servant knows, in the words of the prayer, that it is not the beginning of a thing that is all-important, but it is the continuing of the same and the bringing of it to a successful conclusion which yields the true glory. 'Be not weary in well doing,' is a lesson that most of us might take to heart.

This kind of service, in contrast to so much which the world offers (patronizing, cold and self-centred as it so often is), is only possible on the basis of a complete surrender to God. 'I have put my Spirit upon him' (v. 1) is the only way in which the true servant of God is made.

43$^{1-6}$. NO SITUATION CAN BE TOO BAD FOR GOD

'But now.' This part of the prophecy is in complete contrast to what has immediately preceded it. In the last verses of chapter 42, it was the judgement of God upon the sins of the people which was the prophet's concern. Now it is God's rescue of His people which is so joyously proclaimed. And this in spite of the fact that there has been no sign of repentance, no turning to God. The truth is, says Isaiah, that God's salvation is completely undeserved. It is not because the people are worthy to be saved that God is intervening. It is because of God's grace. He will save His people simply because they are His people and therefore He loves them—'Fear not, for I have redeemed thee; I have called thee by thy name, thou art mine' (43^1).

So, no matter through what dangers the nation will pass (fire and water stand for the very worst perils that could befall), God will be with His own.

This conviction that God is specially with His own in trial and suffering has always been strong with the Jews, and it is one which we can certainly encourage in our own people. We shall avoid the materialistic notions which have gathered around the doctrine of God's providence, as shown in the prayer of the Member of Parliament for Weymouth in 1727 which was expressed in these terms: 'O Lord, Thou knowest that I have nine houses in the city of London and that I have lately purchased an estate in Essex; I beseech Thee to preserve the two counties of Middlesex and Essex from fires and earthquakes.' But we shall assert that, whatever happens, God is always with His children. He may not keep them from danger in exactly the way that Isaiah puts it here, but, 'When thou passest through the waters, *I will be with thee*' (43^2); that is the vital truth of all God's dealing with us.

We are His and therefore He will see us through the very worst, not only as far as our physical life is concerned, but also in respect of our soul's welfare. If Isaiah knew this, how much more certain of it should we be, who have the Cross to remind us that God has betrothed Himself to the human race for ever and ever—'for better, for worse, for richer, for poorer', as Russell Maltby used to quote the marriage service. Nothing can part us from God if we are in Christ, 'neither death nor life . . . nor things present, nor things to come . . . nor height nor depth, nor any other creature shall be able to separate us from the love of God which is in Christ Jesus our Lord' (Rom 8$^{38\ f}$).

45¹⁻⁷. GOD IS NEARER THAN WE KNOW

'I girded thee, though thou hast not known me'—this is what our prophet dares to put into the mouth of God in respect of Cyrus of all people. For Cyrus, as we have seen, was a devotee of heathen gods and as far as we know, remained so all his life. To the surrounding nations, but especially to the Jews, Cyrus was a problem. How was it that he was so singularly successful? Isaiah knows. Cyrus is successful because God wants him to be—Cyrus is God's anointed. God has set him apart, as even the best of the kings of Israel itself were set apart, for the doing of God's will and purpose.

But Cyrus himself would be the last man to recognize this, least of all to be aware of God in his life and thought.

It is worth drawing attention to the fact that we do not always know that God is with us. There are many folk who doubt the great truths of religion because, as they say, they never feel any different. Our feelings are no guide as to the presence of God with us. Sometimes, when we feel at our worst, we may be nearest God. There can be no doubt that when our Lord was on the Cross, He was never closer to the Father, because it was then that He came to the climax of the Father's plan of salvation; but it was in that moment that Jesus felt cut off from His Father completely. 'My God, my God, why hast thou forsaken me?' (Mk 15³⁴). The Bible is not concerned with our feelings, but with the tremendous fact that God is with us whether we recognize Him or not.

There are so many people to whom God would say in our day, 'I girded thee, though thou hast not known me'—social reformers, workers for peace, philanthropists, scientists, doctors, and surgeons, and the quite ordinary men and women who practise goodness and love. Sometimes they are cited as evidence that religion is not the only method by which men can lead good lives, but the Christian preacher must take the initiative here and claim these people, even as Isaiah claimed Cyrus—for God. They are men and women who do not know God, but God knows them. Even when they go so far as to deny God, it is still true that God has girded them and their lives are proof positive that He has. As Dr Jacks said of a shoemaker friend of his: 'He spent his breath in proving that God did not exist, but spent his life in proving that He did.'

We have to call on men to recognize that they are personally related to God, without whom they could not be as they are, nor do what they are able.

45[15]. GOD NEVER THRUSTS HIMSELF

Whilst the Bible is the book in which God reveals Himself, it is also the book in which men often complain that God is difficult to find. 'My God, my God, why hast thou forsaken me? Why art thou so far from helping me and from the words of my roaring? O my God, I cry in the day-time, but thou answerest not.' Thus the Psalmist (22[1-2]). Job puts his famous question, 'O that I knew where I might find him', and Isaiah here roundly asserts: 'Verily thou art a God that hidest thyself, O God of Israel the Saviour.'

We who know God would be the first to confess that there is at the same time a sense in which we do not know Him; that He remains 'In light inaccessible hid from our eyes'. In every way that God is revealed, He also remains hidden.

Nature which is made by God and tells us so much of God, yet leaves us at the point where we would like to know more. The good things of life which come from God ought to convince us of His reality, but it takes a constant effort of the mind to realize that 'every good and perfect gift is from above'. The varied events of life ought to show us God at work in our midst, but it is only rare souls like Isaiah of Babylon who see God's activity in all that takes place.

God wants to be known of men and waits to be known by them, but the astonishing thing is that He is not easy to find. Why is this?

In part it must be because we could not bear that He should be fully obvious. Whenever in the Old Testament there are recorded experiences of God manifesting Himself, the writers are always insistent that He was only partially glimpsed, and the implication is that mortals could not endure the complete vision of One who is wholly other than we are.

Again, this side of eternity at any rate, there must always remain a mystery concerning the being of God. If this were not so, we could not worship Him. If we knew all that could be known about Him, if we could understand Him, then He would not be as we know Him to be—Infinite and therefore always to be approached in humility and reverence.

Neither would there be that trust which is the essential thing in the relationship of God to His children, if His existence could be finally and completely demonstrated. 'He that cometh to God, must believe that he is and that he is a rewarder of them that seek after him' (Heb 11⁶)—this must always characterize our approach to God. He does not thrust Himself upon us. It is given to men 'to take the Kingdom of Heaven by violence', but not so will He take our hearts.

46⁹. MEMORY CAN OPEN A DOOR TO GOD

'Remember the former things of old: for I am God and there is none else; I am God and there is none like me.' Isaiah appeals to the fact that all the former prophecies of God have been ful-filled, and he challenges the heathen devotees by insisting that in their religion they can point to nothing comparable. In one passage after another he draws attention to the fact that God is a God of His word (41²⁶, 42⁹, 43⁹, 44⁷, 45²¹).

There is a great deal of religion in this one word 'Remember', and it is significant that the central rite of Christian worship has at the very heart of it the words: 'This do in remembrance of me.' It is when we look back that we become aware of all that God has done.

It is not always easy to recognize God at work in the present. This is especially true today when our lives are lived at such a hectic pace, and one reason why so many in our day are irreligious is because they never allow memory to play its proper part in their lives. Lord Grey of Falloden, that nature-lover, philosopher, and statesman of the first world war, describes in one place how every angler can look back on days so full of happiness that they stand out, as he says, 'as peaks in the landscape of recollection'.

We all have peaks in the landscape of recollection and, if only we would look back on them, we should know a great deal more than we do about the goodness of God. We should be convinced of this fact, for example, that God has been much kinder to us than we deserve. There are many of the older folk in our churches who say, 'You know, God has been very good to me', and they are passing the only possible verdict on life once we begin to look back the way we have come. God has ministered to us in every conceivable way, even when we could not know that He was doing so:

> Unnumbered comforts on my soul
> Thy tender care bestowed,
> Before my infant heart conceived
> From whom those comforts flowed. (MHB 413)

It is also when we look back that we become aware of the tremendous amount of joy and comfort there is in our lives, and how small by comparison is the pain and the suffering. When suffering strikes, we are so apt to think that that is the whole of life and we tend to pass an unfair verdict upon it all; but when we look back we can see that our joy is only *touched* with pain, not smothered by it, that shadows *fall* on brightest hours, they do not obliterate them.

It is when we look back, too, that we are led to trust God. It is when we 'praise Him for all that is past' that we learn to 'trust Him for all that's to come'.

His love in time past forbids me to think
He'll leave me at last in trouble to sink,
While each Ebenezer I have in review
Confirms His good pleasure to see me quite through. (*MHB* 511)

'Remember the former things of old,' says God through Isaiah, and He desires to say it through us also.

49⁴. OUR FAILURES ARE OFTEN GOD'S SUCCESSES

Here, in the second of the Servant Songs, the Servant is the speaker and from the point of view of the impact he has made on his people he is conscious of failure. It is an experience common to all God's servants. The great Old Testament prophets, for example, felt again and again that their strength had been spent for nothing. And in proportion as the world reckons success, that would appear very largely to be true. What could be said of our Lord's ministry from a worldly point of view, except that failure must be written across it ? The religious folk of His day hounded Him to death, the crowds who had loved Him changed their 'Hosanna' to 'Crucify' at the eleventh hour, and even His intimate band of disciples 'all forsook him and fled', when the Cross finally became a reality.

But the Servant knows that failure with men is often counted success with God, and he is contented to leave the issue with God rather than accept the situation at its face value. 'Yet surely my judgement is with the Lord and my recompense with my God'.

This is a word for all engaged in the service of God. If we perform it in our own strength and judge it from the world's point of view, then failure is certain to be the last word about it; but if we serve in the strength of God and leave the results to Him, then what looks like failure is helping God to achieve His victory. We can in other words be quite wrong in our pessimism concerning the work of God, and if we have not seen as the Servant had seen, that it is better to fail with God than to succeed with men, then there is something radically wrong with us.

The Servant is here anticipating the glorious passages in 52^{12-15}: 'Like as many were astonished at thee (his visage was so marred more than any man and his form more than the sons of men) so shall he sprinkle many nations', and 53^{11}: 'He shall see of the travail of his soul and shall be satisfied.'

52^{7-9}. GOD'S MESSENGERS

Here we share in the arrival in Jerusalem of the long-awaited news that the Jews have been liberated from Babylon, that they are actually on their way home with God at their head. This exciting news is conveyed by an evangelist or herald. It was a quite common practice that someone should go before the King to proclaim his advent, but the scene is an uncommon one as Isaiah portrays it. His enthusiasm carries him away, and in lyrical tones he shows us first the herald approaching the city, the watch-men standing on the walls to hear his tidings, and then the people seeing God 'eye to eye', which means that they see Him clearly, even as in the past the Lord had spoken to Moses 'mouth to mouth' (Num 12^8) and 'face to face' (Exod 33^{11}).

C. R. North, in the *Torch Commentary* on this passage, has caught the spirit of it in these words: 'The threefold "That publisheth peace, that bringeth good tidings of good, that pub-lisheth salvation" suggests the picture of the messenger at first descried upon a distant hill, then descending into the valley that separated it from one nearer the city, reappearing and once more disappearing, until he comes within earshot upon the nearest eminence and cries: "Thy God reigneth!" The cry is taken up by the watchmen on the dilapidated walls.'

The words 'Thy God reigneth' bear the meaning that He who is King is, with the return of the exiles, now assuming His active reign.

It is worth noting that the attractiveness of the messengers ('How beautiful upon the mountains are the feet of him that bringeth good tidings') derives simply and solely from the message they bear, namely that God is coming to His people and that His Kingdom is established. They have no excellence of their own, but only that which arises from the importance of their tidings.

This must always be so with the Church of God. Its function is to proclaim the kingly rule of God. It has no merit, except that which is derived from its message. It points men to God, not to itself, and must be judged by the extent to which it enables men to see Him and Him alone. Mere ecclesiasticism has nothing to commend it, nor fellowship, nor social life within the Church, unless it is all the time opening up the Kingdom of God for men to enter. When this happens the result is always the joy of which Isaiah speaks in verse 9 of this chapter.

53¹⁻³. THE REDEEMER WE DO NOT WANT

If, as is likely, the prophet thinks of the nation collectively when he speaks of 'The Servant', then it is not to be wondered at that the Gentiles, who are represented as speaking here, should find the notion of Israel being a Redeemer or Deliverer completely unattractive. The Jews had never been popular with their neighbours at any period of their history, but after years of harrowing exile, they would be less so than at any previous period. They would look more in need of being saved themselves than of being capable of saving others. Israel, having been grown in the unfriendly soil of Babylon, was but a tender plant and a root that had been starved of nourishment.

Neither is it at all surprising that our Lord Jesus should be likewise despised when He deliberately shaped His ministry on the basis of vicarious suffering, as Isaiah develops that doctrine in the later verses of this chapter. Some people reject the view that Isaiah was consciously prophesying the coming of Christ, on the grounds that the Servant is depicted as being 'without form or comeliness' and as having 'no beauty that we should desire him'. Jesus, so it is argued, was surely attractive in so many ways. There is force in this; yet it still remains true that His ministry of suffering does not commend itself to men. Men do not see anything at all attractive in the Cross.

The fact is we still feel that, in some way or another, suffering is a mark of the displeasure of God. We cling to the old belief that God's Servant should be kept from that kind of thing, largely because even the sight of suffering interrupts our own enjoyment and satisfaction. It gives us an uneasy feeling and so we fall back on the human weakness of letting the eye 'cheat the heart and the conscience'. We judge by looks, and consequently Christ and His Church are rejected by the vast majority. We would prefer a more attractive type of deliverer.

But when God comes to save, He comes to suffer, simply because there is no other way.

53⁴⁻⁶. GOD'S REMEDY FOR SIN

'Surely he hath borne our griefs.' The Gentiles, represented by the prophet in these verses, did not come to this conclusion easily, as we saw in the previous verses. In the first place they had been bewildered by the Servant's sufferings and could not understand them. Then they came to the conclusion that his sufferings were contemptible. Still dwelling on them, they began to seek a moral reason for the suffering and found it eventually in this, that the Servant *suffers for them*.

We are here at the heart of things. We cannot pretend to understand all that is involved, but the fact remains that in vicarious suffering (as we term suffering on behalf of others) there is a power that saves from sin. It is when we see what another is prepared to endure, rather than that we should have to bear the consequences of sin, that, as nowhere else, we are moved to forsake our evil ways. Our prophet has been granted a degree of inspiration experienced by no other, and his conception of one suffering for the sake of others has become the great theme of the Christian Faith, for our Lord Jesus saw that no other way could bring us to God and offered Himself to this end.

In other words, Christianity derives from this, that Jesus has borne something for us which we should have borne ourselves. However much we may dislike the idea of someone suffering on our behalf (is it pride that causes us to dislike the notion ?), if we try to take this away from Christianity, we have not a great deal left.

What is it that Jesus bears ? What are the consequences of sin ? The consequences of sin must be nothing less than separation from God, for God, who is 'of purer eyes than to behold evil', can have no dealings with sin in respect of fellowship. This separation is represented in the Bible in various ways—the doctrine of Hell and the notion that sin brings death to the soul ('the soul that sinneth it shall die': Ezek 18⁴) are the main conceptions of the fate of the wicked in the Old Testament and the Inter-Testamental literature.

Neither can there be doubt as to the serious views of the consequences of sin which were held by Jesus Himself. Again and again He uses words like 'perish' and 'die' to depict the fate of those who are in sin, and in His frequent allusions to 'life' there is always the implication that men and women have not the life which He comes to bring. Indeed, before they can have it, they must be born again.

It is to save them from dying as spiritual beings that Jesus dies on Calvary. He embraces the fate of sinful men and women and, in His physical death, dies the death of the soul which is the consequence of sin.

And the necessity for this was seen by Isaiah of Babylon! This prophet is a true herald of Christianity, and to the forefront in the line of that evangelical succession which runs through Paul, Augustine, Luther, and Wesley, and through all who can sing:

> My pardon I claim;
> For a sinner I am,
> A sinner believing in Jesus's name.
> He purchased the grace
> Which now I embrace;
> O Father, Thou knowest He hath died in my place.
>
> (MHB 188)

This is God's remedy for sin.

53⁷⁻⁹. THE SECRET OF THE REDEEMER

Here is something in complete contrast to most of what had gone before in Israel—here is silence under suffering. Israel's sufferers had not hesitated to protest and to protest vehemently at that which had been laid on them. Job and Jeremiah leap to the mind as instances, and the *Psalms* are full of agonizing cries against the injustices of pain and loss. But Isaiah's Servant is afflicted and he 'opens not his mouth'.

The reason for the contrast is that formerly it had been held that suffering was the direct outcome of sin, God's way of punishing the evil-doer. But Isaiah, by his tremendous 53rd chapter, does a great deal to change that mistaken view. From the Exile onwards it is remarkable how often suffering was endured meekly and in silence.

When we study the silence of Jesus, who fulfilled this Servant prophecy, an even deeper truth emerges. Jesus is silent because He has no sin. It is for other people's sins that He suffers and His silence is the product of His Messianic consciousness. He has a secret that His persecutors cannot wrest from Him, try as they will. The secret is that 'for the transgression of my people was he stricken'. The silence of Christ at His trial was one of the most eloquent things about His whole ministry and, when we understand it, we know what He has come to do for us. In the words of Adam Smith: 'Why was this Servant the unique and solitary instance of silence under suffering? Because he had a secret which they had not. It had been said of him, "My servant shall deal wisely or intelligently", shall know what he is about. He had no guilt of his own, no doubts of his God. But he was conscious of the end God had in his pain, an end not to be served in any other way, and with all his heart he had given himself to it. It was not punishment he was enduring . . . it was a service he was performing—a service laid on him by God, a service for man's redemption, a service sure of results and of glory'. It was because our Lord so perfectly aligned Himself with Isaiah's Suffering Servant, especially as here in His great silence, that we have come to know Him as the Lamb of God. The ewe mother was kept for her wool and for lambs yet to be born, but the lamb itself, as the Jewish ritual required, was led to the slaughter; and Jesus is the 'Lamb of God slain from the foundation of the world'.

53¹⁰⁻¹². THE TRIUMPH OF THE REDEEMER

The reason for the terrible fate of the Servant is now made plain. It was not that he had in any way deserved it. It was all part of God's redeeming purpose. God makes the Servant's soul 'an offering for sin'.

The notion of substitutionary sacrifice goes far back in primitive religion, as in Jewish. With the Jews, the guilt-offering stood for damages or the payment which a transgressor had to make to some person he had offended. So we find it in *Numbers*. In *Leviticus* there has been a development, and the guilt-offering has become the ram exacted over and above the damages to the injured party for satisfaction to God's law. By this guilt-offering, the priest made atonement for the sinner and the forgiveness of God was mediated. Isaiah regards the Servant's death as being in line with this; it is that by which the Servant does homage to the law of God.

How the Cross answers this insight of Isaiah's! What a perfect offering is the offering of Christ! And it is this Christ that the Christian preacher has to offer to men; not Christ the Example (though He will always be the example for us all), not Christ the Teacher (though His ethics surpass all others), but Christ who is the Sacrifice for the sins of the whole world. He dies our death and, through His death, we have eternal life.

That multitudes have found this eternal life that Jesus secured for all in His death is the proof of His victory. It is this which enables Him to 'see of the travail of his soul and be satisfied'. It is not that He undergoes the suffering of the Cross for suffering's sake. It is that through suffering He sees the only way to make Himself one with sinners. He Himself was a man of joys and acquainted with laughter, but He became a man of sorrows and acquainted with grief to pay, once and for all, the price of sin. And all who have entered into redeeming love are part of the harvest of His Cross. He reigns from the tree!

55¹⁻⁶. WHOSOEVER WILL MAY COME

The prophet now seeks to bring His message to a close and, true evangelist that he is, he does so by offering the blessings of salvation, not to those who are fit to receive them, nor to those who will promise to try to be good enough for them, but to anyone who will take them. They cannot be purchased, they can only be received.

He presents them under the form of satisfaction for hunger and thirst, because he knows that they constitute the very necessities of life. There have always been those (and never more so than today) who regard religion as one of the luxuries of life. Religion is commonly conceived as 'all right for those who like that sort of thing'; but not so with Isaiah. Water, bread, wine, and milk represent the food and drink by which men live, and without them they do not live at all.

A. E. Whitham in one place speaks of Christ in this way: 'He is *suitable*, He is *necessary* to human nature: He is Bread and Water. Are you staggering, faint, and weary? Eat of this bread. Are you footsore with the devil's miles you have to cover? Turn aside to this spring. It is Bread and Water, purposed and provided for men who have long journeys to foot, big tasks to discharge, much sin to con fess, heavy burdens to carry. If it is for such—God knows it is for *you*.'

And this is how every preacher must offer Christ; as the One without whom there is no true life at all, as the One who can be received for the asking. It is noteworthy that Jesus offered Himself to men very much in the way that Isaiah here offers salvation. To the Samaritan woman: 'If thou knewest the gift of God and who it is that saith to thee, Give me to drink; thou wouldest have asked of him and he would have given thee the living water' (Jn 4[10]). To the crowds who followed Him : 'I am the bread of life: he that cometh to me shall never hunger and he that believeth on me shall never thirst' (Jn 6[35]).

55[6–7]. COME WHILE YOU CAN!

Here are the notes of the true evangelist. The imperatives, 'seek, call, forsake, return', would make excellent headings for what we often call a 'Gospel sermon'. (Incidentally every sermon should be a Gospel sermon, even if its primary purpose is instruction.) These verses are worthy to stand by the side of our Lord's gracious invitation: 'Come unto me, all ye that labour and are heavy laden . . .' (Mt 11[28 f]).

But the prophet's stress falls on the urgency of the matter. Come *now !* God is always waiting for men to return, but there are with men special times when the invitation can be accepted. In the case of the Jews, the coming of Cyrus provided an excellent opportunity. Release from captivity with Jerusalem in prospect was too good a chance to miss. Isaiah's people should leave the old ways and embrace God's pardon for all their sins.

The doctrine preached here is that of repentance, and the prophet rightly emphasizes the joyous aspect of the matter. Too often in the popular mind repentance has gloomy associations and does not commend itself to men. But the word itself means what Isaiah says here; it is a turning away from self to God. It means to get a new outlook on life, to see it from God's angle instead of our own. It is to change our way of thinking and as such it is to find God and release from the bondage of self.

The fact that this chance to find forgiveness is always available is one of the things that keep men and women from it. They know it is there, so they do not feel the urgency to accept it. But Isaiah knows that delay may be fatal. We can so put off the moment of acceptance that we may reach the stage where we no longer desire it. This is the worst sin of all. It is what Paul had in mind when he wrote: 'Shall we continue in sin that grace may abound' ?

(Rom 6[1]), and the writer of *Hebrews* (3[7]), when he quotes from Ps 95[7-11], 'Today if ye shall hear his voice, harden not your hearts, as in the provocation'.

55[8-13]. INSTEAD

The prophet brings his word to a glorious crescendo. Instead of a life centred in self, concerned all the time with the business of getting and spending and making a living, men can find themselves centred in God whose thoughts are so far beyond the thoughts of men. In this way they will see life as God intended it to be lived, and they will be lifted into that heavenly life which is God's purpose for us all.

Instead of the apathy which takes it for granted that God's purpose will never be realized, they can come to a strong faith in the availability of God's way of life for all. The situation simply cannot be measured by man's despairing thoughts. God is able to bring in His Kingdom. As the natural order fulfils His sovereign will, the rain and the snow bringing forth bread for the eater, so He has the power to make His word accomplish His whole purpose for man.

The entire contrast can only be expressed in a change from the barren life of the desert to the lush vegetation of a parkland, where the fir-tree and the myrtle commemorate for ever the mighty name and power of God. All nature shall rejoice with the returning exiles, the hills will break forth into singing and all the trees of the field will clap their hands.

2. On John 1–4

By the Rev. OWEN E. EVANS, M.A., B.D.

INTRODUCTION

THE purpose of the following commentary is to suggest themes for preaching from the opening chapters of the Fourth Gospel. It is assumed that the student will be familiar with the material contained in Study Six of *ANT* (*paras.* 287–306), and that he will have access to a good commentary on the English text of the Gospel. The best available commentaries are: *The Fourth Gospel: Its Significance and Environment*, by R. H. Strachan (S.C.M., 1941), and *St John's Gospel, A Commentary*, by R. H. Lightfoot, edited by C. F. Evans (Oxford, 1956). The preacher will also derive great benefit from the use of the late Archbishop William Temple's classic devotional commentary, *Readings in St. John's Gospel* (Macmillan). For those who read Greek, by far the best commentary is *The Gospel according to St. John, an Introduction with Commentary and Notes on the Greek Text*, by C. K. Barrett (S.P.C.K.). For the study of the many problems of critical introduction to the Gospel, the student is referred (in addition to the relevant paragraphs of *ANT*) to Vincent Taylor's treatment in *The Gospels, a Short Introduction* (Epworth), pp. 84–109, and F. B. Clogg's in *An Introduction to the New Testament* (University of London Press), pp. 255–74. More advanced students will find an exhaustive and up-to-date treatment of these problems in C. K. Barrett's recent revision of the late W. F. Howard's Fernley Lecture, *The Fourth Gospel in Recent Criticism and Interpretation* (Epworth, 1955).

With regard to these questions of introduction, the position adopted in these notes may be briefly summarized as follows. The Evangelist was a disciple of the Apostle John and based his work on the teaching and testimony of his venerated master. He wrote his Gospel at Ephesus during the last decade of the first century AD. He was acquainted with the earlier Gospels of Mark and Luke, and part of his purpose was to supplement the material contained in those Gospels by recording the special tradition which he had derived from the Apostle John (particularly tradition concerning the activity and teaching of Jesus in Jerusalem and Judea). His main purpose, however, was not so much a *historical* as a *theological* one. He regarded the works of Jesus which he selected for inclusion in his Gospel as 'signs' (*see* below on 2^{1-11}), each of which symbolized some deep spiritual truth, and his concern was not merely to relate the bare facts, but to *interpret* the facts so as to bring out, under the inspiration of the Holy Spirit (cf. 16^{13-14}), their true and abiding significance. He wrote primarily for Gentile readers, desiring to commend the Christian Faith—a Faith deeply rooted in the soil of his own native Jewish thought—to a pagan world that was under the dominance of Greek ways of thinking. He transposed, so to speak, the Palestinian Gospel into a Hellenistic key, and succeeded in doing so without obscuring or distorting the original tune. He was thus the prototype of all Christian preachers of every age, in that he sought to interpret, to his own age and environment, the eternal spiritual meaning and significance of those historical events in which Christianity is rooted and grounded. Accordingly, it may well be said that the Fourth Gospel is pre-eminently 'the preacher's Gospel'.

The chapters to be dealt with may be analysed as follows:

The Prologue. 1^{1-18}.
John the Baptist and Jesus (1). 1^{19-34}.
Jesus and His Disciples. 1^{35-51}.
The Sign at Cana. 2^{1-11}.
The Cleansing of the Temple. 2^{12-25}.
Jesus and Nicodemus. 3^{1-21}.
John the Baptist and Jesus (2). 3^{22-36}.
Jesus and the Woman of Samaria. 4^{1-42}.
Jesus and the Gentile Nobleman. 4^{43-54}.

COMMENTARY

1^{1-18}. THE PROLOGUE

Logos (translated 'Word') was an important term in Greek philosophy and was widely current in the Hellenistic world of the first century. It stood for the rational principle that was the basis of all things. John takes this familiar term (thus, in the manner of the true preacher, arresting the attention of his readers at the very outset) and makes it the vehicle of his teaching about the nature and significance of the Person of Jesus Christ. The term commends itself to him, however, not only on account of its familiarity to his contemporaries who are influenced by Greek ways

of thinking, but also because of its eminent suitability for con-
veying the fundamentally Jewish idea of God's self-expression in
creation and revelation. The OT teaches that the universe was
created 'by the *word* of the Lord' (*see* Ps 33[6]; cf. Gen 1[3], etc.),
and that the message of the prophets which contains the revelation
of God is 'the *word* of the Lord' (*see* Hos 1[1], Jer 1[4], etc.). The
concept of 'Wisdom' in later Judaism (*see* Prov 8[22-31], and the
Books of *Ecclesiasticus* and *Wisdom of Solomon*) is also part of
the background of John's use of the term *Logos*. 'Wisdom' was
thought of in more or less personal terms as the mediator between
God and His creation. Hellenistic Judaism had already adopted
the Greek idea of *Logos* and developed it along the lines of the
Jewish concept of 'Wisdom'. John, however, carries this development a great deal farther by claiming, not only that the *Logos* is
fully *personal*, but that the *Logos* actually became *incarnate* in the
historical person of Jesus of Nazareth. The Prologue reaches its
glorious, and startlingly original, climax in *v.* 14: 'The Word
became *flesh*, and dwelt among us.'

One of the questions that perennially exercise the minds of
men and women is the question whether they can *know* what God
is like and what His purposes are for their lives. It is part of the
duty, and privilege, of the Christian preacher to answer this age-
old question clearly and confidently, and for this purpose he will
find no passage of Scripture more relevant than the Prologue of
John. On the basis of this majestic passage he can assure his
hearers, not only that the God of the Bible is a God who speaks
to men (i.e. makes known to them His mind, His character, and
His purposes)—a truth which is abundantly illustrated throughout the OT—but that He has spoken His final and all-sufficient
Word in the Incarnation of His eternal Son (cf. Heb 1[1-2]). The
God whom 'no man hath seen at any time' has been perfectly
made known (*v.* 18) because His Only-begotten Son came to
dwell upon earth as a fully human person (*v.* 14, where the term
'flesh' implies full humanity). How could God ever be made known
except by One who was, from all eternity (cf. *vv.* 1-2), united
with Him in the most intimate possible relationship (in His
'bosom', *v.* 18; cf. the use of the same figure in 13[23] to describe a
specially intimate personal relationship)—One who Himself,
indeed, shares fully in the divine nature (*v.* 1, 'the Word was
God'; cf. *v.* 18, where the original reading was probably 'the
Only-begotten, who is God')? And how could such a One ever
bring the revelation within the reach of men except by descending

into their midst and sojourning with them ('dwelt' in *v.* 14 = 'pitched His tent')? In Jesus Christ, His eternal Word made flesh, God has told men all that He wishes them to know, and all that they need to know, about Himself. To learn what God is like, and what His purposes for us are, all we need do is look at, and listen to, Jesus Christ; and that is something that we all may do by reading the Gospels, which contain the testimony of those who, like the author of this Gospel, were able to say: 'We beheld his glory' (*v.* 14).

The Incarnation of the Word means that the true Light (*v.* 9) has shone into the darkness of the world. There is here both a message of comfort and a message of challenge which the preacher may proclaim. The comfort lies in the fact that the Light is ever shining in the midst of the world's darkness and can never be extinguished (that is part of the meaning of 'the darkness apprehended it not' in *v.* 5—*see* RVmg and *ANT, para.* 292). The challenge, on the other hand, lies in the fact that it is possible for men to remain in darkness in spite of the fact that the Light is shining (that is the other part of the meaning of *v.* 5—see AV). This tragedy of the rejection of the Light of God's perfect self-revelation in Christ is illustrated from the history of the Jews in *v.* 11 ('His own *home* . . . his own *people*'—*see ANT, para.* 294). That which was true of the Jews, however, is no less true, generally speaking, of the rest of mankind. For men to 'sit in darkness and the shadow of death' (*see* Lk 1[79]; cf. Isa 9[2]) is tragic enough, but for them to go on doing so when the Light is shining upon them, and all they have to do is open their minds and hearts to receive it, is doubly tragic. To drive this point home can be the basis of a strong and effective appeal to men to accept the Light of Christ by believing in Him.

The wonderful privilege of Christian believers is another theme worthy of every preacher's attention, and he will find it strongly emphasized in the later verses of the Prologue. *Vv.* 12–13 remind us that it is those who receive Christ by believing in Him who are given 'the right to become children of God'. This means that men are not by nature children of God; all men, indeed, are *potential* children of God, but it is only by faith in Christ that the potential becomes *actual*. A man is born into God's family not by any physical or natural process of birth, but by a spiritual and supernatural re-birth (*v.* 13; cf. the fuller statement of this truth in 3[1–7]). This is essentially the same truth as Paul teaches by using the metaphor of adoption (*see* Gal 4[4–6] and Rom 8[14–17]), but

John's metaphor of a new birth is warmer and more personal, and so likely to be of more universal appeal, than Paul's rather cold and legal metaphor. To be a child of God is not just a matter of privileged *status;* it is to share in the very nature and life of God Himself. Just as the 'Only-begotten from the Father' partakes fully and perfectly of the Father's nature, so those who receive Him in faith partake of the same divine nature. The Only-begotten (*v.* 14) reflects the divine glory ('glory' is one of the great words of the Fourth Gospel, and denotes all the richness of the character and personal, redeeming activity of God), and is 'full of grace and truth' (which in the OT are attributes of God—*see* Ex 34⁶ and Ps 25¹⁰). Christian believers (the 'we' of *vv.* 14 and 16) have not only been privileged to behold the glory in the face of Jesus Christ (*v.* 14; cf. Paul's words in 2 Cor 4⁶), but have also themselves received 'of his fulness' of grace and truth (*v.* 16). Thus to be a Christian does not mean to strive, in one's own strength, to imitate an ideal of life set before one in Jesus Christ, but rather to receive from Him a share in His own life. This new and higher quality of life which Christ imparts to all who believe in Him is the dominant theme that runs through the whole of John's Gospel (*see* especially 3¹⁶, 10¹⁰, 20³¹).

The expression 'grace for grace' in *v.* 16, when properly understood, is full of suggestion for the preacher. Literally it means 'grace in place of grace'; not, however, the grace of the Gospel in place of the grace of the Law—for the following verse implies that grace does not belong to the Law. The meaning is that the Christian receives, as it were, wave upon wave of divine grace. Each experience of God's grace in Christ which we accept leads on to a further and richer experience thereof. Grace is abounding and inexhaustible, and the Christian life is a matter of grace from beginning to end.

Finally, before leaving the Prologue, we may note the contrast between the Old and New Dispensations suggested by *v.* 17. 'The law *was given* by Moses'—or rather 'through Moses' (*see* RVmg); Moses was not the author and giver of the Law, but merely the human mediator through whom it was given by God. By contrast, the grace and truth which are the marks of the New Dispensation '*came* by Jesus Christ'; He is not merely the Mediator, but the actual source of grace and truth (cf. *v.* 14). Moses offered men a Law and bade them keep it, that they might live thereby (cf. Rom 10⁵); Christ offers men Himself and bids them believe, and in believing find life in Him (cf. 20³¹).

1^{19-34}. JOHN THE BAPTIST AND JESUS (1)

Like the earlier evangelists, and following the pattern of the apostolic preaching (cf. Acts 10^{37}), John makes the ministry of John the Baptist the starting-point of his account of the ministry of Jesus. The Fourth Gospel portrays the Baptist exclusively as a witness to Christ, and loses no opportunity of stressing the fact that he is subordinate to Christ (cf. the two incidental references which have already been introduced in the Prologue, *vv*. 6–8 and 15). It is probable that the Evangelist wished to correct a tendency to over-exalt the Baptist which appears to have been characteristic of Ephesus (*see* Acts 19^{1-7}).

This subordination of the Baptist to Christ is a prominent feature of the account given in *vv*. 19–28 of the conversation between John and a deputation which the religious authorities at Jerusalem sent to question him about his unorthodox preaching and practices. The questions asked of John reflect the Messianic expectations of the time. 'The Christ' in *v*. 20 is the Greek equivalent of the Hebrew 'Messiah' (= 'Anointed one'); 'Elijah' (*v*. 21) was expected to return to the world as the forerunner of the Messiah (*see* Mal 4^5, and cf. Mt 11^{14}, 17^{12-13}); 'the Prophet' in *v*. 21 is an allusion to the promise of Moses in Deut 18^{15} (cf. Jn 6^{14}, 7^{40}; Acts 3^{22}, 7^{37}). John, however, denies that he is any of these. He disclaims any Messianic status for himself and consistently directs attention away from himself to the Greater One who is to come after him. He is content to describe himself, in words quoted from Isa 40^3, as a mere 'voice'. 'We see his growing irritation in the increasing abruptness of his replies. "I am not the Christ"; "I am not"; "No". It is not who he is, but what he says, that matters. He is a voice' (Temple). In this humble self-effacement, John stands as a shining example to everyone whose task it is, whether in the pulpit or out of it, to witness for Christ. How fatally easy it is to draw men's attention to ourselves rather than to the message we proclaim and the Saviour we commend! The preacher whose congregation goes away thinking what a fine preacher he is has failed; he ought to send them away thinking what a wonderful Saviour Jesus is. It is Jesus who is the 'Word' (*see* the Prologue); the witness is a mere 'voice', whose privilege it is to speak that 'Word', and to make straight His way into the hearts of his hearers.

The humility of John the Baptist appears again in his words in *v*. 27 (cf. Mk 1^7). He could not possibly have expressed more emphatically his own subordination to Christ than by saying that he was not worthy to unloose the latchet of His shoes, for that was reckoned to be the most menial even of a slave's duties. There was a Rabbinic saying to the effect that a disciple might perform for his master any duty proper to a slave *except* that of untying his sandals. Every Christian is the bond-servant of Christ, and there is no task, however humble, that it is not his unspeakable privilege to perform in his Master's service. We are not *worthy* to perform even the lowliest service in His name.

The Jewish authorities objected to John's ministry of baptism (*see v.* 25) on two grounds: (i) because he administered baptism to *Jews* (such a rite of purification was all very well for proselytes being received into the Jewish faith, but 'the sons of Abraham' had no need of it!), and (ii) because he had, on his own admission, no official status, and so had no right to baptize. They looked askance at this prophet, and at the new movement which he had initiated, because he dared to disturb their own religious complacence, and because he did not conform to their own preconceived ideas of what a prophet should be and do. There are still those who are in danger of thinking, as they sit at ease in Zion, that their traditional association with the Church is a substitute for a real evangelical conversion. And official Christendom has often been guilty of a conservative suspicion of new and unorthodox methods (one has only to think of the attitude of the Established Church towards John Wesley and his preachers, and the attitude of official Wesleyanism later on towards the early Primitive Methodists). The new and unconventional is not *necessarily* right and commendable, but the Church should always be wary of condemning out of hand the prophet who arises from without its official ranks. It is not without significance that 'in the high-priesthood of Annas and Caiaphas, the word of God came', not to *them* in Jerusalem, but 'unto John the son of Zacharias *in the wilderness*' (Lk 3$^{1-2}$). In this, as in other respects, 'the Spirit bloweth where He listeth', and the sure test is always that advocated by Gamaliel in Acts 5$^{38-9}$. There are themes here which the preacher will sometimes feel constrained to develop.

The content of John the Baptist's witness to Jesus appears in *vv.* 29-34. He claims to have recognized Jesus as the Messiah (= Son of God) on the occasion of His baptism (the Baptism of Jesus, as such, is nowhere related in this Gospel, but its occasion is clearly alluded to in *vv.* 31-34—cf. Mk 1$^{9-11}$). John would not, however, have so recognized Jesus, had not the truth been divinely revealed to him (v. 33). No one can recognize Jesus as the Son of God save by the illumination and inspiration of the Holy Spirit (see 15²⁶, 16¹⁴, and cf. 1 Cor. 12³ᵇ and *MHB* 363). This is something which the preacher needs to stress, especially when speaking to those who have intellectual difficulties about believing in the divinity of our Lord. Ultimately it is not the 'flesh and blood' of unaided reason that will convince anyone of the truth about the Person of Jesus, but the revelation received from the 'Father which is in heaven' (cf. Mt 16¹⁷).

In v. 32 we read that the Spirit not only descended upon Jesus at His baptism, but '*abode* upon him'. The prophets of the OT were visited by the Spirit from time to time, but Jesus' possession of the Spirit was constant and unbroken. It was in perfect communion with the Holy Spirit, and under His inspiration and guidance, that Jesus fulfilled His ministry (cf. Mk 1¹², etc.). How much more do those who would follow Him depend constantly and completely upon the inspiration and guidance of the same Spirit! And what a comfort to know that Jesus Himself has promised to give us the Spirit, 'that he may be with you for ever' (see 14¹⁶). As the Spirit *abode* on Him, so He will abide on us—if we let Him!

I have left to the last the best-known and best-loved text in the present section. Every preacher, sooner or later, will want to preach on Jn 1²⁹. More than one OT idea underlies the title here applied to Jesus—'the lamb of God'. The fundamental idea is probably that of the Paschal lamb of Exod 12 (note that in 19³⁶ Jesus is again identified with that lamb). This idea, however, does not by itself provide an adequate interpretation, since it does not account for the clause 'that taketh away the sin of the world' (the Paschal lamb was not spoken of as taking away sin). In Isa 53 the Suffering Servant is described as 'a lamb' (v. 7) and as 'bearing the sin of many' (v. 12).★ This suggests that in our text the idea of the Servant is fused with that of the Paschal lamb (and possibly with other sacrificial ideas also, such as the sin-offering of the Day of Atonement, see Lev 16). Thus the meaning is that Jesus is the Servant whom God sent to offer Himself as a new Passover sacrifice (cf. 1 Cor 5⁷) in order to make an end of sin (cf. Heb 9²⁶). This thought of the death of Christ as an atoning sacrifice is the very heart of the Gospel which we are privileged to preach. *Why* such a sacrifice should have been necessary before men could be delivered from sin and reconciled to God is a

★ *See* also pp. 146 ff.

question that no preacher will ever be able adequately to answer. He can, however, point out that when one considers 'of what great weight is sin' on the one hand, and the awe-full holiness of God on the other hand, one ought not to be *surprised* that atonement should have involved the payment of such a terrible price. We speculate in vain as to who required the price to be paid. What we may be quite sure about, and proclaim with glad passion, is the glorious news that the price *has* been paid on our behalf— paid by God Himself. The necessary sacrifice has been offered, once for all. The Victim Divine was the Lamb of *God*—the Lamb which God Himself, of His infinite mercy, provided to effect that atonement which 'not all the blood of beasts on Jewish altars slain' (*MHB* 234) could ever effect. 'Worthy is the lamb that hath been slain to receive the power, and riches, and wisdom, and might, and honour, and glory, and blessing' (Rev 5[12]).

1[35-51]. JESUS AND HIS DISCIPLES

The tradition preserved in this passage suggests that some members of the Twelve were formerly adherents of John the Baptist, and that they first came into contact with Jesus at the scene of the Baptist's ministry. Later, in Galilee, Jesus called them to leave their occupations and become His full-time disciples (*see* Mk 1[16-20]). There is no contradiction between John and the Synoptics regarding the occasion of the disciples' call, provided that the call related here by John is understood as being of a preliminary nature (*see ANT*, paras. 104, 298).

The self-abnegating humility of the Baptist (*see* previous section) appears again in the fact that he allows two of his own disciples to leave him and attach themselves to Jesus; indeed he encourages them to do so, by pointing them to Jesus as 'the lamb of God' (*v.* 36, cf. *v.* 29 above). We learn from *v.* 40 that one of these two first followers of Jesus was Andrew. The other is not named, but there are good reasons for supposing that he was John, the son of Zebedee (*see ANT*, paras. 288, 298). If this identification is correct, *v.* 41 (especially if one possible Greek reading is followed) may imply that this unnamed disciple emulated Andrew and in turn found *his* brother; i.e. John found James, thus completing the same group of four—two sets of brothers—which, according to the Synoptics, constituted the earliest disciples of Jesus. In this event, too, the precise note of time in *v.* 39 ('the tenth hour' = 4 p.m. by our reckoning) becomes specially significant as deriving from the personal testimony of John. We may well believe that John, like many another Christian, never forgot the exact hour at which he met this Master for the first time.

At first these disciples see Jesus as a teacher, and address Him as such ('Rabbi', v. 38). There is more in their question, 'Where abidest thou?' than a mere request for an address; they wish to go home with Him to discuss matters at a deeper level than would be possible by the wayside. Similarly there is more in the answer 'Come, and ye shall see' than the mere promise of a view of Jesus' lodgings; the verb translated 'see' is one which is often used of spiritual vision (it occurs again in vv. 50–51). This seemingly simple statement of Jesus implies the far deeper truth that all who follow Him will have their eyes opened to spiritual realities. That this proves to be the case for the two disciples is shown by the conviction which they are soon expressing—'We have found the Messiah' (v. 41). Beginning with the conviction that He is a great Teacher, and being attracted to Him and willing to learn of Him, they soon come to believe in Him as Messiah. There are still those whose experience may follow similar lines, and part of the task of the preacher is to invite those who regard, and revere, Jesus as the supreme Teacher (but have not yet seen anything more in Him than that) to follow Him obediently and learn of Him, that they may be led to a fuller understanding and experience of all that He is and means to men.

We learn more about Andrew from this Gospel than from any other. His outstanding characteristic is his concern to introduce others to Jesus (cf. 6⁸⁻⁹, 12²²). He was a missionary by nature—as every true disciple of Christ should be. And he began bearing his witness—as every Christian should—in his own home, among his own family. He brought 'his own brother Simon' to Jesus. No text can serve as a better basis for an appeal for personal evangelism—and no appeal that the preacher can make to the fully-committed members of his congregation is more relevant to the needs of our time. It is clear from v. 42 that Jesus immediately took a special interest in 'Simon the son of John'. He gave him a new name, *Cephas* (an Aramaic word, the Greek equivalent of which is *petros*, meaning 'rock'). The Fourth Gospel does not attempt to explain the reason for the bestowal of this particular name (as does Mt 16¹⁸, where Peter is said to be the 'rock' on which the Church is to be built). Perhaps Jesus was setting before Simon an ideal after which he must aspire. We know how often Peter failed to live up to his new name, but Jesus saw beyond his failures to the fulfilment of the great possibilities that lay in the man. Peter was destined to become the outstanding figure among the Apostles of Christ—and yet he would not have come to the Master at all, had it not been for his far less prominent brother Andrew. Even so, the obscure Christian in every age, who faithfully bears his witness in his own limited sphere, may be the means of bringing to Jesus someone whose influence and leadership will prove mighty and far-extending.

It may be, as we have seen, that the unnamed companion of Andrew (if he was in fact John) also became a missionary at once. Certainly Philip, the next disciple called by Jesus, did; he set out immediately (*v.* 45) to fetch his friend Nathanael. Andrew and Philip seem to have had a good deal in common, for they appear together again in 6⁵⁻⁹ (where they both display concern that the multitude should be fed), and in 12²⁰⁻²² (where they co-operate to introduce 'certain Greeks' to Jesus). They exemplify the thoughtful, practical-minded type of Christian, who is always concerned about the needs of his fellow-men.

Nathanael is an admirable example of the pious Israelite ('an Israelite indeed', the Israelite at his best), whose 'delight is in the law of the Lord' (cf. Ps 1²). He was one of those devout Jews who longed for the coming of the Messiah foretold in Scripture (cf. the description of Simeon in Lk 2²⁵). It was customary for such Jews to sit 'under the fig tree' (which symbolized the peace and privacy of a man's house—cf. 1 Kings 4²⁵, Mic 4⁴) to meditate upon and discuss the Law. This is a picture that Christian families might well be urged to ponder. Nathanael receives from Philip what must be, for him, the wonderful news that the One 'of whom Moses, in the law, and the prophets, did write' has appeared at last. When, however, Philip mentions Nazareth as the home of Jesus, Nathanael's scepticism is understandable, for Nazareth is not even mentioned, let alone connected with the Messiah, in the OT. It is significant that Philip does not argue with him, but simply invites him to come and see for himself (cf. Jesus' own invitation in *v.* 39). When, as preachers, we meet a sceptical attitude towards our claims regarding the Person and significance of Jesus Christ, it is not so much the cogency of our reasoning as the strength of our conviction and the directness of our personal testimony that is likely to prove effective. We must tell men what *we* have found in Jesus, and invite them to come to Him in the faith that they too may find the same.

Jesus recognizes the sincerity of Nathanael's piety (*v.* 47; cf. Ps 32²), and reveals that He had His eyes upon him before ever Philip found him. How many Christians, looking back to the time of their conversion and the experiences that led up to it, have realized that, long before they became aware of Him and His call, Christ was aware of them and was preparing to lay His hand upon them! It is never we who choose Him, but always He who chooses us (cf. 15¹⁶). To realize this is to become lost in wonder, and to confess our faith in Him—as Nathanael does in *v.* 49.

In *v.* 50 Jesus warns Nathanael that his present faith, though real and valuable, is immature, being based solely upon the wondering realization that Jesus instinctively knew all about his character and his past. He promises him that he will find a firmer basis for his faith as he grows to understand more fully the significance of Jesus. This promise to Nathanael in *v.* 50 merges into the more general promise in *v.* 51 (note the transition from the singular 'thou' to the plural 'ye'), which the Evangelist interprets as a promise to all who believe in Jesus, and one of great significance (it is prefaced by the formula 'Verily, verily, I say unto you', which regularly in this Gospel introduces solemn pronouncements of Jesus). The language of *v.* 51 clearly echoes the description of Jacob's dream in Gen 28¹². Just as Jacob's ladder extended from heaven to earth, so believers are here assured that they will see in 'the Son of Man' (Jesus' favourite title for Himself, *see ANT, para.* 107) the true Mediator between heaven (now 'opened') and earth, and the true Way (cf. 14⁶) along which they may rise from the latter to the former. As a result of the Incarnation, Ministry, Death, and Resurrection of Jesus, 'Jacob's ladder' is now 'pitched betwixt heaven and Charing Cross' (see Francis Thompson's poem, 'O world invisible')—and every other corner of the earth as well.

2¹⁻¹¹. THE SIGN AT CANA

'Sign' is one of the most important words in the vocabulary of the Fourth Gospel. It is regularly used (as in the present passage) of the miracles of Jesus, but the miraculous element is not essential to the idea of a 'sign'. Essentially, a 'sign' is something that points beyond itself to some greater and more important reality. In the Bible the word usually stands for a symbolical action—an action the true meaning of which lies not in itself, but in that which it signifies (*see,* e.g. Ezek 4¹⁻³). To John, the works of Jesus are 'signs' in this sense; each one symbolizes a spiritual truth, and is recorded, not for its own sake, but for the sake of the truth which it signifies. Accordingly the events which he has selected for inclusion in his Gospel are just those events which serve to signify the particular theological truths which he desires to impress upon his readers.

The first such 'sign' which John records ('this beginning of his signs', *v.* 11) took place at a wedding at Cana in Galilee. Whatever doubts one may have about the historicity of the *miraculous* element in this narrative (*see ANT, para.* 299), there is no good reason for doubting the historicity of the wedding as such; the wealth of vivid details which it contains suggests that the actual reminiscences of an eye-witness underlie the narrative. We may believe, then, that Jesus and His disciples did in fact attend a wedding-feast at Cana. This fact in itself is significant. Not only does it mean that Christ (in the familiar words of the marriage service) 'sanctioned and adorned with His presence' the 'holy estate of matrimony', but also that, by entering actively into the festivities of the occasion, He showed that there is a legitimate place, in the Christian life, for healthy and happy social intercourse. Christianity never involves a kill-joy attitude towards life. Our Lord was not above enjoying Himself in the company of His friends, and helping them too to enjoy themselves. He is able, and anxious, to enter into the joys, as well as the sorrows, of His followers. It is not irreverent to think of Him as being, as no doubt He was on this particular occasion, 'the life and soul of the party'. The wine which He supplied was better (*v.* 10) than any of that previously tasted. Thus the joyous experiences of life are enhanced and purified, and made infinitely more precious when He is allowed to take control of them. This is a theme deserving of the preacher's attention, and one that arises naturally out of this lovely story.

The true significance of the event, however, goes deeper than this. As the first 'sign' of Jesus' ministry, the Evangelist attaches to it special importance as defining the meaning of His mission. He came to replace the 'water' of Judaism (symbolized by the waterpots, *v.* 6) by the 'wine' of the Christian Gospel. The emphasis is upon the newness of the Gospel, and its superiority as compared with the Old Dispensation (cf. the teaching of Jesus in Mk 2[19-22], where the metaphors of wedding-feast and wine are also used with the same effect). The story perfectly illustrates the tremendous difference that Jesus makes to life, whenever and wherever He is received into it. It is like the difference between colourless, tasteless, stagnant water and colourful, tasteful, sparkling, and stimulating wine. The life to which Jesus calls us, and which He makes possible for us, is no dull, monotonous, negative round of existence; it is a gloriously positive, purposeful, exciting and adventurous way of living. As preachers, we are called to bear witness to this transformation of the ordinary and humdrum that Jesus is able to effect for all who respond to His call and accept His offer. And we must never cease to remind ourselves, and our fellow-Christians, that if our witness is to be effective and convincing, the transformation of which we speak must be manifestly exemplified in the lives of those who claim to know and follow Christ.

For John, the sign at Cana constituted a manifestation (v. 11) of the glory of Jesus (for 'glory', cf. 1^{14} above). His glory lies in His power to transform life. The manifestation of His glory to be seen in 'this beginning of his signs', however, is only a partial and preliminary manifestation. So much is implied in Jesus' words to His mother in v. 4—'Mine hour is not yet come'. On the surface, He seems to be referring to the time at which He intends to deal with the embarrassing situation in hand at the wedding. For John, however, the words have a deeper significance than that. He often refers to the 'hour' of Jesus (cf. 7^{30}, 8^{20}, etc.), by which he means the hour of His glorification through death and resurrection. For John it is the Death and Resurrection of Jesus that constitute the full manifestation of His glory (cf. 17^1, where, under the shadow of the Cross, Jesus is able to say 'Father, the hour is come; glorify thy Son'). It was by His triumphant redemptive act upon the Cross, upon which the Resurrection set its perfect seal, that Christ effected the supreme transformation of human life. In view of this, it may well be not without symbolical significance that John records that it was on 'the third day' that Jesus performed the sign at Cana (on this point, *see The Interpretation of the Fourth Gospel*, by C. H. Dodd, pp. 299 f.). John tells us (v. 11) that the partial and preliminary manifestation of Jesus' glory at Cana awakened faith in His disciples, who 'believed on him'. Even so, it is the supreme manifestation of His glory in the Cross and Resurrection that awakens faith in men and women of all ages, and the heart of the preacher's task is to set forth, as vividly as he possibly can, before the minds and hearts of his hearers the vision of Christ Crucified and Risen on their behalf.

2¹²⁻²⁵. THE CLEANSING OF THE TEMPLE

Most scholars accept the Synoptic rather than the Johannine dating of the Cleansing of the Temple (*see ANT, Appendix A*). John has no doubt brought his account of the incident forward, for theological reasons, to the beginning of his Gospel. It forms, with the narrative of the sign at Cana, a pair of what Strachan (p. 125) calls 'title-page vignettes to the story of the ministry that follows'. As the Cana incident symbolizes the truth that Jesus transforms the 'water' of Judaism into the 'wine' of the Christian Gospel, so the Cleansing symbolizes the complementary truth that the Jewish Temple is to give way to the Church which is the Body of Christ. That this, for John, is the significance of Jesus' act in the Temple (which is thus a 'sign', though not miraculous) is clear from *vv.* 19-22. The saying in *v.* 19 is one that was quoted against Jesus by His enemies (cf. Mk 14⁵⁸ and 15²⁹). It is certain that Jesus foresaw the final destruction of the Jerusalem Temple (cf. Mk 13², Lk 19⁴¹⁻⁴⁴, etc.), and that He promised to raise up another Temple to supersede it. This new Temple, however, was to be one 'made without hands' (Mk 14⁵⁸), and Jesus promised to raise it 'in three days'. This means (as *v.* 21 explains) that the new Temple was to be none other than the Resurrection Body of Christ Himself—a point which the Jews, by taking Jesus' words literally, completely missed (*v.* 20), and which the disciples themselves only grasped at a later date, after the Resurrection (*v.* 22). The Pauline conceptions of the Church as the Body of Christ (cf. 1 Cor 12¹²⁻²⁷, etc.) and as the Temple of God (1 Cor 3¹⁶, etc.) represent a natural development of this idea. The Christian Church has thus replaced the Jewish Temple as the centre of the true worship of God. As a result, the worship of God has ceased to be localized at any particular place, and has become more spiritual in character (*see* later on, 4²¹⁻²⁴). Moreover, this true worship has been universalized so that Gentiles as well as Jews may participate in it (cf. Mk 11¹⁷, where Jesus, having cleansed the Temple, says 'My house shall be called a house of prayer *for all the nations*'). In view of this, it is significant that the part of the Temple which Jesus cleansed (i.e. the part in which the animal-traders and money-changers conducted their business) was the Court of the Gentiles, the outer court into which alone non-Jews were allowed to enter. The trading did not interfere with the worship of Jews, who were allowed to enter the holier parts of the Temple, but it did interfere with the prayers of God-fearing Gentiles who came to the Temple—and Jesus was concerned with *their* rights, in anticipation of the new order in which Gentiles would participate on equal terms with Jews in the worship of the Temple which was His Body.

Thus for Jesus every part of the Temple was sacred, and no part was to be used as 'a house of merchandise' (*v.* 16). His action is prompted, partly by the dishonesty and merciless exploitation of the public which no doubt characterized the trading and money-changing businesses (in Mk 11[17] He accuses them of turning God's House into a 'den of robbers'), but also by His zeal for His Father's House and His desire to preserve its sanctity (*v.* 17). There are two clear implications here: (i) Dishonesty and exploitation are always despicable, but never more so than when practised under the cloak of religion; and (ii) Everything that is not consonant with true devotion and worship must be cast out of the sanctuary.

It is not clear whether Jesus used the scourge of cords (*v.* 15) on the men as well as on the animals. Jerome, in a famous passage, says that the moral power of 'the fiery and starry light that flashed in His eyes, and the glory of the Godhead that shone in His face' was quite sufficient to drive the guilty traders away. However that may be, the incident clearly reveals that there was room, in the divine character of our Lord, for fiery anger—not indeed a capricious and undisciplined rage, but the righteous indignation that arises out of zeal for the holy, the just, and the good. True zeal for righteousness is inevitably accompanied by wrath against all forms of unrighteousness.

The Jews considered that the right to cleanse the Temple belonged exclusively to the Messiah (cf. Mal 3[1-5]). Moreover, the quotation in *v.* 17 is from Ps 69[9], a passage which the early Church understood as referring to the Messiah, so that John, in introducing the quotation at this point, probably means to suggest that the Cleansing confirmed the disciples' belief in the Messiahship of Jesus. The Jewish authorities also regarded Jesus' action as implying a Messianic claim; accordingly they challenge Him to prove His authority for making such a claim by performing a 'sign' (*v.* 18). They use the term, of course, in the sense of 'miracle'; the Jews were prone to 'ask for signs' to authenticate any claim to divine truth or revelation (cf. 1 Cor 1[22]; Mk 8[11-13], etc.). They do not realize that the Cleansing of the Temple was itself a 'sign' (in the Johannine sense—*see* above), and that they are, in fact, asking for what has already been granted. Jesus, consistently with the decision He took in the wilderness (*see ANT, para.* 191), refuses to give them the miracles for which they ask. He will not *compel* men to believe in Him, because compulsion of that kind is no adequate basis for Christian faith.

This inadequacy of a faith based on miracles alone is emphasized in the short paragraph (*vv.* 23-25) which forms a transition from the present section of the Gospel to the next. There were those who believed in Him as a result of the miracles He performed in Jerusalem during the Passover feast. Jesus, however, did not set much store by such faith. There is a play upon words in *vv.* 23-24, for the same Greek verb is translated 'believe' in *v.* 23 and 'trust' in *v.* 24. These people had faith of a kind in Jesus; but Jesus had not much faith in their faith! John adds a comment (*v.* 25) on Jesus' infallible knowledge and understanding of human nature; He can read all minds and hearts, as He read Nathanael's (*see* 1^{47-50}). There is comfort and challenge in this thought. Whatever human experience we may be passing through, we may take heart from the knowledge that He understands, for He Himself was Man, and 'He hath felt the same' (*see MHB* 236). On the other hand, we must never forget that we can never deceive Him; everything in us, including our faith (*v.* 24), is subject to His all-seeing scrutiny. Every Christian needs at times to examine the basis of his faith in Christ, and to ask, honestly and sincerely, whether it is the kind of faith in which Jesus can trust, and on which He can depend.

The 'transition paragraph' (as we have styled *vv.* 23-25) serves as a fitting introduction to chapters 3 and 4, in which we see Jesus coming into contact with three very different persons, and knowing exactly how to deal with each. These three persons are respectively a Jew (Nicodemus), a Samaritan (the woman at the well), and a Gentile (the nobleman, who is probably to be identified with the Roman centurion of Mt 8^{5-13} and Lk 7^{1-10}). By describing the three contacts in this order, John seems to be emphasizing the universality of the interest, and the appeal, of Jesus.

3^{1-21}. JESUS AND NICODEMUS

This section, like the preceding one, illustrates the conflict between the old order and the new. As a Pharisee and 'ruler of the Jews' (i.e. member of the Sanhedrin), who is also a renowned teacher (Jesus in *v.* 10 calls him '*the* teacher of Israel'), Nicodemus exemplifies the religion of the Old Dispensation at its best.

The character of Nicodemus himself is noteworthy. He is not mentioned in the Synoptics, but appears on three occasions in the Fourth Gospel (here, in 7[50-51], and in 19[39]). His attitude to Jesus shows him to be a man of humble and magnanimous spirit. Prominent members of a profession (even the clerical profession!) are not always prepared to listen to the opinions of those whom they regard as 'laymen'. This prominent Rabbi, however, acknowledges Jesus, in spite of His obscure origin and lack of official training and status (*see* 7[15]), not only as a fellow-Rabbi but as a prophet (one 'come from God', *v.* 2). His magnanimity appears again in his words at 7[51]. It arose, no doubt, out of a passionate religious zeal and an unbigoted desire to know the truth; this made him willing, and anxious, to enter into discussion even with an unorthodox and unrecognized Rabbi like Jesus. The fact that he comes to Jesus 'by night' is not necessarily an indication of cowardice on his part (his words to the Sanhedrin in 7[51] are hardly the words of a coward who wishes to keep secret his sympathy towards Jesus). It was customary for Rabbis to study and discuss the Law at night-time; and in any case that would be the most convenient time to seek a quiet interview with Jesus. Moreover, John probably sees symbolical significance in the fact that the conversation took place 'by night' (he often uses the word 'night' in a symbolical sense—cf. 9[4], 11[10], and 13[30]). He may well be suggesting that Nicodemus, for all the sincerity of his religious zeal, was in spiritual darkness, and that out of that darkness he came into the presence of 'the true Light' (cf. 1[9]). In this connexion, it is significant that the figures of 'light' and 'darkness' are prominent in the closing verses (19-21) of the present section. It is this darkness that prevents Nicodemus from understanding the import of Jesus' words (*see vv.* 4 and 9). The mistaken religious preconceptions of men often form a barrier to their understanding and acceptance of the true Gospel.

Jesus presents Nicodemus suddenly with a statement of the fundamental principle of the new religion, namely the necessity for a man to be born again. The word translated 'anew' (RV) can mean either 'again' or 'from above', and both these meanings are combined in *v.* 3. The reference is to a *second* birth that comes *from above*. It is further described in *v.* 5 as being 'of water and the Spirit'. 'Water' here is a reference to the sacrament of Baptism. In the early Church, Baptism was always the accompaniment of regeneration. This did not mean that the sacrament *effected* the regeneration—the Holy Spirit alone could do that—

but that it *signified* the fact that a man was reborn. The great difference between the baptism of John the Baptist and that of Jesus was that the Holy Spirit was associated with the latter (*see* the Baptist's words in 1^{26} and 1^{33}, and cf. Acts 19^{1-7}); John's was a baptism 'with water', Jesus' a baptism 'with water and the Spirit'.

The term 'Kingdom of God', so common in the Synoptics, occurs in the Fourth Gospel only at $3^{3,\ 5}$. John usually uses the phrase 'Eternal Life' to express the same idea (*see ANT, para.* $290(f)$ (iv)). To see, or enter into, the Kingdom of God = to inherit Eternal Life = to become a child of God (cf. 1^{12-13}, where, as we saw, the necessity of a spiritual and supernatural rebirth has already been touched upon). We have here three equivalent ways of describing the true end of religion. The doctrine of 'the New Birth' means that this end is not reached by means of any process of nature. No man is *by nature* fit for the Kingdom of God—not even the Jew, who belongs physically to the chosen race (Nicodemus would assume that, as a true 'son of Abraham', his place in the Kingdom of God, when it was established, would be assured). Before a man can enter the Kingdom, his nature must be radically changed; he must be raised by a supernatural creative act to an entirely new level of life. We are familiar with different levels of life in nature—e.g. plant life, animal life, human life—and we know that there is no *natural* process of development from one level to another. A flower could never be turned into an animal, nor an animal turned into a man, except by a new, creative act of God. The life of the Kingdom of God (i.e. Eternal Life) is not just the highest *degree* of human life; it is a different *kind*, a different level, of life. And man cannot *grow* into it by any natural process; rather must he be remade by a supernatural, creative act of God.* The distinctively Christian life is so different from ordinary, natural human life ('that which is born of the flesh', *v.* 6) that the transition from the latter to the former can only adequately be expressed in terms of a new *birth*. This teaching has its counterpart in Paul's stress on the 'new creation' in 2 Cor 5^{17}, Gal 6^{15}, etc.)

Regeneration does not have to be fully *explained* in order to be *experienced*, any more than the origin and nature of the wind needs to be explained for its effects to be observed (or, to take a

---

* I owe this illustration to the Rev. E. Tegla Davies's *Dechrau'r Daith*—a little book, unfortunately not available in English, which is by far the best manual of preparation for Church membership that I know.

modern illustration, any more than the working of a power like
electricity has to be explained before we benefit from its effects).
For all its mysterious nature, we know the reality of the wind
(v. 8) because we experience its effects. Likewise we may know
the reality of the Spirit's work because we see its results in the
lives of those who are born of Him. The point of this comparison
is heightened by the fact that in Greek the same word (*pneuma*)
is used for both 'wind' and 'Spirit'. Nicodemus, and those in all
ages to whom the Gospel is preached, may not be able to understand how such a radical change in human nature is possible
(v. 9; cf. the timeworn tag, 'Human nature cannot be changed').
The reply of the Church (the 'we' of v. 11) must always be that
we know it is possible, because we have known it happen. The
ultimate proof of the power of the Gospel is the transformed lives
of those who have believed in it.

Verses 12-15 show that the deep secrets of heaven can only be
known by revelation from above. 'No man hath ascended into
heaven' to discover them, but 'the Son of Man' (who is the true
Mediator between heaven and earth—*see* above on 1^{51}) has
'descended out of heaven' to reveal them. *Verse* 14 introduces the
idea (which is prominent in this Gospel) of the 'lifting up' of the
Son of Man. The word used has both a literal and a metaphorical
meaning (the latter in the sense of exaltation or glorification), and
is always used by John with reference to the Crucifixion (cf. 8^{28},
12$^{32\,f}$). Here in 3^{14}, the lifting up of Jesus upon the Cross (which is
His true path to glory) is compared with the lifting up of the
brazen serpent by Moses in the wilderness (*see* Num 21$^{4-9}$). As
the children of Israel looked up at the serpent on the standard,
their minds were directed towards God, and they were saved from
the bites of the fiery serpents that plagued them. Likewise,
salvation and eternal life come to believers as they look at Him
who was lifted up on the Cross, and put their trust in Him. The
'must' of v. 14 is full of significance; the Cross is an essential
element in the economy of salvation as it was conceived in the
eternal counsels of God (cf. Mk 8^{31}; Lk 24^{26}; Acts 2^{23}, etc.).

This allusion to the Cross, and the redemptive purpose fulfilled therein, prepares the way for v. 16. This verse is surely the
most golden of all the golden texts which the Bible contains for
the Christian preacher. In so far as it is possible to compress the
whole rich content of the Christian Gospel into a single sentence,
John has succeeded in doing so in this majestic and unforgettable
verse We are reminded here that the Cross was the outcome of the

amazing and boundless love of God. The purpose of the sacrifice on Calvary was not the appeasement of an angry God, for it was God Himself who prepared and offered the sacrifice ('He *gave*'). To do so involved for Him the greatest cost imaginable, for it meant giving His beloved, His Only-begotten (*see on* 1[14, 18]) Son. This love of God has for its object the whole world, and that means that it is both all-embracing and undeserved (the term 'world' in *John* means the world that is sinful and in rebellion against God—cf. 1 John 2[16], 5[9], and *see ANT, para.* 302). The purpose of this redeeming love of God for sinful men is to save them from perishing or destruction, and bring them to Eternal Life. Eternal Life is life of the same nature and quality as the life of God Himself. It is the life of 'the world to come', but a man may enter upon it here and now in this present world, on the sole condition of believing in Christ, i.e. believing that He is the Son of God, and trusting implicitly in His redemptive act for men upon the Cross.

This classic expression of the love of God is followed by a treatment, in *vv.* 17–21, of the related theme of the judgement of God. Salvation and judgement are the opposite sides of one and the same process. The Son of God did not come to judge the world but to save it (*v.* 17). Nevertheless, His coming inevitably results in judgement for some men—namely those who refuse to believe in Him and so reject the salvation which He offers. John treats judgement, as he does salvation, not as something reserved for the future, but as something that is taking place *here and now* (the ideas of a *future* judgement and resurrection to Eternal Life are not, however, absent from his thought—*see* 5[28–29], 6[40], etc.). Whether the coming of Christ means salvation or judgement for a man (for it must mean one or the other—no man can just ignore the fact of Christ and say 'It doesn't concern *me* in the least') depends entirely upon the response he makes to Christ. The man who believes in Christ inherits Eternal Life (*v.* 16) and so escapes judgement. The man who rejects Christ, on the other hand, is judged already, for he brings judgement upon himself (just as a man who fails to appreciate a great work of art judges, not the work of art, but himself). This theme is worked out in *vv.* 19–21 by means of the imagery of light and darkness. The tragedy of the world's rejection of Christ is nowhere more poignantly expressed than in *v.* 19 (cf. what was said on 1[9–11]). For a man to perish in darkness, when all he has to do is throw open the shutters to let in the light that is waiting to shine in upon him and give him life is the height of tragedy, and a terrible judgement on the man himself.

John traces men's rejection of the light of Christ to their love of their own sinful practices, and their unwillingness to have them exposed (v. 20, see Moffatt). Men still reject Christ and resolutely shut Him out from their lives, because they are not prepared to face the consequences of accepting Him. They know that it will involve giving up many practices and pleasures which they regard as precious. They need to be reminded that, if they will but take the plunge of faith, they will not only receive something infinitely more precious than that which they will have to forgo, but that their values will be so changed that, far from feeling the loss of what they have forfeited, they will regard themselves as well rid of it all.

There is a significant phrase in v. 21: 'he that *doeth* the truth.' Truth, for John, is not merely something to be believed, but something to be *done*—there is an ethical element in it. A man must live out the implications of the truth which he believes. When he does so, he rejoices in the light of Christ, which shows clearly that his actions have been 'wrought in God', i.e. in communion with God and in accordance with His will.

3^{22-36}. JOHN THE BAPTIST AND JESUS (2)

This section reveals that for a period, prior to the arrest of John the Baptist, Jesus exercised a ministry parallel to that of John in Judea, near the river Jordan. It was later, after the Baptist's arrest, that the Galilean ministry of Jesus opened (*see* Mk 1^{14}). It seems that the ministry of Jesus met with an increasing success and popularity, at the expense of that of John. This fact led to a certain amount of jealousy on the part of the Baptist's disciples, which they express to their master (v. 26). As is so often the case, the master is more tolerant and less prone to envy than are his disciples. John reminds them (v. 27) that the success which attends every mission is given 'from heaven'. If Jesus' mission is succeeding, John is well content, for his own mission is merely preparatory and subordinate. This incident shows John, not only acknowledging the superiority of Jesus (cf. 1^{19-34}), but *rejoicing* in it—as the best man at a wedding rejoices in the happiness of the bridegroom upon whom he waits (v. 29). It is possible to acknowledge the superiority, and greater degree of success, that belong to someone else, but to do so grudgingly and without very good grace. Even preachers and Church officials sometimes show this kind of spirit when they hear of the success attending the work of other preachers or churches. John's words in *vv.* 27–30 remind us that the only thing that should count with us is whether the cause of Christ is going forward or not. If it is, our joy should be fulfilled, whether or not we personally have had any part in the success. The words of *v.* 30, with which John the Baptist makes his final exit from the Evangelist's stage, not only sum up that self-effacing attitude which, in this Gospel, is his outstanding characteristic; they also provide a 'golden rule' for everyone who sets out to witness for Christ. We must always be prepared to keep ourselves out of the picture in order that Christ may take His rightful place in the centre of the picture.

Vv. 31–36 are not a continuation of the Baptist's words, but rather the inspired meditation of the Evangelist himself on the themes which have been treated in the earlier parts of the chapter. *V.* 33 contains a suggestive idea, namely that the believer, by receiving the witness of Jesus (i.e. the revelation which He has brought from heaven—cf. *vv.* 12–13), thereby sets his seal to the truth of that revelation (the source of which, of course, is God). He personally attests that it is true. There is a counterpart to this idea in I Jn 5[10], where it is stated that the man who 'hath not believed in the witness that God hath borne concerning his Son' makes God 'a liar'. The words of Jesus are to be accepted as the words of God (*v.* 34), because God has given Him the Spirit in the fullest possible sense, and not 'by measure' (cf. 1[32], 'it abode upon him'). The perfect relationship of love and trust between the Father and the Son which is described in *v.* 35 is the theme of the great discourse found later in ch. 5.

4[1–42]. JESUS AND THE WOMAN OF SAMARIA

Here we see Jesus passing through Samaria, and 'being wearied with his journey' (a detail which bears striking witness to the fact that He entered fully into all the experiences of humanity—*see* on 1[14]), sitting down to rest at midday ('the sixth hour') beside Jacob's well near Sychar, while His disciples depart to the city to buy food. By entering into conversation with the Samaritan woman, Jesus rises above two deep-seated prejudices that were common in His day—the prejudices of sex and religion. It was considered unseemly for a Jewish Rabbi to address a woman in public. Hence the surprise of the disciples in *v.* 27, and that of the woman herself in *v.* 9. The woman's surprise has an additional cause in view of the fact (noted by the Evangelist in the parenthetical comment at the end of *v.* 9) that 'Jews have no dealings with Samaritans'. This does not mean that Jews avoided all contact with Samaritans (the fact that the disciples had gone to a Samaritan town to buy food indicates that commercial dealings between the two peoples were not impossible). The verb translated 'have no dealings with' probably means 'do not use together with'. Jews regarded Samaritans (and particularly their women) as unclean, and would consequently shrink with horror from the thought of sharing with them the use of anything like a vessel for eating or drinking (on the background of the ill-feeling between Jew and Samaritan *see ANT, paras.* 3 and 8). That Jesus should ask for a drink from the Samaritan woman's vessel thus becomes all the more astonishing. Conventions and prejudices meant nothing to Him when He was confronted with a human being in need.

The manner of Jesus' approach to the woman is significant. He begins by asking a favour of her (cf. His approach to Zacchaeus in Lk 19[5]). It is often the case that the best way to win the friendship and confidence of a person whom one wishes to help (and there is little hope of helping a person until such a relationship of friendship and confidence has been established) is not to offer one's service to him, but to ask a service of him. Moreover, the request for a drink of water enables Him to lead the conversation on to the higher, spiritual level of the 'living water' which He Himself has to offer. Jesus always adapts His teaching to the terms of the actual situation in which He finds His hearers.

The way in which the conversation develops is also interesting. Jesus asks the woman for water (*v.* 7). She expresses surprise at His request (*v.* 9). He points out that He has better water to offer, and that she ought to have requested it from Him (*v.* 10). She refuses to believe that Jesus can supply any water, and certainly no better water than that supplied by 'our father Jacob' (*vv.* 11–12). Jesus explains Himself further (*vv.* 13–14), and then the woman does at last ask for His gift (*v.* 15). She makes the request in a somewhat jocular and sceptical manner that reveals a complete misunderstanding of the meaning of Jesus' offer, but it is at least an advance on her previous attitude. And so Jesus leads her on, step by step, until she realizes who He is and becomes a witness to His Messiahship (*vv.* 28–29 and 39). There are still those who, beginning in complete scepticism as to whether

Christ has anything to offer them, later begin to look to Him for certain benefits (material things that will spare them trouble and worry in this world—cf. *v.* 15), without realizing what the great and precious spiritual gift is that He is offering them. But the fact that they are prepared to look to Christ at all, even in this unworthy way, provides an opportunity for the Church to lead them on to a fuller understanding of what He can do for them.

In countries with a hot, dry climate (such as Palestine), water is the prime necessity of life, and it was natural for the Jews to liken the deepest cravings of the human spirit to the physical thirst for water (cf. Ps 42$^{1-2}$, Jer 2^{13}, etc.). Thus Jesus, in this context, describes His gift of Eternal Life (*see* on 3^{16}) in terms of 'living water'. The term 'living water' was commonly used of running (as opposed to stagnant) water, but here it has, in addition, the deeper meaning of 'water that gives and sustains life'. In every man's soul there is a thirst for life—a life that can really satisfy, and set his heart at rest. Men seek to slake this thirst by various means—pleasure, culture, philosophy, religion, etc. These things may *seem* to satisfy for a while, but they are man-hewn cisterns, 'broken cisterns that can hold no water' (Jer 2^{13}). By contrast, Jesus offers to implant in man's soul a well of living water—a perennial spring that will never run dry—'springing up unto eternal life' (*v.* 14). His gift alone can satisfy, completely and permanently, the deepest needs and longings of the soul. 'Our hearts are restless till they find their rest in Thee' (Augustine); 'From the best bliss that earth imparts we turn *unfilled* to Thee again' (Bernard of Clairvaux, *MHB* 109).

The conversation between Jesus and the woman takes a fresh turn in *v.* 16. Jesus reveals that He is fully aware of the woman's immoral life, and thus, no doubt, awakens in her a sense of sin which predisposes her for a discussion of specifically religious matters. Perceiving that He is 'a prophet' (and thus advancing a further step in her recognition of His true identity), the woman raises the burning question (that was the subject of continuous dispute between Jews and Samaritans) as to whether God should be worshipped at Jerusalem or at Gerizim. This leads to what is the classic expression of Christian teaching about the essential nature of true worship (*vv.* 21–24).

Jesus tells the woman that the problem which she has raised is one that is no longer of any relevance. What matters henceforth is not the *place* at which worship is offered but the *spirit* in which it is offered. The essence of true worship is that it is offered 'in spirit and truth', and that because God whom we worship is Spirit. This means not only that God is non-material and therefore not confined to any time or place, but also that He is the Living God, the Almighty and ever-active Creator and Sustainer of all life. To worship in spirit and truth means, not only to be genuinely sincere in our worship, but to have a clear and true conception of the nature of the God we are worshipping, and, most important of all, to be in harmony with, and under the inspiration and guidance of, the Holy Spirit Himself. We can only worship 'in *spirit and truth*' when our minds and hearts are possessed by 'the *Spirit of Truth*' (as the Holy Spirit is called in 14¹⁷).

There is a further suggestive idea in the words 'for such doth the Father seek to be his worshippers' (*v.* 23). Not only is God *worthy* to receive our worship (which in itself is a sufficient reason why we should offer it to Him), but He also *desires* it and rejoices in it. To realize this must surely heighten our sense of wonder at the priceless privilege of being counted amongst His worshippers.

After Jesus has revealed Himself to her as the Messiah (*v.* 26), the woman immediately turns missionary (as did the disciples in 1⁴¹, ⁴⁵). In her anxiety to bring her fellow-citizens to Jesus, she forgets everything else, even her waterpot (*v.* 28). Her understanding of the significance of Jesus is still very imperfect, as her words in *v.* 29 show, but something strange has happened to her as a result of her encounter with Him, and she is anxious to share the experience with others. One does not have to wait until one *understands* everything about Jesus before one may begin to seek to bring others to Him. The Samaritans of Sychar respond to her message (*v.* 30). They begin by believing in Jesus on the basis of the woman's testimony (*v.* 39), but they are not content with a second-hand experience. They seek Him for themselves, inviting Him to stay to preach to them. Thus they reach a firmer basis for their faith, which they express in no uncertain terms in *v.* 42. To accept the testimony of others is often the *beginning* of Christian faith, but it must only be a beginning. We must never be content until we have entered into a personal relationship with Christ. And the preacher must never be content that his hearers should 'take his word for' the truth of the Gospel; he must always seek to lead them to this personal encounter with Christ Himself.

While the woman is on her mission to the city, Jesus converses with His disciples, who have in the meantime returned to the well (*vv.* 27, 31–38). When they invite Him to partake of the food which they have brought from the city, He takes up the figure of food (just as, in the conversation with the woman, He took up that of water) and uses it in a spiritual sense. He reminds them (as He reminded the Tempter in the wilderness) that 'Man shall not live by bread alone, but by every word that proceedeth out of the mouth of God' (Mt 4⁴; cf. Deut 8³). Jesus is saying (in *vv*. 32 and 34) that, in the deep spiritual satisfaction that has come to Him in the fulfilment of His mission, the physical weariness and hunger which He felt earlier have disappeared. To lose oneself in the devoted fulfilment of a spiritual task can lead to the renewal of physical strength. This is not, of course, meant to imply that the needs of the body are to be ignored, but it is a salutary reminder that man needs food other than the physical kind (cf. 6²⁷, and the whole discourse on 'the Bread of Life'). The idea of Christ's 'accomplishing' (the word means to finish, completely and perfectly) His Father's work is a prominent one in this Gospel (*v.* 34; cf. 17⁴ and 19²⁸, ³⁰). The redemptive work of Christ which it is the privilege of every preacher to proclaim is a *finished* work, a work that has been perfectly accomplished, once and for all.

The results of this work which Jesus has accomplished at the well-side, and the fulfilment of which has brought Him such renewal and satisfaction, begin to appear in *vv*. 35-38. Jesus describes these results in terms of seed-time and harvest. He reminds His disciples of the words of a well-known proverb to the effect that a farmer has to wait four months from the time of sowing before he can reap his harvest. The words of *v.* 35a do not imply that this incident in Samaria took place at a date four months before the harvest season; it is more likely that the harvest season itself was approaching and that the sight of cornfields around them which were 'white already unto harvest' (*v.* 35b) was what actually suggested the illustration to our Lord's mind. The point of the illustration, as He uses it, is that what is true in the natural world is not necessarily true in the spiritual realm. The farmer has to wait four months for *his* harvest, but the fruit of *Jesus*' sowing of His word in the heart of the woman at the well is already appearing, in the persons of the Samaritans whom she has urged to come to Him, and who can already be seen approaching; they are 'the fields . . . white already unto harvest' at which Jesus bids His disciples look. The work of reaping this spiritual harvest is already beginning (*v.* 36, RVmg). The sowing was done by Jesus alone, but the disciples are to share in the work of reaping (*vv*. 37-38). In doing so, they will receive 'wages' (the reward that belongs to all faithful servants of the Kingdom of God—a reward that consists of the joy of performing the service as such—the reward 'of knowing that we do Thy will'). Moreover, they will be 'gathering fruit unto life eternal,' for Eternal Life is the inheritance of all believers whom the Christian mission gathers into the Kingdom of God.

In v. 37, Jesus quotes another proverbial saying, and proceeds in v. 38 to apply it to the situation of His disciples. It is equally applicable to Christians of all ages. Each generation reaps the benefit of the labour and service of previous generations. It is our privilege to reap what our forefathers have sown. It is equally our privilege, and our responsibility, to sow what those who come after us may reap. We may spend our lives in Christian service and evangelistic work without ever seeing much fruit to our labours, but that need not discourage us, for we may take heart in the assurance that our 'labour is not vain in the Lord' (1 Cor 15[58]). In God's universe, no good seed is ever sown in vain (cf. Gal 6[7], which applies to *good* seed as well as *bad*). It does not really matter whether the Lord calls us to the work of sowing or that of reaping, or to a little of each. All is the work of the One Lord, and our highest privilege is to be allowed a part in His work at all. And in the end it will be true in the case of His labourers that 'he that soweth and he that reapeth' will rejoice together (v. 36).

4[43-54]. JESUS AND THE GENTILE NOBLEMAN

This section describes a second sign performed by Jesus at Cana in Galilee. The Evangelist seems anxious to point to a connexion between the two signs (*see v.* 46, and cf. *v.* 54 with 2[11]). The truth symbolized by this sign represents a development of that of 2[1-11]. There we saw that Jesus transforms and enriches life; here we learn that He is able to rescue a life that is on the point of extinction (*see v.* 47). Later, in ch. 11, this development reaches its climax in the greatest of all Jesus' signs, the raising of Lazarus, where we see that He is able even to revive a life that has already been extinguished. There is no limit to the life-giving power of Christ. No man, however hopeless and helpless his situation may appear to be, is beyond the power of Christ to save. The wonderful nature of Christ's healing power is further heightened by the fact that the cure is wrought at a distance (that between Cana and Capernaum) from the sufferer. He has only to speak a word (v. 50), and the saving act is performed (cf. Lk 7[7]). The narrative also illustrates the universal scope of the saving work of Jesus, since the nobleman was a Gentile (the word translated 'nobleman' is one that was used of military officials in the service of Herod, so that he is in all probability to be identified with the centurion of Lk 7$^{1-10}$ and Mt 8$^{5-13}$).

A striking feature of the story is the different levels of faith which are mentioned in it. Jesus meets the nobleman's request with words which appear to contain a rebuke. We feel that the nobleman scarcely merited such a rebuke, and it may well be that the words of v. 48 were meant for bystanders (note the plural 'ye') rather than for the nobleman personally. However that may be, Jesus here (as in 2^{24}) deprecates a faith that requires miracles as its basis. It is to the nobleman's credit that he refuses to be discouraged by Jesus' words. The urgency of his repeated request (v. 49) shows him to be in deadly earnest, as everyone must be who expects the help of Jesus. Jesus then, being satisfied that the man's faith is genuine (cf. Mt 8^{10}), speaks the word, and the nobleman immediately takes Him at His word, and obeys His command to return home. This is the second level of faith seen in the story—the willingness to accept confidently what Jesus says as true. Later, after receiving news of his son's recovery at the precise hour in which Jesus assured him thereof, the nobleman reaches the third, and highest, level of faith. 'He believed' (v. 53), in the full sense in which that term is used in the Gospel, i.e. he believed that Jesus was the Christ, and surrendered himself to Him in full trust and commitment. Christian faith usually begins as a simple, unquestioning willingness to take Jesus at His word, and accept what he says as true. He who so believes, and acts on the basis of such an acceptance, invariably finds that experience confirms the reality of Jesus' promises, and so he is led on to that fuller understanding, commitment, and trust that is mature Christian faith. John adds the further significant detail that the 'whole house' of the nobleman believed with him. It is so often the case that the conversion of the head of a family leads naturally to the conversion of the whole family.